American Cinema and Hollywood

American Cinema and Hollywood

Critical Approaches

Edited by

JOHN HILL and **PAMELA CHURCH GIBSON**

Consultant Editors

Richard Dyer   E. Ann Kaplan   Paul Willemen

OXFORD
UNIVERSITY PRESS
2000

OXFORD

UNIVERSITY PRESS

Great Clarendon Street, Oxford OX2 6DP

Oxford University Press is a department of the University of Oxford.
It furthers the University's objective of excellence in research, scholarship,
and education by publishing worldwide in

Oxford New York

Athens Auckland Bangkok Bogotá Buenos Aires Calcutta
Cape Town Chennai Dar es Salaam Delhi Florence Hong Kong Istanbul
Karachi Kuala Lumpar Madrid Melbourne Mexico City Mumbai
Nairobi Paris São Paulo Singapore Taipei Tokyo Toronto Warsaw

with associated companies in Berlin Ibadan

Oxford is a registered trade mark of Oxford University Press
in the UK and in certain other countries

Published in the United States
by Oxford University Press Inc., New York

British Library Cataloguing in Publication Data

Data available

Library of Congress Cataloging in Publication Data

Data available

ISBN 0-19-874281-9

1 3 5 7 9 10 8 6 4 2

Typeset by J&L Composition Ltd, Filey, North Yorkshire
Printed in Great Britain
on acid-free paper by
Bookcraft Ltd., Midsomer Norton, Somerset

Acknowledgements

We would like to thank a number of people who have helped in the preparation of this book. We are, of course, grateful to all our contributors, some of whom worked to particularly tight deadlines. We would also like to thank our consultant editors— Richard Dyer, Ann Kaplan and Paul Willemen—for their assistance and advice. Geoffrey Nowell-Smith also provided good advice and suggestions at an early stage.

At Oxford University Press, we would particularly like to thank our editor Andrew Lockett for his constant support and enthusiasm for the book, Tania Pickering for her invaluable assistance and Mick Belson and Ruth Marshall for their help and efficiency in preparing the manuscript for publication.

We are also grateful to Roma Gibson, Celia Britton, and Stella Bruzzi for their help. John Hill is also indebted to his colleagues David Butler, Dan Fleming and Martin McLoone at the University of Ulster for their support for the project and to the Faculty of Humanities for a well-timed period of leave of absence. Thanks also to the staff at BFI Stills.

J. H. and P. C. G.

Contents

Contributors

EDITORS

John Hill is Professor of Media Studies at the University of Ulster at Coleraine. He is the author of *Sex, Class and Realism: British Cinema 1956–63* (1986) and *British Cinema in the 1980s* (1999), co-author of *Cinema and Ireland* (1987), and co-editor of *Border Crossing: Film in Ireland, Britain and Europe* (1994), and *Big Picture, Small Screen: The Relations Between Film and Television* (1996).

Pamela Church Gibson is a Senior Lecturer in Contextual and Cultural Studies at the London College of Fashion, a constituent college of the London Institute. She is the co-editor of *Dirty Looks: Women, Pornography, Power* (1993) and has written on heritage film both for *British Cinema in the Nineties* (ed. Murphy, 1999) and for the French journal *1895*. She has a chapter on the *Alien* cycle of films in *Popular Film and Cultural Studies* (forthcoming) and is currently working with Stella Bruzzi on a collection of essays tentatively entitled *Fashion and Culture: Theories and Explorations*.

CONSULTANT EDITORS

Richard Dyer is Professor of Film Studies at the University of Warwick. He is the author of a number of books including *Stars* (1979), *Heavenly Bodies* (1986), *The Matter of Images* (1993), *Now You See It* (1990) and *White: Essays on Race and Culture* (1997).

E. Ann Kaplan teaches at the Department of English at the Humanities Institute at Stony Brook, New York. She is the author of a number of books including *Women and Film: Both Sides of the Camera* (1983), *Motherhood and Representation: The Mother in Popular Culture and Melodrama* (1992), and *Looking For The Other: Feminism, Film, and the Imperial Gaze* (1997).

Paul Willemen is Professor of Critical Studies at Napier University, Edinburgh. He has published widely on film theory and is the author of a number of books, including *Looks and Frictions: Essays in Cultural Studies and Film Theory* (1994) and co-editor of *Questions of Third Cinema* (1989) and the *Encyclopaedia of Indian Cinema* (1994).

CONTRIBUTORS

John Belton teaches film at the English Department at Rutgers University and is author of *Widescreen Cinema* (1992) and *American Cinema/American Culture* (1994).

Jeremy G. Butler is an Associate Professor in the Telecommunication and Film Department of the University of Alabama. He is the editor of *Star Texts: Image and Performance in Film and Television* (1991) and the author of *Television: Critical Methods and Applications*. He also created *Screensite*, a World Wide Web site devoted to film studies: http://www.sa.ua.edu/ScreenSite.

Stephen Crofts has taught Film and Television Studies in universities in the UK, the USA, and Australia. He has published extensively, including books on Australian cinema and on televisual constructions of politics. His research includes work on the internationally cross-cultural export and reception of film and television.

Douglas Gomery teaches at the University of Maryland where he lectures on the economics and history of the mass media. His work on cinema history and Hollywood can be found in *The Hollywood Studio System* (1986) *Shared Pleasures* (1992) and *Media in America* (1998).

Tom Gunning teaches in the Art Department at the University of Chicago. He has published widely on early cinema and is author of *D. W. Griffith and the Origins of Narrative Film* (1991).

CONTRIBUTORS

Douglas Kellner is Professor of Philosophy at the University of Texas at Austin. He is the author and co-author of numerous books on social theory, poltics, history, and culture, including *Camera Politica: The Politics and Ideology of Contemporary Hollywood Film* (with Michael Ryan, 1998), *Jean Baudrillard* (1989) and *Critical Theory, Marxism and Modernity* (1989). He is currently working on the impact of new information and entertainment technologies on society and culture.

Peter Kramer teaches Film Studies at the University of East Anglia (UK). He has co-edited *Screen Acting* (1999) and contributed essays on American film history to *Screen*, *The Velvet Light Trap*, *Theatre History Studies*, the *Historical Journal of Film, Radio and Television*, and *History Today* as well as numerous edited collections. He is currently working on a book on contemporary Hollywood cinema.

Toby Miller is Associate Professor in the Department of Cinema Studies at the Tisch School of the Arts, New York University. He is author *of The Well-Tempered Self: Citizenship, Culture, and the Postmodern Subject* (1993), *Contemporary Australian Television* (with Stuart Cunningham, 1994), *The Avengers* (1997), *Technologies of Truth: Cultural Citizenship and the Popular Media* (1998), and *Popular Culture and Everyday Life* (1998). He is co-editor of *SportCult* (1999), *Film and Theory* (1999) and *A Companion to Film Theory* (1999).

Albert Moran is a Senior Research Fellow in the Faculty of Humanities, Griffith University, Brisbane. He is author of *Projecting Australia* (1991) *and Moran's Guide to Australian TV Series* (1993) and editor of *Film Policy: International, National, and Regional Perspectives* (1996).

Duncan Petrie teaches at the School of English and American Studies at the University of Exeter and is author of *Creativity and Constraint in the British Film Industry* (1991) and *The British Cinematographer* (1996).

Tom Ryall is a Reader in Film Studies at the School of Cultural Studies, Sheffield Hallam University. He is author of *Alfred Hitchcock and the British Cinema* (1986) and is currently working on a study of the interrelationships between the British and American cinemas.

List of illustrations

General Introduction

John Hill

In 1995, the cinema celebrated its centenary. Since 1895, the cinema has grown and spread globally and, despite an actual decline in cinema attendances worldwide, the watching of films is now more popular than ever thanks to television and video. Although new communication technologies and forms of entertainment have undoubtedly affected the social and cultural role of cinema, the cinema nonetheless retains a huge importance as an economic, cultural, and artistic activity. As such, film continues to attract enormous critical attention and commentary in both popular discourses and academic fields of study.

This is particularly so of Hollywood which, as Douglas Gomery suggests in his chapter, is currently stronger than ever. Since the end of World War One, the U.S. film industry has been the dominant cinema in the world and it has often been in relation to Hollywood that other cinemas have had to define themselves (through either competition, differentiation or opposition). It is not surprising, therefore, that it is Hollywood which has been the major focus of interest for film studies as well. Accordingly, it is the various ways in which North American film and Hollywood have been studied and accounted for which is the central concern of this book. (A companion volume—*World Cinema—Critical Approaches*—is devoted to non-Hollywood cinemas).

As the book's title suggests, the emphasis is on *critical approaches* and *debates* in the study of North American cinema rather than on the detailed provision of factual information. Its interest, therefore, is with the key theoretical frameworks, concepts and arguments that have been employed in relation to American/Hollywood cinema. In doing so, the book aims to suggest some of the central issues which have been a feature of the study of American cinema and what is at stake in them. In this way, it is planned that the reader should gain a sense of each topic not simply as a body of agreed knowledge but as a site of continuing debate and discussion. In this respect, the book does not adopt one 'line' or advocate one critical approach above others (even if individual authors sometimes argue for particular theoretical frameworks or critical preferences).

The structure of the book is as follows. The first section—'American Cinema: History, Industry and Interpretation'—looks at the various approaches which have been adopted in relation to the study of American film history. John Belton identifies the various historical frameworks that have been employed in the study of American cinema and reviews the changing agendas of film historians. Duncan Petrie develops Belton's arguments by examining how the role of film technology has been discussed by film historians while Douglas Gomery looks at Hollywood as an industry and assesses the various explanations of how Hollywood has succeeded in maintaining its economic dominance.

Gomery also looks at how the structure of American cinema has changed historically and his concern with periodization is carried over into the three essays that follow. Tom Gunning assesses the study of early (pre-Hollywood) American cinema and the various critical debates—relating to film form, exhibition and audiences, and socio-cultural significance—which this work has generated. A key concept that has governed the study of Hollywood has been that of the 'classical' and Gunning discusses the historical juncture at which a 'classical cinema' may be said to have been consolidated. Ann Kaplan then looks at the history of how the term 'classical' has been used in critical debates and assesses how far conceptualizations of 'classical cinema' are complicated by Hollywood's reliance upon the conventions of melodrama. The final chapter in this section, by Peter Kramer, develops these arguments in relation to the 'new Hollywood' and assesses the ways in which it is possible to describe contemporary American filmmaking as 'post-classical'. In all these discussions, there is a concern to consider not only the textual characteristics of the relevant films but also the whole matrix of economic, technological, social and cultural circumstances in which films are produced and consumed.

The second section—'Critical concepts'—carries on the discussion by looking at some of the key ideas and methods that have been involved in the study of American films. Stephen Crofts looks at authorship study and the various ways in which the role of the Hollywood director has been theorized and analysed. Tom Ryall examines the concept of genre and assesses its value in accounting for the aesthetic and socio-cultural workings of popular films, while Jeremy Butler looks at star studies and assesses the various accounts of the role of stars that film scholars have provided.

The third section—'Politics and Society'—develops the arguments about the social and political role of Hollywood further. Douglas Kellner looks at the ways in which Hollywood films have addressed American society and may be said to have performed an ideological role. Albert Moran examines the neglected area of film policy and assesses the role that the U.S. argument has played in relation to Hollywood. Toby Miller looks at Hollywoood in an international context and assesses the various economic and cultural arguments that have been used to explain the sources and consequences of Hollywood's increasingly global power.

Each chapter is intended to lay out and assess the history and meaning(s) of key critical terms, issues and debates. In some cases, there are also additional 'readings' of individual films that are designed to illustrate how different theories or critical perspectives have been applied to particular examples. Thus, the readings on *Casablanca* illustrate the consequences of arguments about 'classicism' and 'melodrama' for an understanding of an individual film. The bibliographies which accompany each chapter not only include full details of the material referred to in each chapter but also certain texts which may not actually be cited but are nonetheless significant texts of relevance to the area. Particularly useful texts, recommended for further reading, are accompanied by an asterisk.

In this way, the book is designed to provoke thought, encourage debate and stimulate further reading and research. The excitement of film studies is that, despite a growing institutionalization, it remains a field in which a variety of approaches coalesce and compete and in which basic questions remain 'unsettled'. If this volume can communicate some of that excitement amongst its readers (be they students, teachers, or those with a general interest in the serious study of film) then it may be judged a success.

American cinema: history, industry, and interpretation

1

American cinema and film history

John Belton

Early film history

Between 1975 and 1985 the writing of film history underwent a modest revolution. Before this period, the standard texts on America (and world) film history tended to construct history according to nineteenth-century models of historiography which were grounded in theories of knowledge that were positivist and empiricist in nature. Events were understood as the consequences of the acts of individual agents, such as inventors, producers, directors, performers exhibitors, and others. There was little or no consideration of the cinema as a *systemic* phenomenon: as an institution determined by overlapping, contradictory, and/or mutually exclusive economic, technological, ideological, and socio-cultural demands.

These pioneering texts provided a linear account of film history, based on first-hand observation of the film industry and on data furnished by film industry personnel, trade magazines, newspaper articles and reviews, and other primary sources. Film historians were themselves often part of the very industry about which they were writing.

The first 'histories' were, in fact, written by and for the film industry. The writing of the history of the American cinema began with descriptions of its invention in the late 1880s and early 1890s. These took the form of patent applications, various articles in scientific journals (such as *Scientific American*), and accounts of the demonstrations of various motion picture cameras, projectors, and viewing mechanisms in newspapers. One of the first deliberate 'histories' of American film was written by an inventor, W. K. L. Dickson. Published in 1895, Dickson's *History of the Kinetograph, Kineto-scope, and Kineto-Phonograph* (co-authored with his sister, Antonia Dickson) recounted his development of the Kinetograph (a camera) and the Kinetoscope (a peepshow viewing device) for Thomas Edison. Published by Raff & Gammon, the distributor of Edison's Kinetoscope, the book served to promote sales of the Kinetoscope to potential customers.

The next major history was Robert Grau's *Theatre of Science* (1914). Grau was a theatrical agent and (later) a writer for the *Moving Picture World*. Grau's work celebrated the achievements of major American exhibitors, producers, directors, actors, screenwriters, and other creative talents. As Robert Allen and Douglas Gomery (1985: 59–60) have noted, Grau's history was published by subscription; the author raised money to publish the book by selling subscriptions to it to members of the film industry, offering them coverage in exchange for advance orders for the book. Like the Dicksons' earlier work, the book was part-history and part-advertisement. In both instances, history was 'in-house': it was written by (and for) the very individuals who were credited with creating it.

The objectivity of subsequent historians was never as severely compromised as that of Dickson and Grau, but the major works of history that followed were none the less products of individuals whose livelihood once (or still) depended upon the film industry. A former journalist, Terry Ramsaye began work in the motion picture industry in 1915, serving as a publicist for the Mutual Film Corporation, where he launched a newsreel series, *Screen Telegram*. During the First World War he produced and edited films for the United States Treasury Department; after the war he was a publicist for Samuel Rothafel's Rialto and Rivoli Theatres in New York City. In 1920 he began writing *A Million and One Nights* (1926), a two-volume history of the motion picture. A considerable portion of this history was commissioned and published in the early 1920s by *Photoplay* magazine, a trade journal that also enjoyed a general readership. At the same time, he wrote and produced films for the Associated Screen News of Canada and edited ethnographic feature films, including *Grass* (1925) and *Simba* (1928). From 1931 to 1949 he was the editor of the trade magazine *Motion Picture Herald*.

Prominent figures within the next few generations of film historians were also personally involved with the film industry, including Benjamin Hampton (1931), Lewis Jacobs (1939), Paul Rotha (1930), Arthur Knight (1957), Kenneth Macgowan (1965), and David Robinson (1973). For these early historians, the writing of film history became an act of affirmation of the cinema's importance as a social, economic, cultural, and/or aesthetic form. These historians were, in effect, too close to the cinema—too much a part of it themselves—to hold it up to a more critical and distanced scrutiny.

Rewriting the history of the American cinema

During the 1970s a new generation of film scholars began to correct the errors of the standard histories and to present new research. A number of these scholars, including Thomas Cripps, Garth Jowett, Daniel Leab, Robert Sklar, and others, had been trained as historians. Others, such as Tino Balio, had extensive prior experience as scholars working with primary source material in the field of English literature. Most of this new generation were academics. The exceptions—independent scholars such as Kevin Brownlow (1968, 1990) and Anthony Slide (1970, 1976, 1978)—played a crucial role in gathering together primary research collections and in rewriting the history of silent American cinema; academics, however, tended to ignore their work because it lacked a clearly articulated theoretical base.

In his discussion of film historiography, Robert Sklar (1990) identifies three generations of film scholars: the self-taught non-academics (journalists, archivists, filmmakers); the academically trained humanists (himself included); and cinema studies doctorates. For Sklar, revisionist historiography is the product of the third generation—cinema studies doctorates, such as Robert Allen and Douglas Gomery (1985) and David Bordwell, Janet Staiger, and Kristin Thompson (1985). Taking issue with these scholars' theoretical and ideological conservativism (i.e. their non-radical, non-Marxist social vision), Sklar complains that revisionists tend to 'emphasize institutions and processes' rather than 'the lived experiences of people' (1990: 28).

The rewriting of traditional history by this second and third generation of historians was indebted, in part, to the recent deposits of primary research materials in American and European archives. Wisconsin-based activities, such as the publication of *The Velvet Light Trap* (1971) and Tino Balio's first two books (1975, 1976), relied extensively on the United Artists Collection, which contained films and production information for United Artists films, as well as for pre-1948 Warner Bros., RKO, and Monogram films. This collection, of which Balio was the curator, was donated to the Wisconsin Center for Film and Theater Research in 1969. Rarely seen archival prints also launched revisionist interest in early cinema ten years later. In 1978, at a film conference held by the International Federation of Film Archives (FIAF) at Brighton, film archivists and film scholars met, watched rare early films made between 1900 and 1906, and began to rethink standard histories of early cinema.

The publication in 1975 of Robert Sklar's *Movie-Made American* led a challenge to the traditional narrative of American film history as told by Ramsaye and others. At the very beginning of his history, Sklar reviews the standard account of factors leading to the film industry's movement from New York to Hollywood in the 1910s. Hampton (1931/1970: 77, 79), Ramsaye (1926: 533–4), and others had insisted that independent filmmakers using unlicensed cameras in violation of exclusive rights held by the Motion Picture Patents Company (MPPC, the Trust) had moved to southern California in order to escape the watchful eye of the MPPC and, when necessary, to flee the Trust's detectives by crossing the border into Mexico. Sklar points out that the Mexican border was not close; it was at least five hours away by car. He also notes that the Trust's subpoenas could just as easily have been served on the New York sales offices of these independent companies. He suggests that the move to California was driven, instead, by climate, which permitted year-round filmmaking; by the terrain, which featured a variety of potential settings (mountains, the desert, the city, the sea); by cheap land for studio space; and by an inexpensive, non-unionized labour force (Sklar 1975: 67–8).

An example of New Left historiography, Sklar's book sought 'to reconstruct a past in which common people struggled to determine their own lives and institutions' (Sklar 1990: 20). The standard film histories, such as those by Hampton and Ramsaye, had described the audiences for early (pre-1914) cinema as composed of lower-class immigrants and blue-collar workers (Ramsaye 1926: 431; Hampton 1931/1970: 47). Sklar reaffirms this argument, linking the rise of the movies to the emergence of a 'new social order' and identifying early audiences as members of 'the lowest and most invisible classes in American society' (1975: 3). However, in the late 1970s revisionist film historians such as Russell Merritt (1973) and Robert C. Allen (1979) used business directories and other demographic data to identify the location of urban nickelodeons in Boston and New York City. Both Merritt and Allen discovered

that most nickelodeons were, in fact, located in middle-class, as well as in lower-class, neighbourhoods. These findings were used to support an argument that the motion picture was, from its beginning, a middle-class amusement and to trace the growing use of the cinema by the middle class to express and reinforce its own bourgeois values.

The 1970s revisionism of Merritt and Allen has recently been subject to yet another revision which Allen (1996) has subsequently dubbed 'postrevisionism'. Using additional primary sources that list more New York City nickelodeons and give more detailed census data, Ben Singer (1995) concludes that immigrants and the working-class population did indeed constitute the majority of moviegoers as late as 1908–10 and that the standard histories 'may not have been as far off the mark as revisionist historians maintain' (28).

New methodologies

Revisionist history is characterized, in part, by its response to attacks, by comtemporary theorists on the methodology employed in traditional film history. These attacks begin to appear in the early 1970s, most notably in Jean-Louis Comolli's multi-part essay 'Technique et idéologie' (1971–2). Comolli argued that traditional film history was both empiricist in method and idealist in concept.

Employing Marxist theories of historical determination, Comolli called, instead, for a 'materialist' historiography. In part, materialist historiography was simply a repudiation of the methods of standard historiography. Traditional histories were regarded as teleological and reliant upon cause-and-effect reasoning. Thus, as André Bazin suggests in 'The Myth of Total Cinema' (1967), silent black-and-white cinema gave way to sound, colour, and widescreen cinema, and the cinema evolved, in Darwinian fashion, towards greater and greater realism. Comolli rejected the concept of linear causality, arguing instead for a non-linear, uneven development in which events are the results of a field of different, often opposing, determinations; change is not continuous but rather is characterized by gaps and delays. Comolli also rejected the notion that the cinema evolves autonomously, independent of technological, economic, and ideological forces. He insisted that its evolution was highly *mediated*; cinematic forms were determined by the often contradictory demands of technology, economics, and ideology. Comolli's 'materialism' thus views history as a non-linear series of ruptures whose uneven process reflects underlying contradictions within the existing social, economic, and cultural institutions that inform it.

Comolli's call for materialist historiography has not yet been fully answered, but the influence of his essays can be seen in the work of Edward Buscombe (1977, 1978), Edward Branigan (1979), James Spellerberg (1979), Kristin Thompson and David Bordwell (1983), Allen and Gomery (1985), and John Belton (1992).

Much as film theory and criticism sought to systematize its study of the cinema by drawing upon the 'sciences' of structural anthropology (Claude Lévi-Strauss), Marxism (Louis Althusser), and psychoanalysis (Sigmund Freud, Jacques Lacan), the new historians also brought scientific method to bear upon historical methodology. Ed Buscombe (1977) invoked Thomas Kuhn's *The Structure of Scientific Revolutions* (1962). At the same time, Allen (1977) and Allen and Gomery (1985) expressed their concern with issues of historio-

graphy and the development of a methodology for conducting film history by referring to E. H. Carr's *What is History?* (1961). While Kuhn pointed out the quasi-subjective nature of scientific observation, Carr noted the role that interpretation played in reading events yet rejected a relativism that would insist that one interpretation of an event was therefore as good as another. Carr viewed history as a 'continuous process of interaction' between events and their interpreters.

Following Kuhn, film historians began to view historiography as a subclass of epistemology. Kuhn problematized empiricist observation, arguing that scientific observation occurs through models, paradigms, and frames of reference, which shape those observations. Science does not explain phenomena; instead, it *constructs* phenomena, filtering it through pre-existing assumptions or conventions. Film historians, ranging from Allen and Gomery to Charles Musser, read Terry Lovell's *Pictures of Reality* (1980) and began to weigh the relative merits of empiricism and conventionalism. As a theory of knowledge, empiricism 'posits a real world which is independent of consciousness and theory, and which is accessible through sense-experience' (Lovell 1980: 10). Empiricism argues that the subjectivity of the observer does not invalidate the knowledge gained from observation. Conventionalism, on the other hand, insists that observation is always subjective, that knowledge is socially produced, and that, because events are necessarily perceived through frames of reference or systems of knowledge that transform them, these events cannot be known or observed.

Robert Allen and Douglas Gomery's book *Film History* (1985) has proved to be one of the seminal texts in the shaping of contemporary film historiography. In it, the authors draw extensively on Kuhn, Carr, and Roy Bhaskar's *A Realist Theory of Science* (1978), from whom (and Rom Harré) they appropriate the concepts of 'generative mechanisms' and 'realism'. Realism, a philosophy of science and history, is empiricist in so far as it acknowledges a world 'out there' that exists independently of the scientist and that can be known. But unlike the empiricist, the realist views observable phenomena as the effects of non-observable processes; though not observable, these processes do exist and are not simply constructions posited by the scientist or historian. It is these processes, or generative mechanisms, that produce observable events. Against this background, Allen and Gomery seek to negotiate the two extremes of empiricism and conventionalism by

Comolli rejected the concept of linear causality, arguing instead for a non-linear, uneven development in which events are the results of a field of different, often opposing, determinations; change is not continuous but rather is characterized by gaps and delays. Comolli also rejected the notion that the cinema evolves autonomously, independent of technological, economic, and ideological forces. He insisted that its evolution was highly *mediated*; cinematic forms were determined by the often contradictory demands of technology, economics, and ideology. Comolli's 'materialism' thus views history as a non-linear series of ruptures whose uneven process reflects underlying contradictions within the existing social, economic, and cultural institutions that inform it.

combining empirical observation with theories of knowledge to identify generative mechanisms that determine historical events.

First, they discuss the approaches which structured traditional histories, breaking them down into aesthetic, technological economic, and social categories. Each of these approaches is seen, in turn, as driven by a single notion of historical change—the agency of the individual (the director, the inventor, etc.). For example, for Allen and Gomery, aesthetic film history can be understood as the history of film masterpieces which had been created by the individual genius of a director, writer, producer, or star. It involves the study of the cinema as an art form and of filmmakers as individual artists whose visions determine the thematic and aesthetic significance of their films.

Allen and Gomery note several problems with this approach. In celebrating the cinema as an art form, historians tended to neglect other aspects of the cinema, such as its identity as an economic, technological, and/or cultural product. Furthermore, the masterpiece tradition dealt with only a small percentage of films, concentrating on a handful of art films and ignoring the great majority of ordinary films produced by the industry. More importantly, this tradition understood the value, meaning, and significance of individual works to be determined by the degree to which they transcended their historical or industrial context. Finally, what determined a masterpiece's uniqueness was the genius of the individual artist whose vision it reflected.

In response to the limited nature of the explanation of historical events found in traditional approaches such as the masterpiece tradition, Allen and Gomery propose that historians consider instead a network of causal elements that determine events. They refer to this system of determinations as generative mechanisms, i.e. forces which can be seen to have a certain explanatory value in accounting for the production of observable events. These mechanisms are, in effect, systemic rather than isolated occurrences. History is the result of specific modes of production, determined by various economic, technological, and ideological demands.

The masterpiece tradition relied extensively on the critical evaluation of films, on the analysis of visual style, and on the identificaton of authorial vision. In their discussion of Sunrise (1927), Allen and Gomery barely mention the film itself, concentrating instead on the film's 'background'. They explore director F. W. Mur-

nau's 'biographical legend', producer William Fox's interest in Murnau and the film in terms of his promotional strategies for elevating the status of his studio, and various public discourses surrounding Murnau and the production and reception of the film. Thus the historical significance of Sunrise is seen to reside not so much in its aesthetic qualities as in its exemplary status as a product of a complex background set of various economic, technological, and social forces.

Historicizing classical Hollywood

The same year that witnessed the publication of Allen and Gomery's book also saw the appearance of David Bordwell, Janet Staiger, and Kristin Thompson's monumental effort The Classical Hollywood Cinema (1985). During the 1970s film theorists, ranging from the editors of Cahiers du cinéma and Screen to individual authors such as Laura Mulvey (1975) and Colin MacCabe (1974), repeatedly referred to a phenomenon called 'classical Hollywood cinema'. But the exact nature of this 'dominant cinema', which they somewhat vaguely characterized as 'illusionistic', 'transparent–invisible', and/or 'patriarchal', was never clearly defined. In their book, Bordwell, Staiger, and Thompson set out to provide a film historian's definition of this phenomenon.

The approach taken by the authors to classical Hollywood cinema is multifaceted. Classical Hollywood cinema is understood, in part, as a 'style' of filmmaking. Its stylistic (and narrative) features are explored in terms of the relationship of those features to sets of other dterminants, chiefly to developments in film technology and changes in the economic structure of the film industry. However, the development of classical Hollywood cinema is not directly driven by the forces of technology and economics; rather these forces are mediated by the entire system (mode of production) of industrial practices, including those of various professional organizations such as the Academy of Motion Picture Arts and Sciences, the American Society of Cinematographers, and the Society of Motion Picture (and Television) Engineers.

The most prominent features of their history illustrate the revisionist nature of their project. Unlike traditional histories, theirs draws not only on films, but on other, previously neglected, bodies of evidence such as manuals for screenwriters and cinematographers, publications of craft guilds and unions, and technical

A silent masterpiece *and* product of complex background forces—Murnau's *Sunrise* (1927)

and trade journals. Their focus is not on a handful of masterpieces but on 'typical' films. Thus their work draws on an 'unbiased sample' of 100 films made during the period 1915–60. Conclusions made from this study were then tested by analysing them against a background set of 200 additional films from the same period. At the same time, while traditional histories focused their discussion of style on first usages of specific devices, Bordwell *et al.* looked instead at usages when a stylistic device had become a norm.

> **The most prominent features of their history illustrate the revisionist nature of their project. Unlike traditional histories, theirs draws not only on films, but on other, previously neglected, bodies of evidence such as manuals for screenwriters and cinematographers, publications of craft guilds and unions, and technical and trade journals. Their focus is not on a handful of masterpieces but on 'typical' films. At the same time, while traditional histories focused their discussion of style on first usages of specific devices, Bordwell *et al.* looked instead at usages when a stylistic device had become a norm.**

For Bordwell, Staiger, and Thompson (1985), classical Hollywood cinema constituted a 'group style' or norm of stylistic practices that had evolved by (roughly) 1917. Prior to 1917 the modes of production and stylistic practices within Hollywood continued to change—from the cameraman system (1896–1907), in which films were made by cameramen; to the director system (1907–9); the director–unit system (1909–14), in which a director, like Griffith, developed and paid his own stock company; to the producer–unit system (1914 on) within which an individual producer co-ordinated the production process. However, once the system had maximized its efficiency as a mode of production, the basic features of the film style that had evolved remained 'constant across decades, genres, studios, and personnel' (1985: 10).

Their history viewed this group style or norm as more or less static from 1917 to 1960. Disruptions of that norm occurred in the form of individual directors, whose work occasionally violated dominant practice, and in the form of film noir, which deviated in terms of stylistic and narrative conventions from earlier Hollywood cinema. Bordwell argued that neither film noir nor auteur films resulted in the creation of a radically new norm. Indeed, even with the advent of sound, colour, and widescreen, the system of classical Hollywood cinema remained more or less constant.

For example, in one of his more elegant arguments, Bordwell notes that the coming of sound posed a threat to the classical paradigm developed during the silent era. The classical mode of narration depended upon a careful breakdown of shots, through editing, to analyse the action of a scene. Yet early sound technology, which was based on the exact synchronization of sound and image (on the same strip of film in two of the three major sound systems), encouraged the use of a single camera filming a scene without interruption. In order to maintain the classical paradigm, the studios introduced the practice of filming with multiple cameras. This gave them different views (in precise sound synchronization) of the same scene, which could then be edited together in the conventional manner (1985: 304–5). Thus stylistic continuity was maintained across the breach created by the new technology.

The chief flaw of the book lies in its insistence upon the resilience and constancy of the classical paradigm to the exclusion of any sense of the significance of the variations within that paradigm from period to period. Thus the disruptive nature of the transitions to sound, colour, and widescreen and the dramatic violation of classical norms by film noir tend to be softened and viewed as moments of continuity rather than discontinuity. In other words, the book pursues the *systemic* nature of classical Hollywood cinema to a fault. Yet, given the extensive time period under investigation (1917–60), classical Hollywood cinema ultimately does enjoy a certain constancy and coherence as a system, especially in comparison to other modes of film practice, such as European art cinema.

Recent developments

In the 1990s the macroscopic perspective of Bordwell, Staiger, and Thompson's *Classical Hollywood Cinema* gives way to more microscopic histories, and the interest in classical Hollywood cinema seen in that work gives way to an interest in early, pre-classical cinema, exemplified in the work of Charles Musser (1990, 1991), Eileen Bowser (1990), Richard Koszarski (1990), Tom Gunning (1991), Miriam Hansen (1991), Gregory Waller (1995), Janet Staiger (1995), David Robinson (1996), and others. Pioneering this approach was Scribner's History of the American Cinema series, which appeared in 1990 with three separate volumes devoted to the silent American cinema. Musser's book dealt with 1895–1907; Bowser's with 1907–15; Koszarski's with 1915–28.

Like *The Classical Hollywood Cinema*, these books draw on primary research conducted by the authors, using trade periodicals, daily and weekly (local) newspapers, national and local archives, Supreme Court and local circuit court records, and various special collections, ranging from scrapbooks to personal and corporate papers housed at regional libraries, museums, and universities. These diverse historical materials are used to provide a technological, economic, and cultural context within which early cinema takes its place as an entertainment practice alongside other contemporary forms of commercial entertainments.

Thus Musser explores the relation of pre-1907 cinema to illustrated lectures, magic-lantern and photographic slide shows, amusement park and fairground attractions, vaudeville, theatre, newspapers, cartoon strips, popular songs, fairy-tales, and other cultural forms. As a result, Musser's history is not 'the history of a product (the films) or of an industry (Hollywood and its precursors) but of a practice' (1990: 495). For Musser, the 'presentational' techniques of pre-existing entertainment practices (such as those of illustrated lectures or lantern slide shows) determined the way an event is presented or a story is told. For example, in turn-of-the-century cinema it was the exhibitor rather than the producer who assembled discrete shots into a coherent entertainment experience and who, thus, maintained editorial control over the narrative.

In a similar manner, Eileen Bowser focuses on general 'practices' rather than on individual pictures. Traditional histories covering her period (1907–15) celebrate film directors, such as D. W. Griffith, and film masterpieces, such as *The Birth of a Nation* (1915). Although 'the names of the director and the film appear in almost every chapter' (1990, p. xii), Bowser's chief interest lies with normative practices

of the period rather than with individual artists or works.

Though Richard Koszarski necessarily foregrounds the emergence of the star system and the feature-length film in examining the period 1915–28, his book also emphasizes industrial context over individual achievement. Like the other books in the series, Koszarski's volume provides a portrait of American cinema as an *institution*, as an industrial (i.e. economic and technological) and socio-cultural entity.

Recent work on American film history follows the institutional approach taken by Bordwell, Staiger, and Thompson and the Scribner series. These books do not construct their histories around individual films, filmmakers, or stars, but around institutional practices. They explore the cinema's status as a mode of production and its significance as a new form of mass consumption, drawing less upon films themselves than upon primary, print-based research materials such as trade journals, studio files, court testimony, censorship records, screenwriting manuals, and other forms of evidence.

Douglas Gomery provides economic analyses of film production (*The Hollywood Studio System*, 1986) and exhibition (*Shared Pleasures*, 1992). Janet Staiger contributes a history of film reception (*Interpreting Films*, 1992) and a cultural study of the representation of female sexuality on the screen between 1907 and 1915 (*Bad Women*, 1995). Using Hays Office memos, Lea Jacobs examines 'fallen woman' films of the 1930s in *The Wages of Sin* (1991). In a similar effort, communications historian Gregory Black consulted studio production records and Production Code Administration files to construct a history of motion picture censorship in the 1930s in *Hollywood Censored* (1994). Tino Balio added another volume and decade (the 1930s) to Scribner's series of institutional histories with *Grand Design* (1993). Columbia University Press has recently published a number of books that examine various aspects of the American cinema. These books integrate recent work in cultural theory, such as the construction of national identity and the representation of race, class, gender, and other forms of social identification, with issues of film historiography. This series looks back to earlier works of cultural history, such as those of Charles Eckert (1978) and Lary May (1980). Yet it also responds to more recent models, integrating Eckert's and May's approach with the institutional model pioneered by Bordwell *et al.* through studies of directors (Sikov 1994), stars (Studlar 1996), genres (Jenkins

1992; Rubin 1993; Doherty 1993; Berenstein 1995; and Paul 1995), and individual films (Bobo 1995).

The writing of American film history reflects the changing landscape of contemporary film studies. As Bowser notes, 'every generation needs its own history, rewritten with a different emphasis and from new viewpoints' (1990, p. xi). Traditional histories, such as Ramsaye's, convey contemporary—or rather, nineteenth-century—attitudes towards the writing of history. Traditional histories attempt to read the twentieth-century reality of rapid industrialization, urbanization, mass production, and the advent of consumer culture in nineteenth-century terms. Historians romanticize history, rewriting the anonymity of mass culture as a saga of individual achievements. Thus, for them, history consists of the individual accomplishments of heroic inventors, showmen, producers, directors, stars, and others.

Prompted by the academicization of film studies, revisionist film history reflects the theoretical turmoil of the 1970s. Influenced by linguistics and structural anthropology, film theorists attempt to view the cinema not in terms of its individual elements but as a 'system'. Events are the products, not of isolatable features of observable reality, but of underlying structures that exist in a complex system of interconnectedness with one other. Allen and Gomery's 'scientific' approach to film history thus seeks to identify the underlying structures, or generative mechanisms, that determine historical events. This notion of 'system' informs subsequent film historiography, which attempts to explore American cinema as a coherent mode of production that results in the creation of a classical paradigm—classical Hollywood cinema—which can be seen to possess a group style. The interest of contemporary historians in classical Hollywood cinema as a mode of production and as a group of stylistic, economic, and industrial practices culminates in the institutional approach to American cinema that has characterized the most recent phase of American film historiography. The relationship of Hollywood as an institution to its role within the larger phenomenon of American culture has emerged as the latest site for the rewriting of film history. In this way, the history of film history reflects the history of film studies and documents our ever-changing understanding of what it means to do film history.

BIBLIOGRAPHY

Allen, Robert (1977), 'Film History: The Narrow Discourse', in Lawton and Staiger (1977).
—— (1979), 'Motion Picture Exhibition in Manhattan, 1906–1912: Beyond the Nickelodeon', *Cinema Journal*, 18/2 (Spring), 2–15.
—— (1996), 'Manhattan Myopia; or, Oh! Iowa!', *Cinema Journal*, 35/3 (Spring), 75–103.
*—— and **Douglas Gomery** (1985), *Film History: Theory and Practice* (New York: Knopf).
Altman, Charles F. (1977), 'Towards a Historiography of American Film', *Cinema Journal*, 16/2 (Spring), 1–25.
Balio, Tino (1975), *United Artists: The Company Built by the Stars* (Madison: University of Wisconsin).
—— (ed.) (1976), *The American Film Industry* (Madison: University of Wisconsin).
—— (1993), *Grand Design: Hollywood as a Modern Business Enterprise 1930–1939* (New York: Scribner's).
Bazin, André (1967), 'The Myth of Total Cinema', in *What is Cinema?*, i (Berkeley: University of California Press).
Belton, John (1992), *Widescreen Cinema* (Cambridge, Mass.: Harvard University Press).
—— (1994), *American Cinema/American Culture* (New York: McGraw-Hill).
Berenstein, Rhona (1995), *Attack of the Leading Ladies: Gender, Sexuality, and Spectatorship in Classic Horror Cinema* (New York: Columbia University Press).
Bhaskar, Roy (1978), *A Realist Theory of Science* (Atlantic Highlands, NJ: Humanities Press).
Black, Gregory (1994), *Hollywood Censored: Morality Codes, Catholics, and the Movies* (New York: Cambridge University Press).
Bobo, Jacqueline (1995), *Black Women as Cultural Readers* (New York: Columbia University Press).
*****Bordwell, David, Janet Staiger,** and **Kristin Thompson** (1985), *The Classical Hollywood Cinema: Film Style and Mode of Production to 1960* (New York: Columbia University Press).
Bowser, Eileen (1990), *The Transformation of Cinema 1907–1915* (New York: Scribner's).
Branigan, Edward (1979), 'Color and Cinema: Problems in the Writing of History', *Film Reader*, 4: 16–34.
Brownlow, Kevin (1968), *The Parade's Gone By* (New York: Ballantine).
—— (1990), *Behind the Mask of Innocence: Sex, Violence, Prejudice, Crime: Films of Social Conscience in the Silent Era* (London: Jonathan Cape).
Buscombe, Ed (1977), 'A New Approach to Film History', in Lawton and Staiger (1977).
—— (1978), 'Sound and Color', *Jump Cut*, 17 (Apr.), 48–52.
Carr, E. H. (1961), *What is History?* (New York: Vintage Books).
Comolli, Jean-Louis (1971–2), 'Technique et idéologie',

Cahiers du cinéma, no. 229 (May–June 1971), 4–21; no. 230 (July 1971), 51–7; no. 231 (Aug.–Sept. 1971), 42–9; nos. 234–5 (Dec.–Jan. 1971–2), 94–100; no. 241 (Sept.–Oct. 1972), 20–4; part 1 trans. Diana Matias in Bill Nichols (ed.), *Movies and Methods*, ii (Berkeley: University of California Press, 1985); parts 3 and 4 trans. Diana Matias in Philip Rosen (ed.), *Narrative, Apparatus, Ideology: A Film Reader* (New York: Columbia University Press, 1985).

Dickson, W. K. L., and **Antonia** (1895/1970), *History of the Kinetograph, Kinetoscope, and Kineto-Phonograph* (Raff & Gammon; repr. New York: Arno Press).

Doherty, Thomas (1993), *Projections of War: Hollywood, American Culture, and World War II* (New York: Columbia University Press).

Eckert, Charles (1978), 'The Carole Lombard in Macy's Window', *Quarterly Review of Film Studies*, 3/1 (Winter) 1–21.

Gomery, Douglas (1986), *The Hollywood Studio System* (New York: St Martin's).

—— (1992), *Shared Pleasures: A History of Movie Presentation in the United States* (Madison: University of Wisconsin Press).

Grau, Robert (1914), *Theatre of Science: A Volume of Progress and Achievement in the Motion Picture Industry* (New York: Broadway).

Gunning, Tom (1991), *D. W. Griffith and the Origins of American Narrative Film: The Years at Biograph* (Urbana: University of Illinois Press).

Hampton, Benjamin (1931/1970), *History of the American Film Industry From its Beginnings to 1931* (repr. New York: Dover).

Hansen, Miriam (1991), *Babel and Babylon: Spectatorship in American Silent Film* (Cambridge: Harvard University Press).

Jacobs, Lea (1991), *The Wages of Sin: Censorship and the Fallen Woman Film 1928–1942* (Madison: University of Wisconsin Press).

Jacobs, Lewis (1939), *The Rise of the American Film* (New York: Columbia University's Teachers College).

Jenkins, Henry (1992), *What Made Pistachio Nuts? Early Sound Comedy and the Vaudeville Aesthetic* (New York: Columbia University Press).

Knight, Arthur (1957), *The Liveliest Art* (New York: New American Library).

Koszarski, Richard (1990), *An Evening's Entertainment: The Age of the Silent Feature Picture 1915–1928* (New York: Scribner's).

Kuhn, Thomas S. (1962), *The Structure of Scientific Revolutions* (Chicago: University of Chicago Press).

Lawton, Ben, and **Janet Staiger** (eds.) (1977), *Film: Historical–Theoretical Speculations, The 1977 Film Studies Annual*, part 2 (New York: Redgrave).

Lovell, Terry (1980), *Pictures of Reality: Aesthetics, Politics, and Pleasure* (London: British Film Institute).

MacCabe, Colin (1974), 'Realism and the Cinema: Notes on some Brechtian Theses', *Screen*, 15/2 (Summer), 7–27.

MacGowan, Kenneth (1965), *Behind the Screen* (New York: Delta).

May, Lary (1980), *Screening Out the Past: The Birth of Mass Culture and the Motion Picture Industry* (New York: Oxford).

Merritt, Russell (1973), 'Nickelodeon Theaters: Building an Audience for the Movies', *AFI Report*, 4/2 (May), 4–8.

Mulvey, Laura (1975), 'Visual Pleasure and Narrative Cinema', *Screen*, 16/3: 6–18.

Musser, Charles (1990), *The Emergence of Cinema: The American Screen to 1907* (New York: Scribner's).

—— (1991), *Before the Nickelodeon: Edwin S. Porter and the Edison Manufacturing Company* (Berkeley: University of California Press).

Paul, William (1995), *Laughing Screaming: Modern Hollywood Horror and Comedy* (New York: Columbia University Press).

Ramsaye, Terry (1926), *A Million and One Nights*, 2 vols. (New York: Simon & Schuster).

Robinson, David (1973), *The History of World Cinema* (New York: Stein & Day).

—— (1996), *From Peepshow to Palace: The Birth of American Film* (New York: Columbia University Press).

Rotha, Paul (1930/1960), *The Film till Now* (London: Spring); rev. with Richard Griffith (New York: Twayne).

Rubin, Martin (1993), *Showstoppers: Busby Berkeley and the Tradition of Spectacle* (New York: Columbia University Press).

Sikov, Ed (1994), *Laughing Hysterically: American Screen Comedy of the 1950s* (New York: Columbia University Press).

Singer, Ben (1995), 'Manhattan Nickelodeons: New Data on Audiences and Exhibitors', *Cinema Journal*, 34/3 5–35.

*Sklar, Robert (1975), *Movie-Made America: A Cultural History of American Movies* (New York: Random House).

—— (1990), 'Oh! Althusser: Historiography and the Rise of Cinema Studies', in Robert Sklar and Charles Musser (eds.), *Resisting Images: Essays on Cinema and History* (Philadelphia: Temple University Press).

Slide, Anthony (1970), *Early American Cinema* (London: A. S. Barnes).

—— (1976), *Early Women Directors* (London: A. S. Barnes).

—— (1978), *Aspects of American Film History Prior to 1920* (Metuchen, NJ: Scarecrow Press).

Spellerberg, James (1979), 'Technology and Ideology in the Cinema', *Quarterly Review of Film Studies*, 2/3 (Aug.), 288–301.

Staiger, Janet (1992), *Interpreting Films: Studies in the Historical Reception of American Cinema* (Princeton: Princeton University Press).

—— (1995), *Bad Women: Regulating Sexuality in Early American Cinema* (Minneapolis: University of Minnesota Press).

Studlar, Gaylyn (1996), *This Mad Masquerade: Stardom and Masculinity in the Jazz Age* (New York: Columbia University Press).

Thompson, Kristin, and **David Bordwell** (1983), 'Linearity, Materialism and the Study of Early American Cinema', *Wide Angle*, 5/3: 4–15.

Waller, Gregory (1995), *Main Street Amusements: Movies and Commercial Entertainment in a Southern City* (Washington: Smithsonian Press).

2

History and cinema technology

Duncan Petrie

The cinema is predicated on machines. Indeed in the early days of the fledgling medium the audience was attracted by the technology rather than the actual material being exhibited. As Stephen Heath notes, 'what is promoted and sold is the experience of the machine, the "apparatus". The Grand Café programme is headed with the announcement of "Le Cinématographe" and is continued with its description . . . only after that description is there mention of the titles of the films to be shown . . . relegated to the bottom of the programme sheet' (Heath 1980: 1).

Raymond Williams makes a useful distinction between two categories frequently treated as interchangeable in discussions of cinema technology. He defines *technical invention* as 'a specific device, developed from practical experience or scientific knowledge and their interaction'. These include pre-cinema devices associated with the development of still photography, and others concerned with the display of moving images including magic lanterns, zoetropes, and other optical entertainments. Such inventions are subsequently 'selected, improved and developed into a *systematic technology* of "film" or "cinema" ' (Williams 1983: 12–13). This implies that technology is necessarily directed towards particular goals or uses. Indeed, the interest most film scholars have in technology is very much in how it relates to aesthetic practice. Their task, therefore, is not only to describe and identify particular inventions, technolo

gies, and techniques, but to account for them within a dynamic perspective grasping the processes of development and change.

> **Technology is necessarily directed towards particular goals or uses. Indeed, the interest most film scholars have in technology is very much in how it relates to aesthetic practice. Their task, therefore, is not only to describe and identify particular inventions, technologies, and techniques, but to account for them within a dynamic perspective grasping the processes of development and change.**

Idealist technological history

Since the formative years of film theory, many discussions of technology have been underpinned by an idealist, evolutionary perspective, characterized by a romantic conception of the autonomous individual subject and a teleological view of historical process. Robert Allen and Douglas Gomery (1985) have identi fied two strands of such evolutionary history. The 'great man' theory is grounded upon an assumption of the autonomous agency of human subjects, regarding technological development as dependent upon the activities of a handful of individual inventors and pioneers. This theoretical perspective underpins such pioneering works of film history as Gordon Hendricks's painstaking investigations (1961, 1964, 1966) into the origins of the cinema in America and John Barnes's similar endeavours (1976, 1983, 1988, 1992) in relation to Britain.

A second evolutionary approach shifts the focus from the creative individual to the technology and its relationship to aesthetic consequences. Raymond Williams describes this approach as involving 'technological determinism': 'new technologies are discovered by an essentially internal process of research and development, which then sets the conditions for social change and progress. The effects of the technologies, whether direct or indirect, foreseen or unforeseen, are, as it were, the rest of history' (Williams 1974: 13).

Such an approach informs the work of the technological historian Raymond Fielding, for whom each technological advance contains within it the seeds of subsequent aesthetic uses by filmmakers. Technology sets the parameters and determines the space within which innovative techniques can occur: 'Just as the painter's art has changed with the introduction of different media and processes, just as the forms of symphonic music have developed with the appearance of new kinds of instruments, so has the elaboration and refinement of film style followed from the introduction of more sophisticated machinery' (Fielding 1967).

But however detailed and compelling as narrative, the shortcomings of such approaches lie in their inability to account adequately for why the cinema developed at the times, in the places, and in the forms it did; and why certain technologies and techniques were adopted and others rejected in the emergence of the new medium. For example, technological determinism cannot explain why the same basic film technology was utilized for widely divergent kinds of filmmaking in the early days of cinema, yet by the mid-1910s the narrative feature film had emerged as the dominant form of filmmaking practice.

The most influential analysis of the development of the cinema within idealist film theory may be found in the seminal writing of André Bazin. More theoretical than empirical in his project, Bazin locates what he terms 'the myth of total cinema' in the minds of the

individuals who invented the medium: 'In their imaginations they saw the cinema as a total and complete representation of reality; they saw in a trice the reconstruction of a perfect illusion of the outside world in sound, colour and relief' (Bazin 1967: 20). The evolution of cinema is viewed as moving towards an ever-increasing verisimilitude, a re-creation of the world in its own image, with each subsequent innovation—from still images, to movement, to sound, to colour—marking a more advanced stage in the process. (This was subsequently extended by Charles Barr (1963) to the introduction of widescreen cinema. Processes like CinemaScope open out the frame, presenting a greater impression of depth which, following Bazin's own discussion of deep focus, preserved the essential ambiguity of the real within the image.) This also gives rise to a history based on 'firsts' or 'founding moments', signposted by such 'innovations' as the first 'projected' film programmes by the Lumière brothers in Paris in 1895; the first 'talkie', *The Jazz Singer*, in 1927 and the first three-colour Technicolor feature, *Becky Sharp*, in 1935; and the first CinemaScope film, *The Robe*, in 1953. Others might include the first use of Dolby stereo sound, *Star Wars*, in 1977, and the first animated feature to be entirely generated by computer, *Toy Story*, in 1996.

The first steps away from evolutionary models of technological development began to emerge in the 1970s. In his examination of the development of deep-focus cinematography in Hollywood in the 1940s, Patrick Ogle (1972) challenges conventional understandings which associated this with innovative 'auteurs' such as Orson Welles and William Wyler. Drawing upon primary source material, including technical journals such as *American Cinematographer*, he identifies a historical lag between the technical possibility of deep focus and its adoption, a gap accounted for by the resistance of Hollywood cinematographers to deviations from the established visual style of soft tonal qualities and shallow depth of field. Unfortunately Ogle does not offer any explanation as to why Hollywood cameramen were so conservative. Moreover, his assertion of the centrality of cinematographer Gregg Toland in the exploitation of the technical possibility of deep focus in films like *The Grapes of Wrath* (1940), *The Long Voyage Home* (1940), and *Citizen Kane* (1941) resurrects an idealist perspective by merely shifting the focus from the director to the technician as creative individual.

Barry Salt's copious writings on the history of film

technology and style (1976, 1983/1992) represent a similar move away from overtly linear models. Salt constructs an avowedly empirical analysis based on dealied examination of primary sources coupled with close viewings of numerous films. Highly critical of deterministic theories, he regards technology as at best a loose pressure on film practice and cites instances where technology can be seen to respond to aesthetic demands such as the trend towards longer shots in 1940s Hollywood, which led to the development of more sophisticated camera dollies. Despite an impressive grasp of historical detail, Salt's unashamed empiricism, a method he terms 'scientific realism', set him increasingly at odds with the major currents of contemporary theoretical development.

Anti-idealist technological history

Under the influence of the twin discourses of Marxism and psychoanalysis, film theory in the 1970s began to shift the focus away from idealistic perspectives towards more materially based analyses concerned with the operation of the various factors underpinning and determining the nature of the cinematic process, including the question of technology. The most obvious 'external' factor, given the highly capitalistic nature of the film business, was the role of economics. Douglas Gomery's (1976) analysis of the coming of sound in Hollywood utilizes neo-classical economic theory to explain technological change via a three-stage model incorporating invention, innovation, and diffusion. The first is dominated by the research and development activities of two corporate giants, the American Telephone and Telegraph Corporation (AT&T) and the Radio Corporation of America (RCA) aimed at developing telephone and radio technology respectively. One side-effect common to both was the perfected capability for sound recording and reproduction. The innovation stage was subsequently driven by the activities of two Hollywood film companies, Warner Bros. and Fox, who adapted the basic technology for practical use in the production and exhibition of sound films. The third and final phase involved the diffusion of such new techniques throughout the industry, with all the other studios embracing sound. At each stage, the overriding concern of the companies concerned was the maximization of long-term profitability.

Edward Buscombe (1977) comments that Gomery's model is very persuasive, but since it does not explain the need for a particular innovation, it suggests the operation of ideological rather than economic concerns. Buscombe proceeds to apply this theory to the development of colour in cinema. According to 'the myth of total cinema', colour would appear to signify a greater realism than black and white, the ideology of realism 'has never been a question of what *is* real but of what is *accepted* as real' (Buscombe 1977: 24). When colour was first introduced it tended to be restricted to 'unreal' genres such as cartoons, musicals, fantasies, and comedies, while the more 'realistic' genres—crime films, war films, documentaries, and newsreels—were predominantly in black and white. The ideological appeal of colour, it seems, was both as a signifier of spectacle and as a self-conscious celebration of the technology itself. Of course, this cannot be divorced from economic considerations, since the association of colour with particular genres aided Hollywood's need for product differentiation.

The role of ideology was given centre-stage even more in subsequent materialist theory. Stephen Heath criticizes historians like Barry Salt for their belief in technology as a self-autonomous instance:

Cinema does not exist in the technological and then become this or that practice in the social; its history is a history of the technological and the social together, a history in which the determinations are not simple but multiple, interacting, in which the ideological is there from the start. (Heath 1980: 6)

In a similar vein, the influential French Marxist critic Jean-Louis Comolli criticizes perspectives which consider technology to be ideologically neutral by attempting to show how the cinematic apparatus is necessarily rooted in ideology—'the machine is always social before it is technical'. Comolli writes:

the historical variation of cinematic techniques, their appearance–disappearance, their phases of convergence, their periods of dominance and decline, seem to me to depend not on a rational-linear order of technological perfectibility nor an autonomous instance of scientific 'progress' but much rather on the offsettings, adjustments, arrangements carried out by a social configuration in order to represent itself, identify itself, and itself produce itself in its representation. (Comolli 1980: 121)

This particular mode of representation, which presents itself as 'natural' rather than ideologically determined, previously underpinned Renaissance painting and photography and is rooted in the invention of artificial perspective, which centres space around the eye. This in turn designates the perceiving subject as the origin of meaning, and hence transcendentally separated from the material world—the autonomous subject of idealist theory. Comolli may share with Bazin a fascination with the relationship between representation and the real, but he regards 'realism' as ideologically constructed, suppressing difference and promoting identity in the interests of the dominant bourgeois order.

While materialist arguments have proved persuasive, Comolli's conception of ideology has been criticized as somewhat monolithic, tending towards the abstract and the ahistorical. John Belton suggests that he 'reduces the complex interaction of various (often conflicting) ideologies to the uniform operation of a single unchanging ideology' (Belton 1988), while James Spellberg notes: 'Dominant ideology is dominant, not total, and the technology as well as the signifying practice of the cinema is created in the field of ideology and is subject to the stresses and contradictions of that field' (Spellerberg 1977: 296).

The materialist idea of technological development has informed less abstract commentaries such as those of Peter Wollen (1980) and Steve Neale (1985). Wollen stresses both the heterogeneity of technology—citing various examples of the interplay of developments in the fields of mechanics, optics, chemistry, and electronics—and the uneven process of technological development, in which innovations in one area can produce conservatism or even retreat in another. The introduction of sound, for example, created obstacles in the fields of lighting and film stocks, enforced a shift from location to studio filming, altered shooting techniques, and led to the automation of the studio laboratory process.

John Belton similarly applies a materialist method to his historical analysis of the introduction of Cinema-Scope. He poses the question why, given the invention of the anamorphic Hypergonar lens in the late 1920s, it was a further twenty-five years before the introduction of CinemaScope as a viable widescreen process. His answer is that while technological and ideological determinants existed in the 1920s to support the introduction of anamorphic cinema, there was no economic interest from either lens manufacturers or the studios. By the 1950s all the economic factors had been reversed, with a declining film industry desperate to find ways to reinvest the cinema with new appeal as a spectacle distinct from the experience offered by television. Belton is at pains to note that this is not an instance of a delayed take-up of an already existing

> **Wollen stresses both the heterogeneity of technology—citing various examples of the interplay of developments in the fields of mechanics, optics, chemistry, and electronics—and the uneven process of technological development, in which innovations in one area can produce conservatism or even retreat in another. The introduction of sound, for example, created obstacles in the fields of lighting and film stocks, enforced a shift from location to studio filming, altered shooting techniques, and led to the automation of the studio laboratory process.**

technology, as empiricist historians would have it. Rather, recent technical developments in the fields of optics, stock design, colour, sound, and screen fabric were crucial to the emergence of anamorphic cinema in the 1950s. Ideology also played a part in how the experience of CinemaScope was differentiated not only from conventional cinema but also from other new formats such as 3-D and Cinerama.

Equally rich in historical data is the consideration by David Bordwell and Janet Staiger of the role of technology within Hollywood cinema, which they regard as 'a distinct mode of film practice with its own cinematic style and industrial conditions of existence' (Bordwell and Staiger 1985, p. xiii). Technological development can be explained by the operation of one or more of three basic factors—production efficiency (economy), product differentiation (novelty), and adherence to standards of quality (aesthetic norms)—with the classical Hollywood stylistic paradigm being constructed in relation to specific ideologies governing narrative, realism, and spectacle. These factors can either complement or collide with one another: for example, change to effect product differentiation may be costly at least in the short run. Differentiation also takes place within defined limits of stylistic standardization.

Within their analysis, Bordwell and Staiger (1985) identify certain historical agents of change, including institutions such as the manufacturing and supply firms Eastman Kodak, Western Electric, and Bell & Howell

The delights of Technicolor CinemaScope as advertised in publicity for *The Ten Commandments* (1956)

and professional associations like the American Society of Cinematographers, the Society of Motion Picture Engineers, and the Academy of Motion Picture Arts and Sciences. Cumulatively these served to transfer the industry's economic structures and aesthetic precepts to the spheres of technological innovation and film form, ensuring that the latter developed within the constraints set by the former. For example, the professional associations played a major role in regulating technical change and linking the production sector with the service industries.

Multideterminate approaches also opened up interesting questions of the diffusion of technological development outside Hollywood. Gomery (1980) extends his discussion of the economics of sound technology to the complex process of Europe's conversion to sound via a consideration of the economic relations between the advanced capitalist countries at the time. Against the historical backdrop of post-Second World War multinational expansion, particularly in the new technological industries such as automobiles and motion pictures, Gomery proceeds to chart a process of economic struggle between the American studios and equipment manufacturers and their European competitors, the latter determined to resist the seemingly overwhelming tide of Hollywood imperialism.

This struggle resulted in the formation of a loose cartel between Western Electric, RCA, and the mainly German-backed conglomerate Tobis-Klanffilm to divide up the world for patent rights. While this cartel was only partially successful, it provides a tangible example of the central role of capitalist expansion and competition in the process of technological diffusion.

Dudley Andrew (1980) examines a similar process of struggle with regard to the introduction of colour in France after the Second World War. His intentions are to demonstrate the role played by self-conscious (as opposed to invisible) ideological discourse in relation to technological and economic determinants in a particular historical context characterized by suspicion and mistrust. He describes the relevant material circumstances of the time: the hegemony of Technicolor, the (limited) potential of new processes derived from the German Agfacolor system, and the hostility towards America felt in France—particularly in the wake of the Blum–Byrnes accord, which limited the extent to which the French cinema industry could resist Hollywood domination, effectively restricting a regeneration of indigenous production. As it transpired, colour was barely used in French production until the mid-1950s owing to a combination of factors including the influence of contradictory ideological discourses. On the one hand, there was an appreciation of the artistic potential of Technicolor, displayed in some British films like *Henry V* (1944). But, because of certain technical and economic factors, Technicolor could not meet the increase in demand, and after the failure of indigenous experiments the French industry adopted the Belgian Geva system. At the same time the strategy adopted by the French industry to resist American domination was the pursuit of a 'quality' aesthetic which, as Andrew puts it, 'would unquestionably have preferred the formal and saturated look of Technicolor to the more casual and documentary look of Agfa processes' (1980: 73). He concludes that these contradictory discourses of a desire and loathing for American technology served to paralyse the development of colour in France until 1953, when, unsettled by rumours of a new danger posed to their industry by television, French producers began to put up the extra finance necessary for colour production.

Perhaps one of the major differences between recent historical accounts and earlier writing is a certain degree of self-reflexivity with regard to theoretical approaches and methods, including the processes of selection and interpretation of data. As Edward Branigan notes, 'categories arranged in a scheme are not just a way of looking at the world but in some sense determine what we see' (Branigan 1979: 16). And, as John Belton argues, materialist histories are as prone to this as idealist histories: 'idealist methodologies will reveal only the essential linearity of history, while materialist methodology will only reveal the essential contradictions and discontinuities that underlie historical change' (Belton 1988: 23). While this contingency might seem to negate any claims to 'truth', it does underline the importance of clarity of purpose and method, of defining terms and categories, and of making the implicit explicit. It has also guided scholars back towards the treasure-trove of historical data, refining our understanding of the complexities of the technologies of cinema and their use in concrete, historically specific contexts.

BIBLIOGRAPHY

Allen, Robert, and Douglas Gomery (1985), *Film History: Theory and Practice* (New York: Kopf).

Andrew, Dudley (1980), 'The Post War Struggle for Colour', in Teresa de Lauretis and Stephen Heath (eds.), *The Cinematic Apparatus* (London: Macmillan).

Barnes, John (1976), *The Beginnings of the Cinema in England* (Newton Abbot: David & Charles).

—— (1983), *The Rise of the Cinema in Great Britain* (London: Bishopsgate).

—— (1988), *Pioneers of the British Film* (London: Bishopsgate).

—— (1992), *Filming the Boer War* (London: Bishopsgate).

Barr, Charles (1963/1974), 'CinemaScope: Before and After', in Gerald Mast and Marshall Cohen (eds.), *Film Theory and Criticism* (Oxford: Oxford University Press).

Bazin, André (1967), 'The Myth of Total Cinema', in *What is Cinema?*, 2 vols., ed. and trans. Hugh Gray, i (Berkeley and Los Angeles: University of California Press).

Belton, John (1988), 'CinemaScope and Historical Methodology', *Cinema Journal*, 28/1: 22–44.

Bordwell, David, and Janet Staiger (1985), 'Technology, Style and Mode of Production', in David Bordwell, Janet Staiger, and Kristin Thompson, *The Classical Hollywood Cinema: Film Style and Mode of Production to 1960* (London: Routledge).

Branigan, Edward (1979), 'Colour and Cinema: Problems in the Writing of History', *Film Reader*, 4: 16–34.

Buscombe, Edward (1977), 'Sound and Colour', *Jump Cut*, 17: 23–5.

Comolli, Jean-Louis (1980), 'Machines of the Visible', in Teresa de Lauretis and Stephen Heath (eds.), *The Cinematic Apparatus* (London: Macmillan).

Fielding, Raymond (ed.) (1967), Introduction, in *A Technological History of Motion Pictures and Television* (Berkeley and Los Angeles: University of California Press).

Gomery, Douglas (1976), 'The Coming of the Talkies: Invention, Innovation Diffusion', in Tino Balio (ed.), *The American Film Industry* (Madison: University of Wisconsin Press).

—— (1980/1985), 'Economic Struggle and Hollywood Imperialism: Europe Converts to Sound', in Elisabeth Weis and John Belton (eds.), *Film Sound: Theory and Practice* (New York: Columbia University Press).

Heath, Stephen (1980), 'The Cinematic Apparatus: Technology as Historical and Cultural Form', in Teresa de Lauretis and Stephen Heath (eds.), *The Cinematic Apparatus* (London: Macmillan).

Hendricks, Gordon (1961), *The Edison Motion Picture Myth* (Berkeley and Los Angeles: University of California Press).

—— (1964), *The Beginnings of the Biograph* (New York: privately published).

—— (1966), *The Kinetoscope* (New York: privately published).

*Neale, Steve (1985), *Cinema and Technology: Image, Sound, Colour* (London: British Film Institute).

Ogle, Patrick (1972), 'Technological and Aesthetic Influences on the Development of Deep Focus Cinematography in the United States', *Screen*, 13/1: 45–72.

Salt, Barry (1976), 'The Evolution of Sound Technology', *Film Quarterly*, 30/1: (Fall), 19–32.

—— (1983/1992), *Film Style and Technology: History and Analysis* (London: Starword).

Spellerberg, James (1977), 'Technology and Ideology in the Cinema', *Quarterly Review of Film Studies*, 2/3: 288–301.

Williams, Raymond (1974), Television: Technology and Cultural Form (London: Fontana).

—— (1983), 'British Film History: New Perspectives', in James Curran and Vincent Porter (eds.), *British Cinema History* (London: Weidenfeld & Nicolson).

Wollen, Peter (1980), 'Cinema and Technology: A Historical Overview', in Teresa de Lauretis and Stephen Heath (eds.), *The Cinematic Apparatus* (London: Macmillan).

3

Hollywood as industry

Douglas Gomery

While the study of film may involve a concern with aesthetics, technology, ideology, and audience, it is the study of film as an industry which remains central and is basic to all other cinema studies. For in most of the world cinema is first of all organized as an industry, that is as a collection of businesses seeking profits through film production, film distribution, and the presentation of movies to audiences (whether in theatres, on television, through video, or by some new method). So, although we may wish that cinema was not a business, we none the less need to study the industrial character of film in order to understand fully the impact and influence of motion pictures.

A central question which most scholars characteristically face is: how does the study of the organization and control of the film industry help to explain the aesthetics, ideology, and reception of film? There is no simple answer to this, but I side with the argument that, while the film industry does not straightforwardly determine the aesthetic and ideological characteristics of film, it none the less sets the constraints within which aesthetics, ideology, and reception must operate. However, the theory linking the study of film as an industry to concerns of aesthetics, ideology, and reception remains to be worked out and will constitute one of the central tasks for film historians.

The study of the film industry itself is complex, but it is simplified by one key historical fact. Since the 1920s—that is, for most of the history of cinema—

one industry, that based in the United States and known as Hollywood, has dominated the world. Thus the locus of study for the history of the film industry properly begins with Hollywood, not because the cinema industry based in the United States has produced the best films (by some criteria) but because it has forced all other national cinemas to begin by dealing with the power of Hollywood as an industry.

First principles

Hollywood is first of all an industry, a collection of profit-maximizing corporations operated from studio headquarters in the United States, and so, like all film industries, it consists of three fundamental components: production, distribution, and presentation of feature films.

Production. Films must be created. Since the early 1910s this has been done in studios in and around Los Angeles in an area generically known as Hollywood. However, it encompasses more than that city section: the Universal Studios, for example, are in Universal City, Warner Bros. in Burbank.

Distribution. Once films are made, Hollywood companies then peddle their films around the world. World-wide distribution has long been the basis of Hollywood's power and no other film industry has been as far-reaching for as long as Hollywood.

Presentation. Finally, movies are watched in theatres and cinemas, and on television at home. Prior to the television age, films were shown principally in theatres which were sometimes vast 6,000-seat movie palaces. Since the 1960s most people see most movies at home on television.

The key question then is: how did a collection of major studio corporations (Hollywood) come to dominate the production, distribution, and exhibition of movies and continue to maintain its control through the coming of sound, the innovation of colour and widescreen images, and the diffusion of television and home video? I shall explore the answers to this question by examining the history of Hollywood as an industry, identifying four key periods:

- the rise of Hollywood, from the late nineteenth century to the coming of sound;
- the studio era of the 1930s and 1940s;
- the television broadcasting age beginning with the rise of television in the 1950s;
- and the era inaugurated by the coming of the feature film blockbuster in the mid-1970s.

The key question then is: how did a collection of major studio corporations (Hollywood) come to dominate the production, distribution, and exhibition of movies and continue to maintain its control through the coming of sound, the innovation of colour and widescreen images, and the diffusion of television and home video?

The rise of Hollywood

The motion picture industry in the United States grew from its origins during the final years of the nineteenth century to consolidation into an oligopoly (that is, control by a few corporations) in 1930, amidst the coming of sound. This initial period of Hollywood history is tainted by an overlay of sadness in that Hollywood has been seen as preventing what might have been—a group of progressive filmmakers serving a working-class audience—adopting instead an overt

profit-maximizing structure (Wasko 1982; Guback 1969). Nevertheless, we need to continue to look at how the remarkable institution of Hollywood came to be.

In the beginning, cinema was just another technology. Through the decade of the 1890s into the early days of the twentieth century inventors worked with the first filmmakers and exhibitors to persuade a sceptical public to embrace the movie show. The study of the introduction of this new technology focuses on a set of businesses formed to exploit the new knowledge in the United States and around the world.

The early inventors and entrepreneurs were not operating in a vacuum, seeking to create some ideal new enterprise, but rather sought to sell their discoveries through the existing entertainment industries. Robert Allen (1985) shows that the vaudeville (or variety) hall provided the first business outlet. However, as Allen (1982) demonstrates for Manhattan, and I have shown for other cities in the United States (Gomery 1992), this model of exhibition soon gave way to the nickelodeons—the thousands of converted store-front theatres—that from 1905 to 1910 presented hour-long all-movie shows; and it was the nickelodeon that formed the basis of the film industry that within a decade became Hollywood.

However, more than a locus for presenting was needed; a system of producing films also had to develop, and Hollywood established a flexible system for regularly producing and distributing feature-length motion pictures, along with short subjects and newsreels (Staiger 1982). It is this process of learning to make movies that would sell on a year-round basis that constitutes part of the analysis of David Bordwell, Janet Staiger, and Kristin Thompson in their highly influential book *The Classical Hollywood Cinema* (1985).

Finally, Hollywood came to stand for world distribution and presentation. The diffusion of the Hollywood cinema throughout the world was successfully completed by the early 1920s, but the achievement of world hegemony was not straightforward. Robert Anderson (1985) shows that a monopoly based on patents was formed by Thomas Edison and others, but then quickly failed, and it was to take flexibility of a different kind to gain long-term control.

This initial period ended with a sudden technical change—the coming of sound. The popularity of the talkies enabled new companies such as Warner Bros. to rise to power and join the small list of major studios including Paramount, Loew's, and other powerful corporations of the silent era, which not only retained but increased their power (Gomery 1980, 1982a).

The studio system

The coming of sound consolidated Hollywood's control over the world market and moved the United States into the studio era in which filmmaking, distribution, and exhibition were dominated by five theatre corporations: Paramount, Loew's (parent company to the more famous MGM), Fox Film (later Twentieth Century-Fox), Warner Bros., and RKO. They ruled Hollywood during the 1930s and 1940s and operated around the world as fully integrated business enterprises.

Historians have struggled to deal with the studio system. We have a number of 'insider' studio histories best exemplified by Bosley Crowther's (1957) authorized history of Loew's Inc. and MGM. Although this is rich in data, it is almost wholly lacking in perspective and method; Lillian Ross's (1952) history of the same studio is far more critical. In recent years a few histories of individual studios and powerful producers have appeared, such as Tino Balio's (1976) history of United Artists and Mathew Bernstein's (1994) study of Walter Wanger. But fine as these two studies are, United Artists and Walter Wanger hardly stood at the centre of the Hollywood industry. In-depth studies of the operations of key studios such as Twentieth Century-Fox and Paramount remain to be done. Gomery (1986) is a general study covering the studio system as a whole, including its major participants. Some of the detail it omits is provided by Kathy Klaprat's (1985) analysis of a single star, Bette Davis, and how she struggled to work within the studio system, and by Ida Jeter's (1986) examination of the attempts to unionize workers with less fame and fortune. More basic building-block studies such as these two are needed.

However, it was theatre ownership rather than studio production which defined the status of Hollywood in this era. By controlling picture palaces in all of the downtown areas across the United States, the major studios took three-quarters of the average box-office receipts. Only after their own theatres had soaked up as much as possible of the initial wave of box-office grosses through first and exclusive runs did the 'Big Five' permit smaller, independent theatres to scramble for the remaining bookings, sometimes months, or even years, after a film's première.

Universal Pictures, Columbia Pictures, and United Artists constituted the studio era's 'Little Three' and led the scramble for these left-over film revenues. While always considered part of the Hollywood studio colossus, these three corporations could never match the economic muscle of the Big Five because they did not own the top (exclusively first-run) theatres. Even less powerful were Monogram and Republic Pictures, the inhabitants of 'Poverty Row', which created low-budget fare for marginal theatres. This type of production was partly fuelled by changes in exhibition practice brought on by the Great Depression. Borrowing thechniques from the dime stores, marginal neighbourhood movie houses began regularly to offer two films for the price of one—the double feature—and thus stimulated the demand for the B movie.

The television broadcasting age

The decline of the studio era was the result of three main factors: the Paramount antitrust decrees, the social transformation of the United States with suburbanization and the baby boom, and the emergence of a moving-image rival, television. In 1948, as a consequence of what became known as the Paramount case, the federal government of the United States forced the Big Five to sell their movie palaces, and suddenly Hollywood lost direct control of and access to the movie market. This legal antitrust case against the Big Five and the Little Three had its origins in the second administration of President Franklin D. Roosevelt (1936–40) which, as Conant (1960, 1985) has shown, turned to enforcement of existing antitrust laws to help bring the nation out of the Great Depression.

This action against the major studios also occurred at a time when cinema audiences were falling. Weekly attendance in movie theatres in the United States peaked in 1946 and then began to drop, so that by the early 1960s it was half of what it had been in the glory days of the Second World War. The causes of this decline have been much debated and television is conventionally identified as the central villain. The common argument is this: once television programming commenced in the United States after the Second World War, movie fans stayed at home, attracted by 'free' (i.e. funded by advertising) television enter-

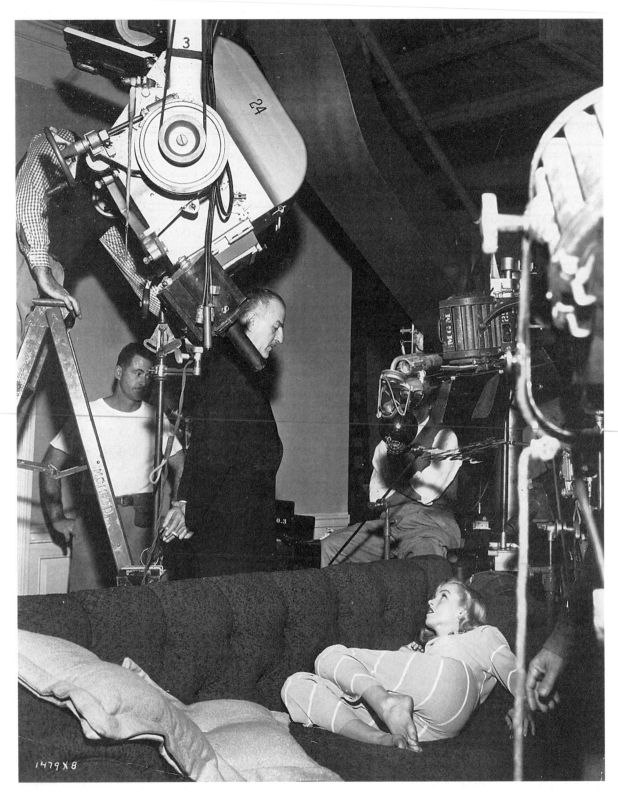

Struggles within the studio system—Marilyn Monroe and Louis Calhern rehearse *The Asphalt Jungle* (1950)

tainment. Going out to the movies suddenly became a relatively expensive night out, requiring a long journey downtown. Television entertainment was so much cheaper that millions of citizens of the United States simply stayed at home.

However, this 'analysis of substitution' ignores that, in most parts of the United States, television signals did not become available until long after the decline in moviegoing had commenced (see Gomery 1992). During the late 1940s and early 1950s only one-third of the nation had sets, but it was precisely then that millions stopped going to the movies. After the Second World War, formerly loyal film fans in the United States began to look for other things to do: starting families, finding nicer homes in the suburbs, buying cars, refrigerators, or the elusive pair of nylons not available during the war. It was therefore suburbanization and the baby boom (and the costs to a family involved) that were probably most responsible for the initial decline in movie attendance in the United States.

During the 1950s and 1960s the film industry adjusted to these new circumstances, first with auto theatres (drive-ins) and then with cinemas in shopping-malls, the long-term solution. In this completely new network of venues Hollywood also differentiated its product from black-and-white television with the development of widescreen and colour images. These and the introduction of Panavision lenses and Eastman Color film stock ought to be judged as important in their day as the coming of sound had been a generation earlier.

The arrival of television transformed Hollywood in expected and unexpected ways. Ever since the 1950s, when citizens of the United States stuffed their homes with television sets, Hollywood has been predicted to lose its power. This, however, has not been the case as the industry has adapted to, and taken advantage of, its changed circumstances. There are too few studies of this era of change. Concerning the corporate level there is Tino Balio's (1987) history of United Artists in the television age, from 1952 to the late 1970s. This company, Balio argues, demonstrated the importance of independent production for future Hollywood filmmaking; but unlike its rivals of the 1950s, the pioneering United Artists did not benefit from its innovations and by the 1980s had been reduced to a minor player in Hollywood.

Balio and others argue that these moves towards independent filmmaking represented a new mode of Hollywood production. Gone were the studios as fac-

tories turning out regular product for their theatre chains. Instead, independent producers put together packages of stars, a story, and production values which they turned into feature films that were distributed by a studio. In this formulation, the studio boss is seen to lose his former power, while that of the director as auteur is seen to increase.

This, however, was not the case. Independent production simply provided the studios with a more flexible, less costly way to fill their quotas of releases. No production was made without the green light from a studio head, whether the director was an auteur or a hired hand from a talent agency. Packagers came and went, but the studios remained all-powerful. Without studio approval, no blockbuster was made.

And while Hollywood may have used the blockbuster to distinguish the cinematic experience from that of television, the film industry also made its peace with broadcast television. This began with the movie made for television and then expanded into the mini-series and novel adapted for television. While these low-budget made-for-television dramas have often been attacked by critics, they are really the successors to Hollywood's B movies of yesteryear and have helped to boost ratings—which is why mini-series such as *Hollywood Wives* (1985) and *The Thorn Birds* (1983) have arrived like clockwork at key ratings-measurement periods.

Today and into the future

By the mid-1970s Hollywood as an industry had adjusted to a new world of flexible film production and the new suburban audiences captured by television. However, as the work of Mayer (1978), Gomery (1993), and Vogel (1995) suggests, a new era for Hollywood as a film industry began in the mid-1970s following the innovation of the blockbuster, exemplified by such films as *Jaws* (1975) and *Star Wars* (1977). Despite the heralded 'end' of moviegoing, theatrical attendance in the United States has remained steady at 1 billion admissions per year. Millions of fans still journey in the summer high season to nearby multiplex cinemas in the shopping-mall to relish Hollywood blockbusters. Indeed Hollywood corporate stock market prices rise and fall with the weekend figures for such films.

Hollywood as an industry has also continued to redefine itself, principally by adding to its technological bag of tricks. Computers in particular have enabled filmmakers to craft special effects to live action and animation in a way which was simply not possible before, and major hits such as *Who Framed Roger Rabbit?* (1988) and *Jurassic Park* (1993) have achieved near-miraculous interaction of live and animated figures. Yet, despite these technological innovations, the process of moviemaking has stayed remarkably constant because the underlying ideology of narrative production has remained unchanged.

This position differs from that of Janet Staiger, who has argued for various periods of production in Hollywood and their key differences (Staiger 1982). Staiger's meticulous work identifies a mutation from independent production to a package system. Yet, looking over the history of production in Hollywood, I find a consistent pattern—with studios always selecting films for production and groups under studio control making them—rather than some fundamental set of transformations. My view, however, is a minority one, and the debate about understanding the history of modes of production in Hollywood is destined to continue.

For me, it is the new ways and places to watch movies—especially cable, satellite, and video—that have defined the era of contemporary cinema. In the mid-1970s Time Inc. changed the world of cable television in the United States for ever with its Home Box Office (HBO), which, for a monthly fee of about $10, offered cable television subscribers recent Hollywood motion pictures—uncut, uninterrupted by commercials, and not sanitized to please network censors. For the first time in the television age a way had been found to make viewers pay for what they watched in their living-rooms. As 'pay television', HBO also lured back the older movie fan who did not want to go out to a theatre but loved watching second-run films on television at home.

But cable television offers the film fan much more than HBO. The entrepreneur Ted Turner took a typical independent television station, complete with its sports, reruns, and old movies, and beamed it to all America via the satellite to create his famous Superstation with half of the schedule filled with old films. By 1995 there were also American Movie Classics and a number of other repertory cable television cinemas in the home, where old Hollywood films, the best and worst, run all day long.

The post-1975 video age achieved its greatest change in the mid-1980s with the home video revolu-

tion. Sony introduced its Betamax half-inch home video cassette recorder in 1975. Originally priced at more tha $1,000, the cost of the Beta machines and their newer rivals from VHS dropped to just over $300 by the mid-1980s. An enthusiastic American public (plus millions in other nations) snapped up so many machines that by 1989 fully two-thirds of American households were equipped to tape off the air or run pre-recorded tapes.

At first the Hollywood moguls loathed the new machine. Jack Valenti, President of the Motion Picture Association of America, declared that the VCR was a parasitical instrument robbing Hollywood's take at the box-office. But quickly enough, during the 1980s, Hollywood found a way to capitalize on the innovation. In 1986 the returns from ancillary video sidelines exceeded the take at the box-office in the United States. During the mid-1980s about 400 new pre-recorded cassettes were being released each month, 70 per cent of which were Hollywood feature films. In the 1990s came 'sell through', by which Hollywood studios, led by Disney with *Aladdin* (1992) and *The Lion King* (1994), sold tapes at prices between $10 and $20 directly to the public, bypassing rental altogether. As Hollywood moved towards the end of the twentieth century, it had fully absorbed the impact of the VCR and had begun to look forward to the next technological change.

This adaptation to the new delivery systems has been accompanied by a change of ownership of the major Hollywood corporations and their emergence as media conglomerates. This process of conglomeratization may be seen to have begun during the television age, as the example of the rise of the Disney operation shows (Gomery 1994). As the age of television began after the Second World War, Disney was a minor player in corporate Hollywood, and indeed nearly went out of business during the early 1950s. But the studio entered television production early on, pioneered theme parks, and later skilfully exploited cable television, home video, and merchandising. Disney became a major Hollywood operation and then a major producer of feature films. Since the mid-1980s this process of conglomeratization has intensified. The owners and operators of the Hollywood of the television era, led by Lew Wasserman at Universal, cashed in, while outsiders—recognizing the advent of a new industrial era characterized by video, multiplying cable television channels, and movies on demand—bought in.

This process began in 1985–6, when Rupert Murdoch took over Twentieth Century Fox (and dropped the hyphen). At the same moment Michael Eisner began to transform and rebuild the Walt Disney Corporation. At the end of the 1980s Japan entered the fray; Sony took over Columbia Pictures, and Matsushita acquired MCA. Time and Warner merged. Viacom took over Paramount, and in 1995 Seagrams bought MCA from Matsushita. As a result, the Hollywood industry today consists of but six multinational media conglomerates: Disney, Murdoch's Twentieth Century Fox, Seagram's Universal, Viacom's Paramount, Sony's Columbia, and Time Warner's Warner Bros.

A key feature of these conglomerates is their involvement in nearly all forms of mass media. Viacom's Paramount division, with its Simon & Schuster division leading the way, is one of the leading book publishers in the world. MCA, Warner, and Sony are all top makers and distributors of recorded music—in cassettes and compact discs and whatever new forms will come. Time Warner is the world's leader in magazines. Disney pioneered theme parks; MCA and Viacom's Paramount are key theme park operators as well. Fox, as part of Rupert Murdoch's News Inc. empire, is allied with leading newspapers around the world. And more media convergence is on the way. The Hollywood media conglomerates presently stand at the centre of the new world of video, computers, and interactive media. Within a decade our homes and workplaces will be wired with fibre optics and will make use of even more of Hollywood's products. As a result, the six media conglomerates are destined to become even more diversified and powerful.

Thus, a handful of companies formed more than a half century ago still have hegemony over the creation of the movies and the distribution of them throughout the world. Since the end of the Second World War the Hollywood major studios have survived the enforced selling of their theatre chains, the rise of network television, the advent of cable and pay television, the video cassette revolution, and the arrival of digitization. These companies may have new owners, but they show no signs of weakening—if anything, they are getting stronger. During the past decade, a number of enterprises have challenged the major studios only to lose millions of dollars and declare bankruptcy. The corporate shells of Orion and New World were always marginal at best; even the once-powerful United Artists is poised to go out of business.

A handful of companies formed more than a half century ago still have hegemony over the creation of the movies and the distribution of them throughout the world. Since the end of the Second World War the Hollywood major studios have survived the enforced selling of their theatre chains, the rise of network television, the advent of cable and pay television, the video cassette revolution, and the arrival of digitization. These companies may have new owners, but they show no signs of weakening—if anything, they are getting stronger.

Critical debates

As this survey suggests, historians continue to tackle the vexing problems of how best to understand the development of Hollywood as an industry. While historians need to work to find better accounts of changes in finance, ownership structure, corporate actions, modes of production, international distribution, and new technologies of presentation, they also need to challenge past 'certainties'. Three areas of debate may be seen to be of particular importance: the significance of the studio system, the explanation of the control of Hollywood, and the identification of the appropriate analytical focus for the study of 'Hollywood'.

The significance of the studio system

It is commonplace to identify the studio system of the 1930s and 1940s as the most important—and interesting—era for film industry study. At that time, it is believed, Hollywood filmmaking was somehow purer and uncompromised by that 'evil of all evils', television. Yet, while the studio era was important, it also represents only one of four fundamental eras in the history of Hollywood as industry.

We like the studio era because it had a defined beginning, middle, and end. The industry was logically organized, transformed only by intrusions from the outside. This studio era began with the invention of sound, which created a peak in attendance. This high point was followed by a decline in demand caused by the Great Depression. The studio era came to a close, transformed by the Paramount antitrust decrees, suburbanization, and the advent of television.

> **The six media conglomerates which dominate contemporary Hollywood now possess a power and cohesion against which the oligopoly of the Hollywood studios during the 1930s and 1940s simply pales in comparison.**

However, we have to be careful not to overestimate the typicality of this one epoch, or to exaggerate its importance. Indeed, in comparison with the contemporary industry, the operations of the studio era, as explained by Bordwell, Staiger, and Thomspon (1985), seem positively quaint. Moreover, the six media conglomerates which dominate contemporary Hollywood now possess a power and cohesion against which the oligopoly of the Hollywood studios during the 1930s and 1940s simply pales in comparison.

The explanation of the control of Hollywood

This second issue is concerned with the question of the control of Hollywood. Historians of Hollywood as industry such as Janet Wasko (1982, 1995) and her mentor Thomas Guback (1969) have argued that the Hollywood industry is controlled by financial institutions. Under this type of Marxist-influenced economics there is no reason to do any further analysis. For, as with all aspects of capitalism in the United States, the mass media industries are shaped by forces found in the investment banking community, commonly known as Wall Street.

This analysis of finance capitalism, as it is known, can be found in its purest form in the argument that Hollywood in the 1930s was controlled by J. P. Morgan and John D. Rockefeller, who, it is suggested, held the balance of power within the eight major studios and their affiliated theatre and distribution channels and thus controlled Hollywood as an indus-

try. In 1937 Klingender and Legg popularized the Morgan and Rockefeller hypothesis, and since then it has served as a corner-stone of the history of Hollywood as an industry.

New work suggests that the Morgan and Rockefeller hypothesis is misleading and that the Great Depression signalled the close, not the continuation, of the epoch of finance capitalism (Gomery 1982). Bankers helped Hollywood studios get started in the 1920s, but were jettisoned as major players with the coming of the studio era, when corporate hegemony replaced control by Wall Street. It is therefore corporations, rather than bankers, that hold the key to power and control in the US motion picture industry. To consider Wall Street as other than an investor since the 1930s is to focus on the wrong issue.

One can best appreciate the power of the corporations by pushing aside corporate propaganda about how tough a competitive environment these companies face and focus instead on how the major studios and their corporate owners co-operate. They have long done this through one of the least-appreciated institutions in Hollywood industry history—the Motion Picture Association of America.

Too often Hollywood historians tell us only about the Motion Picture Association of America as an agent of restraint, first through the Hays Code and today with movie ratings. But the Association is better understood as a co-operative agency, or trade association, set up to maintain corporate power. This has meant lobbying for favourable rules in its own market of the United States and the elimination of all regulations in foreign markets.

The Motion Picture Association of America was the agent that the major studios used to work for an open US market in negotiations required by the National Recovery Act in the 1930s and for an open Europe through the General Agreement on Tariffs and Trade (GATT) talks in the 1990s (Gomery 1982). In both cases—and most times in between—the Association has skilfully protected its corporate owners. Indeed, protected by the Association, the Hollywood industry has demonstrated remarkable continuity. The corporations that controlled Hollywood in 1930, as the Great Depression commenced, have remained as the top corporations to the end of the century—and will probably continue to do so. No new corporation as a major studio has been created, although many have tried. Hollywood as an industry is thus best analysed and understood as one of the most enduring and powerful corporate oligopolies in the history of world business.

The analytical focus of Hollywood

Although this seems a straightforward issue, it is not. Generally, the US film industry has been seen to have a simple analytical focus, the Detroit of the movie business—Hollywood. However, this argument reduces the film industry from three functions (production, distribution, and presentation) to one, filmmaking.

To take Hollywood as a single industrial centre therefore is misleading. The centre of power of the film industry based in Hollywood has, since the close of the First World War, rested with its control over international distribution. The Hollywood industry has long dominated bookings around the globe, and film box-office figures in the United States, even with blockbusters, are small in comparison with the total take from all sources around the world. By taking advantage of sizeable economies of scale, Hollywood corporations have been able to spread production over dozens of films and amortize the costs of multi-million-dollar production budgets and a global network of offices. This has also meant that their distribution costs per film have been far lower than competitors. Moreover, unlike in the United States, Hollywood companies have been able to work together abroad to ensure the distribution of their films. Through various alliances, individual foreign film companies have not simply faced a Warner Bros. or Twentieth Century Fox, but the two companies (sometimes three or more) working in tandem: if films are not booked from the major Hollywood companies, under their terms, the chance of any Hollywood blockbuster may be lost (Thompson 1985; Guback 1969).

> **To take Hollywood as a single industrial centre is misleading. The centre of power of the film industry based in Hollywood has, since the close of the First World War, rested with its control over international distribution. The Hollywood industry has long dominated bookings around the globe, and film box-office figures in the United States, even with blockbusters, are small in comparison with the total take from all sources around the world.**

However, if the core of Hollywood's power has been its international control of distribution, this has inspired proportionally little scholarly research. Distribution, sadly, is the least analysed part of the industry; there are no fascinating movies to consider, only dry, dull figures, both numerical and executive, defining and producing raw power. This is why Thompson and Guback ought to be praised for the path-breaking character of their work.

Conclusion: Hollywood and economic power

If the economic power of Hollywood derives from control of not just the production of feature films but their distribution and exhibition, it would still be wrong to exaggerate their economic might. For, despite the size of these vast empires, they generate revenue figures that pale beside a truly big business such as Exxon or General Motors. As poorly as IBM has done in the 1990s, it could absorb all of Hollywood and these mighty media conglomerates would remain but a small division.

This is, perhaps, not recognized because Hollywood's products have always taken up large portions of people's leisure time. People in the United States watch a lot of television and film, and once we pile up all those minutes, the time commitment comes to 250 billion hours per year. If we take the average hourly wage in the United States to be about $10, we come to a couple of trillion dollars of time invested. However, since this is not the actual amount paid for the pleasure, Hollywood as industry must ultimately be understood as a medium-sized, though highly profitable, and very influential, set of business enterprises.

BIBLIOGRAPHY

Allen, Robert C. (1982), 'Motion Picture Exhibition in Manhattan 1906–1912', in Gorham Kindem (ed.), *American Film Industry: A Case Studies Approach* (Carbondale: Southern Illinois University Press.

—— (1985), 'The Movies in Vaudeville: Historical Context of the Movies as Popular Entertainment', in Tino Balio (ed.), *The American Film Industry: An Anthology of Readings* (Madison: University of Wisconsin Press.

Anderson, Robert (1985), 'The Motion Picture Patents Company: A Reevaluation', in Tino Balio (ed.), *The*

American Film Industry: An Anthology of Readings (Madison: University of Wisconsin Press).

Balio, Tino (1976), *United Artists: The Company Built by the Stars* (Madison: University of Wisconsin Press).

—— (1987), *United Artists: The Company that Changed the Film Industry* (Madison: University of Wisconsin Press).

Bernstein, Mathew (1994), *Walter Wanger: Hollywood Independent* (Berkeley: University of California Press).

Bordwell, David, Janet Staiger, and Kristin Thompson (1985), *The Classical Hollywood Cinema* (New York: Columbia University Press).

Conant, Michael (1960), *Antitrust in the Motion Picture Industry* (Berkeley: University of California Press).

—— (1985), 'The Paramount Decrees Reconsidered', in Tino Balio (ed.), *The American Film Industry: An Anthology of Readings* (Madison: University of Wisconsin Press).

Crowther, Bosley (1957), *The Lion's Share: The Story of an Entertainment Empire* (New York: Dutton).

Gomery, Douglas (1980), 'Hollywood Converts to Sound: Chaos or Order?', in Evan William Cameron (ed.), *Sound and the Cinema* (Pleasantville, NY: Redgrave).

—— (1982a), 'Hollywood, the National Recovery Administration, and the Question of Monopoly Power', in Gorham Kindem (ed.), *American Film Industry: A Case Studies Approach* (Carbondale: Southern Illinois University Press).

—— (1982b), 'Warner Bros. Innovates Sound: A Business History', in Gerald Mast (ed.), *The Movies in our Midst* (Chicago: University of Chicago Press).

*—— (1986), *The Hollywood Studio System* (New York: St Martin's Press).

*—— (1992), *Shared Pleasures: A History of Motion Picture Presentation* (Madison: University of Wisconsin Press).

—— (1993), 'The Contemporary Movie Industry', in Alison Alexander, James Owers, and Rodney Carveth (eds.), *Media Economics* (Hillsdale, NJ: Lawrence Erlbaum Associates).

—— (1994), 'Disney's Business History: A Re-interpretation', in Eric Smoodin (ed.), *Disney Discourse: Producing the Magic Kingdom* (New York: Routledge).

Guback, Thomas H. (1969), *The International Film Industry* (Bloomington: Indiana University Press).

Jeter, Ida (1986), 'The Collapse of the Federated Motion Picture Crafts: A Case Class Collaboration', in Paul Kerr (ed.), *The Hollywood Film Industry: A Reader* (London: Routledge & Kegan Paul).

Klaprat, Cathy (1985), 'The Star as Market Strategy: Bette Davis in Another Light', in Tino Balio (ed.), *The American Film Industry: An Anthology of Readings* (Madison: University of Wisconsin Press).

Klingender, F. D., and Stuart Legg (1937), *Money behind the Screen* (London: Lawrence & Wishart).

Mayer, Michael (1978), *The Film Industries*, 2nd edn. (New York: Hastings House).

Ross, Lillian (1952), *Picture* (New York: Rinehart).

Staiger, Janet (1982), 'Dividing Labor for Production Control: Thomas Ince and the Rise of the Studio System', in Gorham Kindem (ed.), *American Film Industry: A Case Studies Approach* (Carbondale: Southern Illinois University Press).

Thompson, Kristin (1985), *Exporting Entertainment: America in the World Film Market 1907–1934* (London: British Film Institute).

Vogel, Harold L. (1995), *Entertainment Industry Economics* (New York: Cambridge Unviersity Press).

Wasko, Janet (1982), *Movies and Money* (Norwood, NJ: Ablex).

*—— (1995), *Hollywood in the Information Age* (Austin: University of Texas Press).

4

Early American film

Tom Gunning

Early cinema as a challenge to film history and theory

Since the early 1970s the study of early American cinema (from its origins until about 1916) has transformed conceptions of film history and of the relation between theory and history. When this research began in the late 1970s film history was a neglected field. Previous film historians had only limited access to films or other primary materials from the early period, and usually operated under implicit teleological assumptions, chronicling film's gradual technical and aesthetic maturation. Cinema's beginnings were viewed as immature babblings, followed by precocious discoveries and a growing mastery of editing and storytelling. Historians who began working in the 1970s questioned this teleological approach, benefiting from increased access to archival collections of films and other primary materials. These scholars abandoned the pejorative connotations of describing early film as 'primitive', maintaining that this era possessed a different approach to filmmaking than that of later cinema, so often considered the norm.

Under the dominance of apparatus theory, which marked film studies in the decade of the 1970s, film theorists tended to view history with suspicion. From an amalgam of Lacanian psychoanalysis and Althusserian critique of ideology, a systematic model of the way cinema operated had been fashioned that owed little to historical research. Film history as it had been practised was viewed as an empirical gathering of facts that could hardly shed light on the deep structures of the way the cinematic apparatus constructed its spectator as subject—a process, theorists claimed, which embodied ideologies endemic to Western thought at least since Plato. How could chronicling changes in industrial practices reveal anything of deep significance?

New approaches to early cinema emerged, however, not so much in opposition to film theory as in dialogue with it, and from a desire to test some of its propositions. Apparatus theory constructed a model of cinema based on a number of assumptions about cinematic form and text–spectator relations: the centring of the film spectator as master of a visual field and decoder of narrative puzzles, and a viewing process in which the spectator remains immobile and loses all sense of surroundings, in thrall to an illusion of reality deriving from psychological regression (Baudry 1986). Investigating early cinema, historians could ask whether these assumptions functioned during cinema's first decades.

Early cinema as a different sort of cinema

Work on early cinema took on historical and theoretical tasks. As models of new research methods and increased rigour, Gordon Hendricks, George C. Pratt, and Jay Leyda provided inspiration for the systematic use of archives, drawing on contemporary documents and looking more thoroughly at archival films. The event which many scholars see as the origin of the rethinking of early cinema, the conference *Cinema 1900–1906* (Holmann 1982), held by the International Federation of Film Archives (FIAF) in Brighton in 1978, was devised by a group of forward-looking archivists (particularly Eileen Bowser, David Francis, and Paul Spehr) to pull early films out of the vault and have them examined by scholars. In many ways the renaissance of early-film studies was begun by film archivists (Cherchi Usai 1994). Around the same time seminal works, such as Robert C. Allen's (1980) dissertation on the interrelation between vaudeville and early film, exemplified new carefully focused research projects.

Realizing that early cinema could offer new theoretical insights was primarily the inspiration of Noël Burch, whose interest in oppositional film practices led him to approach early films in a radical manner (Burch 1990). Burch located the significance of early film in its differences from the way films were made and understood within the dominant mode of filmmaking, which he termed the IMR, the institutional mode of representation, exemplified by Hollywood film, but international in scope. He described early cinema as an alternative approach, a PMR, or primitive mode of representation. The PMR consisted of a number of unfamiliar structures: a spatial approach combining frontality with non-centred composition and distant camera placement to create a 'primitive externality'; a lack of narrative coherence, linearity, and closure; and an underdevelopment of character.

Burch's view of the relation of this PMR to the later IMR was complex and ambivalent. At points, he related the different approaches of early films to the working-class background of early cinema's audience and of at least some of its showmen producers. The IMR, in contrast, introduced bourgeois values of coherence and subjectivity into this originally primitive and popular mode of entertainment. Burch raised what has remained a vexed issue in the history of early cinema: the role of class in its development and the class make-up of its audiences. However, he stressed that his interest in the PMR lay primarily in the light it could shed on the IMR, the dominant cinema as it was described by apparatus theory. As a contrast to IMR, PMR allowed Burch to denaturalize this dominant mode, revealing it as the product of historical development rather than the discovery of the natural language of cinema, as teleological film history had assumed. In this respect, Burch launched a strong critique of linear teleological film history. But he also resisted any conception of early cinema as a 'lost paradise', claiming (particularly in his later work) that early cinema was less rich and complex than IMR. For Burch an assumption of progressive development remained, and he retained the term 'primitive' partly to indicate that in his view this early mode remained underdeveloped. Burch's analysis of early film often does not stress its difference from the IMR as much as the way early film techniques anticipate many of IMR's basic assumptions in a primitive fashion. He therefore saw early cinema as rehearsing a variety of elements essential to IMR and the apparatus theory of the cinema. Thus, the evolution of early cinema strove to *overcome* the primitive externality that marks the PMR. The centred masterful spectator of apparatus theory appeared in the PMR in a number of precocious yet underdeveloped ways. This classical spectator acted as a goal which impelled the development of centred compositions and continuity editing strategies, but it also appeared in a number of seemingly deviant features, as later practices appeared in 'infantile' versions. For instance, Burch claimed that the frequent theme in trick films of a body that explodes into fragments (as in Cecil Hepworth's *Explosion of a Motor Car*, 1900) anticipated the later schema of fragmentation through editing. Following from the assumptions of the apparatus theory that the cinema in its basic apparatuses (the camera, the projector, and the movie theatre) reproduces the Western ideology of subject formation, Burch found that early cinema already held the seeds for these later structures. Although he added a historical dimension to his analysis, the determination of theoretical structures provided the ultimate significance of early cinema.

Burch's approach to early cinema received swift criticism from David Bordwell and Kristin Thompson (1983). The authors offered a critique of the linear and teleological assumptions of traditional film history, inspired by Jean-Louis Comolli's call for a materialist history of film, based on discontinuities and ruptures rather than a schema of evolution. While Comolli never supplied an example of materialist history, the authors found that Burch attempted one, but, in their view, failed. Much of their criticism targeted a cavalier attitude towards research and verification in Burch's work, but they also criticized his theoretical assumptions. The authors questioned the role of working-class culture in early cinema's formal difference from traditonal bourgeois forms, pointing out that the first audiences for film in the United States were in vaudeville theatres, a basically middle-class form, while the working-class nickelodeon appeared only as the codes of the IMR were emerging. In addition, Bordwell and Thompson noted Burch's return to linearity in his belief that the basic assumptions of the IMR are present in embryonic form in early film.

In a key work in revisionist film history *The Classical Hollywood Cinema* (1985), written jointly by David Bordwell, Janet Staiger, and Kristin Thompson, Thompson developed a view of early film which also accentuated its difference from later filmmaking practice. Maintaining that from 1917 until the 1960s American mainstream commercial cinema shows a remarkable stability in its style and mode of production (the 'classical Hollywood cinema' of the title), Thompson saw the age of early cinema as a time when films were 'so fundamentally different as to be incomprehensible' (Bordwell *et al.* 1985: 157). Early cinema can be understood as 'pre-classical', standing in varying degrees outside the codes of spatial and temporal relations that define the stability of the classical Hollywood film. The authors' definition of the classical system, although in some ways parallel to (and possibly inspired by) Burch's IMR, made little use of the apparatus theory of subject construction. Instead, Thompson placed storytelling at the centre of the classical system and saw primitive cinema struggling to harness cinematic space and time to this dominant function. Thompson's emphasis on narrative allowed the difference between early cinema and classical cinema to gain more clarity. Since the basic apparatus, the camera, the projector, the darkened room, was the same in both periods, an approach founded in the ideological effect of the basic apparatus would be hard-pressed to discover significant differences between periods.

Thompson applied the principles articulated in Bordwell and Thompson (1983), and investigated the transformation between primitive cinema (she retained this term, although with misgivings) and classical Hollywood forms by investigating the economic and cultural determinants of this change. Retaining

Burch's description of the exteriority of early cinema, she related this to the dominant influence of vaudeville on early cinema both economically and as a model. Thompson claims primitive cinema transformed itself by taking up the task of storytelling, overcoming the exteriority of the vaudeville spectator and replacing it by a spectator immersed in the narrative space of the film.

My own work also defined the difference between early cinema and the later classical mode in terms of its relation to narrative. The work of my colleague and collaborator André Gaudreault, analysing the structures of early cinema through structuralist narrative theory, differentiated cinematic *narrators* (cinematic devices which narrated a story) and *monstrators* who, instead of telling a story, displayed or showed things (Gaudreault 1988, 1990). For Gaudreault, these two different functions in cinema corresponded to the narrating function of an edited sequence and the monstrative display of the single shot. Early cinema, particularly in its very earliest period in which films most often consisted of a single shot (before 1904), related more to monstration than to narration. In my work, this contrast between formal devices of storytelling and display became less a matter of a contrast between the single shot and the edited sequence than a broadly based address to the spectator in early cinema, which I termed the cinema of attractions (Gunning 1990).

While Thompson had shown that early cinema differed from the classical model primarily through its lack of narrative dominance, there remained the question of how to describe what early cinema *was*, rather than what it *wasn't*. Burch's ideas about exteriority and Gaudreault's concept of monstration were useful guides. Taking a cue from Sergei Eisenstein's theatrical work in the 1920s, I felt that the essential gesture of early cinema (which could not be described simply as an incomplete mastery of the task of storytelling) lay in its aggressive address to the spectator's attention. The spectator addressed by early cinema was very different from the spectator of classical cinema, absorbed in a coherent fictional world, attentive to character cues and immersed in following a story. The exteriority noted by Burch and Thompson corresponded to an outward address of the films themselves, a sort of hailing of the viewer, most obvious in the look at the camera and the bows and gestures directed at the audience so common in early cinema (as in such films as *From Show Girl to Burlesque Queen*, Biograph,

1903, or nearly any Méliès films, e.g. *The Man with the Rubber Head*, 1902) but taboo in most genres in classical cinema.

The exteriority of early cinema expresses the basis of the cinema of attractions: the act of display of something to a viewer. The attraction itself is aware of the viewer's gaze, is constructed to attract it. Rather than narrative development based on active characters within detailed fictional environments, the cinema of attractions presented a series of curious or novel views to a spectator. These views could be non-fictional actualities (current events, human oddities, natural wonders), vaudeville acts (dances, acrobatics, gags), famous fragments (peak moments from famous plays, realizations of well-known paintings), or trick films (magical transformations and illusions). In contrast to the temporal development inherent in narrative, the cinema of attractions presented bursts of interest, such as the rapid transformations in a magic film, or the succession of sights in a scenic film (Gunning 1995a). In this cinema, characterization was unimportant and the spatial and temporal relations essential to narrative development were basically irrelevant.

> **The exteriority of early cinema expresses the basis of the cinema of attractions: the act of display of something to a viewer. The attraction itself is aware of the viewer's gaze, is constructed to attract it. Rather than narrative development based on active characters within detailed fictional environments, the cinema of attractions presented a series of curious or novel views to a spectator. These views could be non-fictional actualities (current events, human oddities, natural wonders), vaudeville acts (dances, acrobatics, gags), famous fragments (peak moments from famous plays, realizations of well-known paintings), or trick films (magical transformations and illusions).**

Although there are differences and even contradictions between these models of early cinema, they all emphasize the difference between the early period of film history and the cinema which eventually became dominant. These models were primarily focused on the formal aspects of early films. Further discoveries came as historians broadened the focus from films to the contexts in which they were shown.

From early film to early cinema: exhibitors, audiences, and the public sphere

The new generation of historians of early film investigated not only the films themselves, but also the way they were shown and understood. This involved a shift, to use the terms suggested by Christian Metz, from early *films* to early *cinema*, the culture surrounding films, including their industry, their theatres, and their audiences. Of course, cinema culture and actual films are inseparable, the one implying and enlightening the other. Charles Musser's (1991) work on Edwin Porter and other early American filmmakers emphasized that simply looking at archival prints of early films, while essential, was not sufficient for a full understanding of early cinema. Not only editing, compositional techniques, and narrative strategies differed in early cinema; classical cinema had also transformed the ways films were presented and the means audiences used for understanding them.

Research into primary sources about the presentation of early film led Musser to stress the role of the exhibitor. In cinema's first decade, particularly before 1903, the person showing the film took over important roles in what is now termed post-production, which would later be under the control of film producers. Since many films consisted of a single shot, the exhibitor assembled them into a programme. This could be done with great ingenuity, joining individual films together to stress similarity or contrast; interspersing other material, such as lantern slides or recitations; adding music or other sound effects; and frequently narrating the whole with a spoken commentary or lecture. The exhibitor therefore endowed each film with aesthetic effects and meanings, becoming the author of the film programme (Musser 1991; Musser and Nelson 1991). Buttressed by research into the importance in this era of the film lecturer (the performer who spoke a commentary as the film was projected) by Gaudreault

(1988), Burch (1990), Martin Sopocy (1978), and others, Musser showed that formal analysis of films alone was not sufficient for understanding the meanings and pleasures derived from them by early audiences.

In contrast to classical films, early film had a more open form. As Burch had indicated, their narratives were not as complete and finalized as the films of the IMR. However, this openness was not an avant-garde love of ambiguity. Narrative coherence was supplied in the act of reception, rather than inherent in the film itself. Filmmakers frequently relied on familiar stories or current events well known to their audiences, who could fill in gaps in the narrative or supply significance. These cultural contexts outside film—like the magic-lantern narratives of fire rescues discussed by Musser (1991) which influenced Porter's *Life of an American Fireman* (1903), or the theatrical performances of the novel *Uncle Tom's Cabin* cited by Janet Staiger (1992) which contextualize Porter's 1903 film *Uncle Tom's Cabin*—could explain some formal differences in early films. Staiger claims that early film narratives were less divergent from classical practices than they may seem—they simply used other means to make themselves comprehensible. However, if audience foreknowledge or other extrafilmic aids did supply narrative coherence, the means of achieving it remained different from classical cinema, which supplies the necessary narrative information within the film itself. Early films seem less aberrant and irrational when foreknowledge or other aids are factored in, but their difference from later practice also becomes highlighted.

The investigation of early cinema must consider the broader cultural context in which films were made, exhibited, and understood. The importance of vaudeville for early cinema, both as an exhibition outlet and as a model, had received renewed attention. But what about the nickelodeon, the theatre of the masses, which traditional histories saw as defining the early American cinematic experience? How did the nickelodeon appear, who was its audience, and how did it relate to changes in early films? The nickelodeon era (which began in 1905, became widespread in 1906, and was ending by 1912) began with the rise of story films, while the end of that era saw the first development of classical traits such as characterization and narrative closure. Did the nickelodeon encourage the growth of story films, or, as Musser (1991) claims, were they a pre-condition for it?

The nickelodeon remains an area of controversy.

Musser has pointed out that, even before the nickelodeon, a range of contexts existed in which films were shown, including not only the middle-class vaudeville palaces, but also fairground exhibitors, travelling tent shows, sponsored entertainments in local opera-houses or other public halls, educational exhibitions in schools and even churches (Musser, 1990). As Robert C. Allen (1980) found, vaudeville possessed a range of levels, moving from palaces to purveyors of 'cheap vaudeville', which also offered motion pictures at a price considerably below that of high-class vaudeville. While the audiences for motion pictures when they premièred as the latest novelties were undoubtedly middle class, patrons of all classes had seen films before 1905. But the nickelodeon, with its low admission price of 5 cents, specifically targeted new entertainment seekers, the working class, whose gains in the early twentieth century of a bit more leisure time and disposable income provided an opportunity for small-time entertainment entrepreneurs. But were the working class the main patrons of the nickelodeon?

Doubt was cast on this traditional thesis by a number of scholars. Russell Merritt (1976), Douglas Gomery (1982), and Robert C. Allen (1983) investigated Boston and New York City and decided that the location of nickelodeons in those cities actually avoided working-class neighbourhoods in favour of more central commercial districts, areas frequented by middle-class shoppers as well as working-class patrons. The patrons of these cheap theatres might well have been more frequently middle class than traditonal histories had assumed. Further, as Merritt in particular emphasized, the nickelodeon operators wooed middle-class patrons, seeming uncomfortable with their identity as 'democracy's theatre', and anxious for middle-class respectability. But scholars have also rushed to revise these revisionists. Robert Sklar objected to Allen's and Merritt's thesis, maintaining the importance of working-class culture to the development of the nickelodeon and to our understanding of the role of film in working-class experience (Sklar 1990). Recently Ben Singer (1995b) has returned to the site of Allen's research, New York City, and found that nickelodeons were more prevalent in working-class neighbourhoods than Allen had indicated. Clearly this is an area of continuing debate, as recent exchanges between Allen and Singer indicate (Allen 1996; Singer 1996).

At issue, however, is more than the accurate description of the class make-up of New York neighbourhoods or the number of film theatres. The effect of class

**The theatre of the masses—
the nickelodeon**

antagonism and class definition on early American cinema remains a vital issue. The work of social historian Roy Rosenzweig showed that the relation between film theatres and working-class culture cannot simply be dismissed as a sentimental myth of traditional historians. It is not necessary to attribute early American cinema to the domain of a single class. Rather, the most valuable approach sees cinema as one of the areas in which turn-of-the-century America defined class relations, culture, and dominance. Preliminary work by

J. A. Lindstrom (1996) on nickelodeons in Chicago has centred less on attributing theatres to specific classes than on the way film theatres inspired new systems of zoning and regulation, as leisure time and entertainment became an aspect of municipal control and class struggle.

The history of film exhibition has become one of the liveliest areas of film scholarship. It occupies important sections of the carefully researched and conceived volumes in the History of American Cinema series by

Musser (1990) and Eileen Bowser (1990) and is exemplified by the fine work of Douglas Gomery (1992), showing early cinema's vanguard position in framing and pursuing innovative questions in film history. Gregory Waller's (1995) work on exhibition in a smaller city, Lexington, Kentucky, demonstrated the value in investigating exhibition contexts beyond the metropolis. His work also investigates African-American exhibition and audience patterns, an area all too often ignored in favour of immigrant populations. Waller places early cinema within pre-existing patterns of entertainment, including not only vaudeville, but the multi-purpose opera-house, the amusement park, and local fairs. Robert Allen (1996) has theorized that such viewing situations in small-town and rural America were different from the urban nickelodeon in tems of class and surroundings.

The most broadly conceived attempt to theorize the class basis of the nickelodeon came in Miriam Hansen's (1991a) conception of the nickelodeon as a working-class public sphere. The concept of the public sphere was introduced by Jurgen Habermas's (1991) consideration of the rise of bourgeois democracy, in which certain contexts of public discussion—coffee-houses, newspapers, literary discussion groups—formed an ideal of equitable exchange and reasonable debate. The public sphere provided Hansen with a historical model of the manner in which institutions and discourse created new forms of subjectivity quite different from the ahistorical model of subject formation offered by apparatus theory. However, for Habermas, the classical public sphere was almost immediately compromised by the rise of capitalism, which undermined the claim of a realm of free discussion divorced from economic power. Further, for Habermas, the modern commercialized technological forms of media have seriously undermined the classical terms of debate and participation through techniques of manipulation and opinion management.

Hansen draws on critical reformulations of Habermas's concept. Emphasizing that the classical public sphere had always excluded certain groups (obviously the working class, but also women), critics such as Negt and Kluge (1993) developed the idea of oppositional or proletarian public spheres. The key issue here is less public discussion or overt political action than what Hansen describes as the 'experience' of the participants, 'that which mediates individual perception with social meaning, conscious with unconscious processes, loss of self with self reflexivity' (Hansen 1991a:

12). Negt and Kluge claim the collective viewing of films, the way they could speak to viewers' experience, opened the possibility of cinema as an oppositional public sphere.

For Hansen this possibility became a historical tool for approaching not only the stylistic alterity of early films (as in her analysis of Porter's 1907 film The 'Teddy' Bears), but also its specific modes of exhibition and relation to its audience. Hansen theorized that early cinema may have provided 'an alternative horizon of experience' for groups excluded from the classical public sphere, such as working-class and immigrant audiences and women. Following the research of social historian Kathy Peiss (1986), Hansen showed that the nickelodeon moved away from a homosocial, gender-specific world of male entertainment which excluded women, to a heterosocial world of commercial entertainment where women not only attended, but frequently made up the majority.

The importance of cinema as a new public sphere for women has become a key issue in early cinema research, with such scholars as Lauren Rabinovitz (1990), Janet Staiger (1995), Judith Mayne (1990), Constance Balides (1993), and Shelley Stamp Lindsey (1996) exploring the role of female spectators and at points testing the feminist understanding of apparatus theory which saw the cinema as embodying a male gaze. While the patriarchal and even sexist content of early cinema is unquestionable (see such films as Thomas Edison's 1901 Trapeze Disrobing Act, or Porter's 1903 film The Gay Shoe Clerk), women patrons attending this new medium could transform these male-oriented films in unexpected ways, as in Hansen's famous example of the women who flocked to early boxing films, breaching a former male bastion.

For Hansen, early cinema's difference from classical cinema reflects its role as an oppositional public sphere, allowing viewer relationships that would become suppressed in the classical paradigm. The diversity of display evident in the cinema of attractions did not entice viewers to lose their sense of being present in a public space. The direct address of the cinema of attractions encouraged a recognition of the viewer as part of an audience, rather than as an atomized consumer absorbed into the coherent fictional world of the classical paradigm. The lack of devices channelling spectator attention into following a narrative meant that the cinema of attractions allowed its viewer more imaginative freedom. Further, the less controlled modes of nickelodeon exhibition, with live music, occasional use of a lecturer, egalitarian seating, variety format, and continuous admission, gave it 'a margin of participation and unpredictability' (Hansen 1991: 43) lacking in classical cinema. The alternative public sphere of the nickelodeon gave way to the domesticating of audience behaviour within the elaborate picture palaces which became the premier show-place for films in the middle to late 1910s. This change in exhibition, along with the adoption of the classical paradigm in the feature film, eliminated most elements of earlier film culture in favour of a universal address to a film spectator unspecific in class or gender.

For Hansen, early cinema's difference from classical cinema reflects its role as an oppositional public sphere, allowing viewer relationships that would become suppressed in the classical paradigm. The diversity of display evident in the cinema of attractions did not entice viewers to lose their sense of being present in a public space. The direct address of the cinema of attractions encouraged a recognition of the viewer as part of an audience, rather than as an atomized consumer absorbed into the coherent fictional world of the classical paradigm. The lack of devices channelling spectator attention into following a narrative meant that the cinema of attractions allowed its viewer more imaginative freedom.

Periodization and transitional stages

However they might differ in dividing them up, scholars of early cinema agree that in a relatively short amount of time (two decades or so) so much change occurs that several distinct periods exist. This stands in stark contrast to the classical Hollywood cinema, which for Bordwell, Staiger, and Thompson (1985) remained stable for more than four decades. The period of early cinema stretches from the origins of motion pictures in the late nineteenth century to around 1916. The year given by Bordwell, Staiger, and Thompson for the consolidation of the classical Hollywood cinema is 1917, so this end-date marks early cinema as pre-classical. Around 1913 to 1915 the American film industry moved definitively to the production of longer feature films (from one to several hours) as the new basis of the industry, exiling one- or two-reel films to marginal theatres, or to 'added attractions' in a feature programme. The middle 1910s witnessed new institutions (feature films, the star system, the picture palace, new studios, and systems of distribution) essential to the classical Hollywood cinema.

Exhibition, production, and distribution underwent a series of reorganizations in the two decades of 'early cinema'. Originally films and projection machines were produced by the same company, and these were offered to vaudeville theatres as a complete package. By the turn of the century, both films and machines were sold publicly, and entrepreneurs acquired them and became exhibitors, marking the first differentiation within the industry. Around 1905 the next essential differentiation occurred as exchanges appeared: middlemen who purchased films from production companies and rented them to exhibitors. This increased the availability of films to an exhibitor and led to the nickelodeon explosion. The multiplication of cheap theatres showing new films on a daily basis created a demand for films the American producers could not initially fulfil, and the French company Pathé took up much of the slack. Around 1909 American producers attempted to seize control of the industry again, and submit the exchanges and exhibitors to a series of regulations. The organ for this was the Motion Picture Patents Company (MPPC), in which Edison and Biograph tried to exert control through their ownership of patents. Opposition to the MPPC arose with 'independent' producers, but even they soon adopted its methods of control over distribution through regulation of release dates and price schedules. By 1913 the power of the MPPC had waned, as well as the popularity of the one-reel film, replaced by longer feature films and the rise of new 'independent' companies, such as Universal, Famous Players in Famous Plays, and Mutual. Exhibition became dominated by large urban picture palaces, some of which were already owned by production studios, paving the way for the later vertical integration of the industry. While changes in film style cannot be neatly tied to all these changes, the volatile nature of the industry explains why there is probably more transformation in the way films were made and conceived (both by producers and audiences) in this period than in the rest of film history.

Changes in film style can be divided into periods partly in terms of the opposition between the cinema of attractions and narrative form. Like all binary oppositions, the contrast between attractions and narrative can lead to unfortunate simplification. These aspects should never be seen as mutually exclusive, but need to be dialectically interrelated. While there are films (particularly in the first decade of cinema) which function purely as attractions with no narrative structure, many early films (especially after 1902) show an interaction between the two aspects. I claim that the cinema of attraction works as a 'dominant' up to about 1905, employing forms of direct address, punctual temporality, and surprise rather than narrative development.

The concept of the dominant comes from the literary analysis of the Russian Formalists and has been applied to film by Kristin Thompson (1988). It recognizes that, though various elements might coexist in a work, one element may organize the others. In the classical style, narrative structures act as the dominant, so that, even though attractions persist (such as special effects, the physical attraction of stars, s͏pᴇcular sets, or musical numbers), they are subordinated to a narrative structure. Likewise, although certain fairy films of Méliès or Pathé, such as *A Trip to the Moon* (1902) or *The Red Spectre* (1907) have stories, they basically serve as show-cases for the dominant attractions of camera tricks, costumes, elaborate sets, and stencil colouring. Certain early films, particularly from the years around 1903 to 1907 (such as Pathé's *A Policeman's Tour of the World* from 1906), appear as almost equal contests between the claims of attractions and narrative, veering from one logic to the other. One basic arc of stylistic transformation traces the increasing dominance of narrative structures, leading to structures that are clear harbingers of later classical forms. From 1906 more films were made with narrative structures as their dominant. By 1908 films became increasing narrativized and were provided with volitional characters. However, 'narrative' is an expansive term, including many styles of storytelling. The difference that early films show when compared to films of the classical style should not be reduced simply to a contrast between narrative and non-narrative forms. Even the narrative films of this early period tell stories differently from the classical paradigm.

The non-classical narrative forms of early cinema make up a series of genres. Closest to the form of attractions are fragment narratives. This minimally narrative genre consisted of a single fragment or series of fragments, often famous moments from a play or famous events, to be completed by the viewer's understanding of previous (non-film) versions. Biograph's 1903 production of the famous temperance play *Ten Nights in a Barroom* consisted simply of five key scenes (or rather moments from the well-known play: *Death of Little Mary*; *Death of Slade*; *The Fatal Blow*; *Murder of Willie*; and *Vision of Mary*)—to someone unfamiliar with the play these brief films would be incomprehensible. Such fragments could be more or less incomplete. The versions of the Passion play produced both in the United States and France showed the range of possibilities, from early discontinuous and highly fragmented films to later, nearly narratively coherent, versions. In their lack of temporal development the fragment narratives are close to attractions.

Perhaps the earliest complete narrative form was the gag, the brief visual joke, often centred around physical pranks, which had a minimum essential narrative development: a set-up for the gag and a pay-off as the gag (usually some minor disaster) takes place, creating the fundamental narrative roles of prankster and victim. Early American companies produced scores of such films, and a few titles from American Mutoscope and Biograph in 1903 give some sense of their flavour: *How Buttons Got Even with the Butler*; *Pulling off the Bed Clothes*; *You will Send me to Bed, Eh?* Their disaster structure gives them a brief and punctual temporality—like an exploding cigar—as well as an often highly visual pay-off which makes them resemble attractions. In the period of multi-shot films, Edison

> **Perhaps the earliest complete narrative form was the gag, the brief visual joke, often centred around physical pranks, which had a minimum essential narrative development: a set-up for the gag and a pay-off as the gag (usually some minor disaster) takes place, creating the fundamental narrative roles of prankster and victim.**

and Biograph reworked such gags into longer films, as a bad boy or other trickster carried out a series of practical jokes (*The Truants*, Biograph, 1907; *The Terrible Kids*, Edison, 1906). This form of concatenation led to another simple narrative form, which I have called 'linked vignettes', consisting of a series of brief gags linked by a common character (Gunning 1994*b*).

As Burch and others have pointed out, the first extended self-contained narrative form in film was the chase. Burch (1990) saw the linearity of the chase as an anticipation of later classical narratives. In its earliest examples (*The Escaped Lunatic*, 1903; *Personal*, 1904, both Biograph) the chase created a continuous fictional space, rendered coherent by its methodical following of a single physical action. While chases often included attractions (such as dogs leaping fences and swimming streams, or ladies revealing legs as they slid down a hill), a single-minded focus on a pursuit through several shots created a new narrative dominance. However, unlike later classical films, the chase remained dependent entirely on physical action for its narrative structure. Figures running through various locales created the continuous geography of the film. The initiation of a pursuit provided the inciting incident of the film and capture marked its completion. This picks out a decidedly non-classical aspect of early film narrative, its lack of characterization or motivation behind action.

Around 1906 a number of films attempted stories with a greater degree of character and less physical action (such as Edison's *The Miller's Daughter*, 1905, or *Fireside Reminiscences*, 1908). Contemporary comments leave no doubt that many character-based films of this era were obscure to their contemporaneous audiences. Basic codes for conveying thoughts and emotions had not yet been devised by filmmakers, nor were they understood by audiences. Perhaps the greatest transformation of early film style came with the adoption of new narrative codes which conveyed character motives and organized storytelling devices. To some extent, this shift in narrative style parallels the attempts to regulate and rationalize the film industry which culminated in the formation of the MPPC in 1908 (Gunning 1991*a*). This large-scale transformation of American filmmaking has frequently been referred to as the 'transitional' period, marking its mediation between the radically different earlier cinema and the establishment of the classical paradigm. Narrative in the transitional period obeyed new rules: interior coherence (lack of reliance on audience foreknow-

ledge or other extra-filmic aids); a strong narrative closure; and, especially, an emphasis on characterization, frequently building stories around changes in character or key decisions whose motivations are indicated within the film. Many of the Griffith one-reel dramas produced for the Biograph company display these qualities (such as *The Drunkard's Reformation*, 1909), as do the films produced by the Vitagraph Company (such as *An Official Appointment*, 1912, so well analysed by Ben Brewster (1991*a*)). This form differs sharply from the earlier forms based primarily in physical action, although many films united the two forms (including Griffith's Biograph melodramas, such as *The Lonedale Operator*, 1911).

However, this transitional period remained volatile and ambivalent, as the term suggests. While new narrative structures were evident in many films (particularly dramas from the Vitagraph, Biograph, and Edison studios), and were praised by trade journals devoted to the film industry (which began to appear around this time), variation occurs. Research by both Ben Singer (1993) and Charles Keil (1995) has stressed that the most advanced films by Griffith are not typical of the period. Films even as late as 1913 sometimes show uncertainty in conveying character psychology or even a coherent plot. Singer (1993) cites an episode from the Thanhouser Company's 1913 serial *Zudora* as an example of pure incoherence.

While actual achievements varied from studio to studio (or film to film), organizing films around clear stories and motivated, volitional characters was, none the less, an acknowledged value in this period. Of course, action genres like westerns and other sensational films still showed the importance of non-narrative attractions, but these were largely absorbed into character-driven plots. At the same time, while the narrative integration of the transitional period certainly looks forward to the later classical style, it maintained a unique style. Ben Brewster (1991*b*) and Charles Keil (1995) have stressed that the one-reel film standard of this period demanded narrative compression and encouraged patterns of recurrence. While these aspects are not contradictory to the classical style, they seem more endemic to short films than to features. Brewster (1991*b*) has pointed out that early features, such as the scandalous *Traffic in Souls* from 1913, often reflected the patterns of individual reels in their structure (partly due to the fact that many theatres owned only one projector, necessitating a pause between reels). Indeed, one of the earliest long film formats, the serial (appearing around 1912–13 with Edison's *What Happened to Mary*), literally spun out its narrative reel by reel, as single-reel instalments were screened every week. The serial, with its strong emphasis on thrilling attractions, its often rather incoherent plotting, and its compromise between the single reel and the feature structure, may, as Singer (1993) claims, stand as an emblem of the often contradictory impulses of the transitional period.

If the transitional period corresponds to an attempt to bring order and regularity to film production and distribution (often through legally dubious practices, as the US courts decided when they ruled against the MPPC in an antitrust action in 1914), how does this new narratively integrated film structure relate to changes in exhibition and audience? A number of scholars, myself included (Gunning 1990), see the cinema of narrative integration as an element in a concerted attempt to attract a middle-class audience and gain respectability for the cinema. Production companies adapted literary classics, while filmmakers devised cinematic codes to tell stories of the type familiar from middle-class forms like the short-story magazine, apparently with such audiences in view.

However, this view of the bourgeoisification of cinema during the transitional period can be exaggerated, particularly if one relies on trade journals, whose desire for the imprimatur of respectability led them to exaggerate the number of middle-class patrons attending movies or the comfort and order of theatres. Careful reading of trade journals and industry publicity reveals a strong desire to retain working-class patrons, while the emphasis on signs of middle-class approval partly served to allay the attacks of reformers suspicious of the new form, rather than indicated real conditions. The only existing survey of film audiences indicates that in New York City the working class still made up nearly three-quarters of the audience in 1910, while a category called 'clerical', referring most likely to office workers (i.e. a newly emerging lower middle class), constituted most of the other quarter (Davis 1911; Singer 1996). However, small-town audiences may have had a different composition, as Allen (1996) stresses.

William Uricchio and Roberta Pearson's (1993) investigation of Vitagraph's 'quality films'—adaptations from Dante or Shakespeare (*Francesca di Rimini*, *Julius Caesar*, both 1908), or films on cultural figures such as Napoleon or Moses (*Napoleon, the Man of Destiny*, 1909; *The Life of Moses*, 1910)—found that while such films aimed at attracting an audience who might scorn typical nickelodeon fare, they were also carefully designed to be accessible to the working-class audience most exhibitors relied upon. This 'dual address' seems typical of this period and should alert us to the dangers of seeing the bourgeoisification of the cinema

A model for future westerns—*The Great Train Robbery* (1903)

at the end of early cinema as an established fact without complexity or resistance. The transitional period appears to be less a gradual fade into the classical paradigm than a period of ambivalence and contestation.

Early cinema and modernity

The study of early cinema has consistently expanded its area of investigation. Research into the exhibition of early films extended into a consideration of audiences and the role the nickelodeon played in American society. Uricchio and Pearson (1993) found that determining what audience producers aimed for, or how widely films were comprehensible to different classes, called for an investigation of the intertextual framework in which images of Napoleon or scenes from Shakespeare circulated outside cinema, from school textbooks to advertising cards.

Perhaps the most far-reaching (and possibly most controversial) extension of the study of early cinema relates techniques of early film, particularly the cinema of attractions, to large-scale transformations of daily experience in the era of urbanization and modernization. This approach draws inspiration from Walter Benjamin (1969) and Siegfried Kracauer (1995) as well as Miriam Hansen's (1987, 1991b, 1993, 1995) discussion of these authors' writings on the cinema. Benjamin, writing in the 1930s, related the shock of the rapidly changing experience of the urban environment and new technology to cinematic techniques, such as rapid montage, slow or fast motion, and huge close-ups. Kracauer, writing in the later 1920s, found that the visual stimulus of the picture palace captured the mechanization and surface character of the modern life as the pursuit of distraction. In my writings (Gunning 1994a, c, 1995b), I have claimed that Benjamin's and Kracauer's analyses could be used to describe the cinema of attractions with its aggressive viewer-confronting address and discontinuous structures.

Early films dealing with the railroad provide a powerful intersection of the aggressive address of the cinema of attractions and the technological transformations of modern life. The many early films taken from trains of the passing landscape (e.g. Biograph's *Into the Heart of the Catskills*, 1906) and the Hales Tours exhibition of films in theatres designed to imitate railroad cars (including sound effects and ticket takers) reveal early cinema's affinity with the railroad. Lynne Kirby's (1996)

work on this subject, as well as works by Mary Ann Doane (1985) and myself (Gunning 1994a, 1995c) drew on the work of a contemporary Benjaminian, Wolfgang Schivelbusch, whose book *The Railway Journey* (1977) claimed that the experience of railway travel, with its speed and potential danger, was emblematic of modern perception. In films shot from moving trains Kirby found a fascination with what Schivelbusch calls 'panoramic perception', a view of the world in motion through a window or other framing device. The shocklike structure of the abrupt transitions and often aggressive imagery of the cinema of attractions also reflected for Kirby the sense of hysteria which the fear of the railway accident brought to modern consciousness. Eileen Bowser (1995), Yuri Tsivian (1994), and Gunning (1991b) have made a similar case for the telephone in early cinema, knitting together distant spaces and creating new dramatic situations.

Following Walter Benjamin's example, writers on early cinema have isolated a number of emblematic instances of modernity besides the railway and the telephone: the World Expositions, the department store, the city streets, the diorama and panorama, urban billboards. Anne Friedberg (1993) has related a number of these to the 'mobilized virtual gaze', the heightened involvement of a viewer in a visual illusion combined with motion which she sees as essential not only to the pre-history of cinema (in devices like the diorama and panorama), but also to the subjectivity of modernity. My writings (Gunning 1994a, b) have emphasized that such relations are embedded in the way early films embraced modern technology or new environments (such as the World Expositions or the amusement park) as subjects for films (Porter's *Coney Island at Night*, 1905; Biograph's *Panorama St Louis Exposition*, 1904). Ben Singer (1995b) has detailed how the most aggressive aspects of the cinema of attractions reflected both the experience of urban life with its threats and danger, and its portrayal in the sensationalist press. Lauren Rabinovitz's (1990) research on Chicago amusement parks sees these mechanized forms of amusement as another example of accelerated modern experience with a stong relation to early cinema, focusing as well on the way amusement parks shed light on female subjectivity, an issue central to many investigations of modernity, including the work of Hansen (1991a), Friedberg (1993), Bruno (1993), and Singer's (1995a) work on the serial queen, the powerful woman protagonist of the films of the serial genre, such as Pathé's *The Perils of Pauline*, from 1914.

Feminist theory has provided a key motive for these investigations on multiple levels, not only as part of the vitally important project of bringing to light the neglected and often suppressed role of women in American history. One could claim that feminist film theory in the late 1970s both adopted the subjectivity of the apparatus theory of cinema and supplied its most radical critique. Laura Mulvey (1975) pointed out that the apparatus as constructed within this theory and as exemplified by classical Hollywood cinema embodied a male gaze. If this were so, not only did it marginalize and problematize female subjectivity, but it also traced a basic fissure in the theory's universal claims if one had to conceive the subject, not as a Platonic entity, but as a gendered being. This introduction of gender difference opened the flood gates for a reconceptualization of the film spectator open to history and the play of gender and ethnic difference. While an attempt to reconcile this historical and cultural investigation of spectatorship with the assumptions of apparatus theory may encounter contradictions in method, the historical investigation of early cinema and modernity has sketched a model of a more fluid concept of subjectivity, along the lines of Hansen's (1991a) treatment of the public sphere of early cinema as providing a ground for processing new experiences.

Art historian Jonathan Crary provides one of the most far-reaching theories of the relation between modernity and historical subjectivities. Crary (1990) investigates psychological theories and accounts of the physiology of perception of the nineteenth century (such as those of Helmholtz and Fechner), claiming that these new models of perception switched focus from the accurate reflection of exterior phenomena to the physiology of the senses. This view found support in the perceptional illusions that optical devices, such as the phenakistiscope and the stereoscope (which are often seen as precursors to the cinema), make visible, but which do not actually exist other than in the observer's sensorium. Crary claims that the breakdown of representation in painting associated with modernism has its roots in this earlier technological and philosophical modernization of vision. Closer to Foucault than to apparatus theory, Crary sees subject formation as a historical process inscribed in techniques and institutions specific to different periods. He locates a major shift in the conception of visuality in the modern period. Although Crary discusses early cinema only in passing, his insights provide a basis for the historicization of perception and visual experience.

What has been termed the 'modernity thesis' has recently been subjected to serious criticism, particularly by David Bordwell (1996a, b). As a cognitivist, Bordwell finds a 'history' of vision, perception, or experience a dubious concept, vague at best and absurd at its most extreme. 'It is highly unlikely that visual perception has changed over recorded human history,' he claims (1996: 23). Bordwell finds that the ultimate failure of the modernity thesis lies in its dubious attempt to tie stylistic aspects of early cinema to modern experience. Developing an objection also raised by Charles Keil (1995), Bordwell asks how one can relate the fragmentary, aggressive form of the cinema of attractions to abrasive modern experience in the street or to new modes of transportation, since these aspects of modernity continued, or even increased during the transitional period, which subordinated the more aggressive aspects of attractions to the coherence of narrative integration.

In many respects such criticism is well taken, but it may reflect irreconcilable positions about the nature of history and experience. Bordwell is aware that no theorist of modernity could responsibly claim a transformation in the perceptual hard wiring of human beings, so some of his objections seem to be based on a disingenuous *reductio ad absurdum*. However, there is no question that terms such as 'experience' or even the use of the word 'perception' remain in need of greater precision and discussion. Crary (1990: 6) states: 'Whether perception or vision actually change is ir-

> **While an attempt to reconcile this historical and cultural investigation of spectatorship with the assumptions of apparatus theory may encounter contradictions in method, the historical investigation of early cinema and modernity has sketched a model of a more fluid concept of subjectivity, along the lines of Hansen's treatment of the public sphere of early cinema as providing a ground for processing new experiences.**

relevant, for they have no autonomous history. What changes are the plural forces and rules composing the field in which perception occurs.' Thus what needs to be made more precise are the social mediations of experience, observable not only in works of art, but in the scientific and political discourse of the period.

Bordwell's contention that the experience of modernity remains irrelevant to the history of film style is more complex. There is no question that the relations drawn between the structures of modernity and those of early film frequently lack specificity and remain on the level of vague analogies. However, in tying the pace and abruptness of early films to modern experience, contemporary critics are not so much inventing an analogy as rediscovering one. Such connections were frequently made by the first commentators on the cinema, who recognized in the new media an experience related to modern city life. As a fact of discourse this is an important element of the history of film reception, one worth careful research and consideration. Bordwell's and Keil's claim that the modernity thesis cannot explain stylistic change is probably correct, but seems to defeat a claim that no scholar of early cinema ever made. The relations between modernity and early film need not be limited to the cinema of attractions. The thrill melodramas of the transitional period, such as Griffith's last-minute rescues in such films as *The Lonely Villa*, 1909, and *The Lonedale Operator*, 1911 (with their use of modern technology such as the telephone, the railway, and the telegraph to convey a new sense of urgency and danger), are prime examples of early film's relation to modernity. Reference to the broader contexts of modernity cannot, and does not desire to, explain everything. Changes in film style derive from many immanent causes: changes in technology, industry realignment, cycles of innovation and canonization, as well as transformations in film's relation to society—relations, I should add, that are fully mediated and traceable in contemporary discourse, and not a matter of a mystical reflection of a *Zeitgeist*.

Topics for further research

While the history of early cinema in the last two decades has seen a sudden growth that almost recalls the nickelodeon explosion, with many more scholars making important contributions than can be included in this summary, there are still many issues to explore. Many of these, such as the relation between social class

and the nickelodeon, or the validity of the relation of early cinema to modernity, have already been discussed. I want briefly to add some others. Since this chapter treats early *American* cinema, I have not dealt with scholarship on early cinema in other countries. While the United States has served as a key area of investigation, it is hard to conceive of early cinema history without the work done on early French cinema by a large number of scholars in France as well as the United States, and increasingly in Italy, Germany, Britain, Denmark, Sweden, and Russia, as well as work on film production and exhibition outside Europe and the United States. The period of early cinema marks a time when films circulated freely across borders and in which the concept of a national cinema was largely unarticulated. Richard Abel's recent research (1995*b*) on the effect of the French production company Pathé on American cinema shows that to examine even American cinema within a narrowly national context leads to distortion. Since Pathé films were the most widely shown and most successful films exhibited in the United States at the beginning of the transitional period (1906–9), Abel's claim that they had a definitive effect on the development of American film seems unquestionable. Pathé's early experiments in parallel editing certainly influenced Griffith's development of this technique at Biograph, as the comparison of Pathé's *Physician of the Castle* (1908) and Griffith's *The Lonely Villa* (1909) undertaken by both myself (Gunning 1991*b*) and Barry Salt (1985) demonstrates. In the transitional period the American film industry tried to define and produce an 'American film' in opposition to Europe, a goal that matched the MPPC's attempt to marginalize European producers. The construction of national cinema cultures began in early cinema and calls for more research.

An area of relative neglect in the study of the early cinema is non-fiction filmmaking. While this has gained more attention from European scholars such as Stephen Bottomore (1988) and the archivists at the Nederlands Filmmuseum (Hertogs and De Klerck 1994), it remains in need of more research and theorization from a US perspective. Until about 1905 the bulk of American production was non-fiction films, but these have not received the investigation that reflects their importance in this period.

The transitional period needs more research. Because of its limited focus my work on Griffith at Biograph during this period, while setting up issues of broad concern, cannot serve as an account of this period in the US generally. Charles Keil's (1995) broader-based survey of the transitional period should answer a number of questions about the techniques of narrative integration. Even more neglected is the end of the transitional period, the era of early features. Perhaps the most important work being produced about this era comes from Ben Brewster and Lea Jacobs's (1997) thorough discussion of early cinema's relation to theatrical practice. Although not restricted to the United States, this work traces the often surprising degree to which theatrical practice (including performance style, lighting techniques, and sensation scenes) inspired early feature films, while also undergoing strong transformations. Rather than repeating the simple account promulgated by Nicholas Vardac (1949), of cinema taking up the visual tradition of nineteenth-century theatre, Brewster and Jacobs tell a much more nuanced and detailed story of cross-media influence. The date that Bordwell, Staiger, and Thompson selected for the beginning of the classical Hollywood cinema—1917—still seems a reasonable one for the period in which most American films show a mastery of the basic codes and conventions of fiction filmmaking. However, the selection of this date, several years after feature films had become the basic product of the American film industry, acknowledges that the early feature period itself saw a gradual spread of the codes of classical narration as well as competing alternatives. Further research on early features will undoubtedly find a number of stylistic approaches in terms of reliance on editing versus deep staging and the relative importance of intra-scene editing versus parallel editing. But by the end of the teens a basic narrative vocabulary is in place meriting Bordwell, Staiger, and Thompson's term 'classical Hollywood cinema'.

Early cinema remains an area which grapples with crucial issues of film study. Besides providing a clearer picture of the earliest era of our medium through new research and historical models, the investigation of early cinema continues to explore and redefine encounters between spectator and screen, audience and film, cinema and social context. From the energy generated by such debates, early cinema has demonstrated that film studies still engages vital issues, and that cinema stands at the core of our understanding of the modern world.

BIBLIOGRAPHY

Abel, Richard (ed.) (1995a), *Silent Cinema* (New Brunswick, NJ: Rutgers University Press).

—— (1995b), 'The Perils of Pathé; or, The Americanization of the American Cinema', in Charney and Schwartz (1995).

Allen, Robert C. (1980), *Vaudeville and Film 1895–1915: A Study in Media Interaction* (New York: Arno Press).

—— (1983), 'Motion Picture Exhibition in Manhattan 1906–1912: Beyond the Nickelodeon', in Fell (1993).

—— (1996), 'Manhattan Myopia; or, Oh! Iowa!', *Cinema Journal*, 35/3: 75–103.

Balides, Constance (1993), 'Scenarios of Exposure in Everyday Life: Women in the Cinema of Attractions', *Screen*, 34/1: 19–31 (Spring).

Baudry, Jean-Louis (1986), 'Ideological Effects of the Basic Cinematographic Apparatus', in Rosen, 'Narrative, Apparatus, Ideology' (New York: Columbia University Press).

Benjamin, Walter (1969), *Illuminations: Essays and Reflections*, ed. Hannah Arendt and trans. Harry Zohn (New York: Schocken Books).

Bordwell, David, (1996a), 'La Nouvelle Mission de Feuillade; or, What was Mise en Scène?', *The Velvet Light Trap*, 37: 10–29.

—— (1996b), *Visions of Cinema: On the History of Film Style* (Cambridge, Mass.: Harvard University Press).

—— and **Kristin Thompson** (1983), 'Linearity, Materialism and the Study of Early American Cinema', *Wide Angle*, 5/3: 4–15.

—— **Janet Staiger,** and **Kristin Thompson** (1985), *The Classical Hollywood Cinema: Film Style and Mode of Production to 1960* (New York: Columbia University Press).

Bottomore, Stephen (1988), 'Shots in the Dark: The Real Origins of Film Editing', *Sight and Sound*, 57/3 (Summer), 200–4.

Bowser, Eileen (1990), *The Transformation of Cinema: History of the American Cinema, ii: 1907–1915* (New York: Scribner's).

—— (1995), 'The Telephone Thriller; or, The Terrors of Modern Technology', lecture given at the British Film Institute.

Brewster, Ben (1991a), 'A Bunch of Violets', paper presented to the Society for Cinema Studies Conference, Washington, June.

—— (1991b), '*Traffic in Souls*: An Experiment in Feature Length Narrative Construction', *Cinema Journal*, 31 (Fall).

*—— and **Lea Jacobs** (1997), *Theatre to Cinema: Stage Pictorialism and the Early Feature Film* (Oxford: Oxford University Press).

Bruno, Giuliana (1993), *Streetwalking On a Ruined Map: Cultural Theory and the City Films of Elvira Notari* (Princeton: Princeton University Press).

Burch, Noël (1990), *Life to those Shadows* (Berkeley: University of California Press).

Charney, Leo, and Vanessa R. Schwartz (eds.) (1995), *Cinema and the Invention of Modern Life* (Berkeley: University of California Press).

Cherchi Usai, Paolo (1994), *Burning Passions: An Introduction to the Study of Silent Cinema* (London: British Film Institute).

Crary, Jonathan (1990), *Techniques of the Observer: On Vision and Modernity in the Nineteenth Century* (Cambridge, Mass.: MIT Press).

Davis, Michael (1911), *The Exploitation of Pleasure: A Study of Commerical Recreations in New York City* (New York: Russell Sage Foundation).

Doane, Mary Ann (1985), 'When the Direction of the Force Acting on the Body is Changed: The Moving Image', *Wide Angle*, 7/2.

*Elsaesser, Thomas (ed.) (1990), *Early Cinema: Space Frame Narrative* (London: British Film Institute).

Fell, John (ed.) (1993), *Film before Griffith* (Berkeley: University of California Press).

Friedberg, Anne (1993), *Window Shopping: Cinema and the Postmodern* (Berkeley: University of California Press).

Gaudreault, André (1988) *Du littéraire au filmique: système du récit* (Paris: Meridians Klincksieck).

—— (1990), 'Film, Narrative, Narration: The Cinema of the Lumière Brothers', in Elsaesser (1990).

Gomery, Douglas (1982), 'Movie Audiences, Urban Geography and the History of American Film', *The Velvet Light Trap*, 19: 23–9.

—— (1992), *Shared Pleasures: A History of Movie Presentation in the United States* (Madison: University of Wisconsin Press).

*Gunning, Tom (1990), 'The Cinema of Attractions: Early Film, its Specator and the Avant-Garde', in Elsaesser (1990).

—— (1991a), *D. W. Griffith and the Origins of American Narrative Film* (Champaign: University of Illinois Press).

—— (1991b), 'Heard over the Phone: *The Lonely Villa* and the De Lorde Tradition of Terrified Communication', *Screen*, 32/2 (Summer), 184–96.

—— (1994a), 'The Whole Town's Gawking: Early Cinema and the Visual Experience of Modernity', *Yale Journal of Criticism*, 7/2 (Fall).

—— (1994b), 'Crazy Machines in the Garden of Forking Paths: Mischief Gags and the Origins of American Film Comedy', in Kristine Karnick and Henry Jenkins (eds.), *Classical Hollywood Comedy* (London: Routledge).

—— (1994c), 'The World as Object Lesson: Cinema Audiences, Visual Culture and the St Louis World's Fair', *Film History* 5/4 (Winter), 422–44.

—— (1995a), 'Now you See it, now you Don't: The Temporality of the Cinema of Attractions', in Richard Abel (ed.), *Silent Cinema* (New Brunswick, NJ: Rutgers University Press).

—— (1995b), 'An Aesthetic of Astonishment: Early Film and the [In]Credulous Spectator', in Linda Williams (ed.), *Viewing Positions: Ways of Seeing Films* (New Brunswick, NJ: Rutgers University Press).

Habermas, Jurgen (1962/1991), *The Structural Transformation of the Public Sphere: An Inquiry into a Category of Bourgeois Society*, trans. Thomas Burger and Frederick Lawrence (Cambridge, Mass.: MIT Press).

Hansen, Miriam (1987), 'Benjamin, Cinema and Experience: The Blue Flower in the Land of Technology', *New German Critique*, 40 (Winter), 179–224.

*—— (1991a), *Babel and Babylon: Spectatorship in American Silent Film* (Cambridge: Mass.: Harvard University Press).

—— (1991b), 'Decentric Perspectives: Kracauer's Early Writings on Film and Mass Culture', *New German Critique*, 54 (Fall), 47–76.

—— (1993), 'Of Mice and Ducks: Benjamin and Adorno on Disney', *South Atlantic Quarterly*, 92/1 (Winter), 27–61.

—— (1995) 'America, Paris, the Alps: Kracauer (and Benjamin) on Cinema and Modernity', in Leo Charney and Vanessa R. Schwartz (eds.), *Cinema and the Invention of Modern Life* (Berkeley: University of California Press).

Hertogs, Daan, and Nico De Klerck (eds.) (1994), *Non-Fiction from the Teens* (Amsterdam: Nederlands Filmmuseum).

Holman, Roger (ed.) (1982), *Cinema 1900–1906: An Analytical Study* (Brussels: FIAF).

*Keil, Charles (1995), 'American Cinema 1907–1913: The Nature of Transition', dissertation, University of Wisconsin at Madison.

*—— (1996), paper presented to the Society for Cinema Studies Conference, New York City, May.

Kirby, Lynne (1996), *Parallel Tracks: The Railroad and Silent Cinema* (Durham, NC: Duke University Press).

Kracauer, Siegfried (1963/1995), *The Mass Ornament: Weimar Essays*, ed. and trans. Thomas Y. Levin (Cambridge, Mass.: Harvard University Press).

Lindsey, Shelley Stamp (1996), *Ladies' Night: Women and Movie Culture in America during the Transitional Era* (Princeton: Princeton University Press).

Lindstrom, J. A. (1996), ' "Class Hatred Seeds Sown": Zoning the Debate about Class and Early Film Exhibition in Chicago', paper presented to the Society for Cinema Studies Conference, New York City, May.

Mayne, Judith (1990) *The Woman at the Keyhole: Feminism and Woman's Cinema* (Bloomington: University of Indiana Press).

Merritt, Russell (1976), 'Nickelodeon Theaters 1905–1914: Building an Audience for the Movies' in Tino Balio (ed.), *The American Film Industry* (Madison: University of Wisconsin Press).

Mulvey, Laura (1975), 'Visual Pleasure and Narrative Cinema', *Screen*, 16/3: 6–27.

*Musser, Charles (1990), *The Emergence of Cinema: The American Screen to 1907, History of the American Cinema*, i (New York: Scribner's).

—— (1991), *Before the Nickelodeon: Edwin S. Porter and the Edison Manufacturing Company* (Berkeley: University of California Press).

—— and **Carol Nelson** (1991), *High Class Motion Pictures: Lyman Howe and the Forgotten Era of Traveling Exhibition 1880–1920* (Princeton: Princeton University Press).

—— (1994), 'Rethinking Early Cinema: Cinema of Attractions and Narrativity', *Yale Journal of Criticism*, 7/2 (Fall), 203–32.

Negt, Oskar, and **Alexander Kluge** (1993), *Public Sphere and Experience: Towards an Analysis of the Bourgeois and Proletarian Public Sphere* (Minneapolis: University of Minnesota Press).

Peiss, Kathy (1986), *Cheap Amusements: Working Women and Leisure in Turn-of-the-Century New York* (Philadelphia: Temple University Press).

Rabinovitz, Lauren (1990), 'Temptations of Pleasure: Nickelodeons, Amusement Parks and the Sights of Female Pleasure', *Camera Obscura*, 23: 71–90.

Rosenzweig, Roy (1983), *Eight Hours for what we Will: Workers and Leisure in an Industrial City 1870–1920* (Cambridge: Cambridge University Press).

Salt, Barry (1985), 'The Physician of the Castle', *Sight and Sound*, 54/4 (Autumn), 284–5.

Schivelbusch, Wolfgang (1977), *The Railway Journey* (New York: Urizen Press).

Singer, Ben (1993), 'Fiction Tie-ins and Narrative Intelligibility 1911–1918', *Film History*, 5/4: 489–504.

—— (1995a), 'Female Power in the Serial Queen Melodrama: The Etiology of an Anomaly', in Richard Abel (ed.), *Silent Cinema* (New Brunswick, NJ: Rutgers University Press).

—— (1995b), 'Manhattan Nickelodeons: New Data on Audiences and Exhibition', *Cinema Journal*, 34/3 (Spring), 5–35.

—— (1995c), 'Modernity, Hyperstimulus and the Rise of Popular Sensationalism', in Charney and Schwartz, (1995).

—— (1996), 'New York, just like I Pictured It . . .', *Cinema Journal*, 35/3: 104–28.

Sklar, Robert (1990), 'Oh! Althusser!: Historiography and the Rise of Cinema Studies', in Robert Sklar and Charles Musser (eds.), *Resisting Images: Essays on Cinema and History* (Philadelphia: Temple University Press).

Sopocy, Martin (1978), 'A Narrated Cinema: The Pioneer Story of James A. Williamson', *Cinema Journal*, 18/1 (Fall), 1–28.

Staiger, Janet (1992), *Interpeting Films: Studies in the Historical Reception of American Cinema* (Princeton: Princeton University Press).

—— (1995), *Bad Women: Controlling Sexuality in Early American Cinema* (Minneapolis: University of Minnesota Press).

Thompson, Kristin (1988), *Breaking the Glass Armour: Neoformalist Film Analysis* (Princeton: Princeton University Press).

Tsivian, Yuri (1994), 'Speeding the Bullet Message: Images of "Elsewheres" in the Age of Electronic Media', paper presented to the Domitor Conference, New York City, June.

Uricchio, William, and **Roberta Pearson** (1993), *Reframing Culture: The Case of the Vitagraph Quality Films* (Princeton: Princeton University Press).

Vardac, Nicholas (1949), *Stage to Screen: Theatrical Method from Garrick to Griffith* (Cambridge, Mass.: Harvard University Press).

Waller, Gregory A. (1995), *Main Street Amusements: Movies and Commerical Entertainment in a Southern City 1896–1930* (Washington: Smithsonian Institution Press).

5

Classical Hollywood film and melodrama

E. Ann Kaplan

In the first half of the twentieth century the classical Hollywood film was the dominant popular form through which the bourgeoisie increasingly represented itself, its values, and the working classes—to whom cinema was earlier largely addressed. This dominant popular form developed out of, and existed alongside, the popular and classical novel and their corollaries—the melodrama and the 'well-made' play—that preceded film and with which it had most affinity (Altman 1992). Indeed, as will be clear in what follows, Hollywood film becomes the site in which notions of the 'classical', developed in relation to drama and the novel as transparent forms reflecting social reality, find themselves in tension with the sensationalism and spectacle of the melodrama.

Geoffrey Nowell-Smith (1977) has argued that theatrical melodrama arose in the late eighteenth century as a form that specifically addressed the new bourgeoisie. As Nowell-Smith puts it, 'Author, audience and subject matter are put on a place of equality,' as against the hierarchical relations implied in the earlier epic and tragic forms. 'Mystified though it may be,' Nowell-Smith notes, 'the address is from one bourgeois to another bourgeois, and the subject matter is the life of the bourgeoisie' (Nowell-Smith 1975: 71). The Greek melodrama, while anticipating some of the modes of hysteria and excess of late eighteenth-century melodrama, is situated in a very different relation to its audience. The characters are far from

mimicking the lives and status of those watching, retaining their mythic and ritualistic dimensions. It is when the monarchic paradigm is overthrown by democratic urges that, first, the melodrama arises and leads, once the camera is invented, to the Hollywood film.

Given these origins of Hollywood cinema, about which theorists of the classical cinema do not basically disagree, it is somewhat paradoxical that such theorists coined the term 'classical cinema' in the first place. As will be clear, the term arose because links were forged (somewhat misleadingly) between cinema and the classical novel rather than with popular theatre. It is precisely this tension between a paradoxical 'classical' (melodramatic) cinematic form and feminist theories of a less 'classical', and therefore possibly subversive, melodramatic mode that I explore below.

Film theorists, then, differ first in their understanding of the 'classical' in cinema, and second in the degree to which they are willing to distinguish classicism from the possibly subversive aspects of the sensationalism and spectacle of melodrama. I first outline differing theories of classical cinema. I will then show how feminist film theorists' interventions in turning to the woman's melodrama (building on the research of Nowell-Smith, Peter Brooks, and Thomas Elsaesser) unwittingly exposed the limitations and blindnesses of both conceptions of classical cinema outlined earlier. I end by offering a position that seems pertinent to the current moment.

Classical cinema

Two main theorizations of classical cinema were developed by film scholars between 1950 and 1980. The first evolved out of French 1950s film criticism—largely through André Bazin, but also, later, through Christian Metz. Bazin's theories were extended in the 1960s in the context of French left politics and under the influence of Althusserian Marxism. The resistances of May 1968 and their aftermath also contributed to the *Cahiers du cinéma* positions outlined below, especially in the work of Jean-Louis Comolli and Jean Narboni. British film scholars in and around the journal *Screen* further developed French theories (e.g. Noël Burch, Stephen Heath, Ben Brewster, and Colin MacCabe). Both the British and the French ideas about classical cinema became part of American scholars' research (see Rosen 1986).

The second conception of classical cinema emerged in reaction to, but still governed by and strangely similar to, these prior theories, mainly through the work on Hollywood narrative by David Bordwell, Janet Staiger, and Kristin Thompson in the 1980s. These theories have become increasingly influential in the 1990s in the wake of students trained in them. In what follows, I detail briefly the development of these two main conceptions of classical cinema from Bazin to Bordwell.

The concept of classical cinema emerged in France through the influence of André Bazin's lectures in the 1950s (collected in Bazin 1967, 1971). Particularly in his essay 'The Evolution of the Language of Cinema', Bazin began to outline the practices of camera-work, editing, and sound that he appreciated in both selected Hollywood and French directors—practices which he claimed as representing cinema at its height (or 'in its essence'). In Bazin's words, seeing films by William Wyler, John Ford, or Marcel Carné, 'one has the feeling that in them an art has found its perfect balance, its ideal form of expression' (Bazin 1967: 29). The necessary practice of montage, which Bazin believed Soviet and German directors fetishized, must be combined with 'the sequence of shots "in depth"'. Citing particularly the films of William Wyler and Orson Welles as exemplary, Bazin argues that 'depth of focus brings the spectator into a relation with the image closer to that which he enjoys with reality' (35). Here, Bazin establishes that narrative coherence and the unity of filmic elements (a kind of classicism in the sense of the French neo-classicism of Racine, for example) define the best in Hollywood cinema.

Although he does not mention the classical novel explicitly, it seems that Bazin has this form in mind as he tries to argue for the kind of cinema that represents its 'highest' mode. Bazin's ideas influenced the *Cahiers du cinéma* collective in the 1960s, but in developing Bazin's ideas in the context of May 1968, the group moved from the concept of Hollywood's aesthetic representing cinema's 'maturity' to a focus on the ideological investment underlying the aesthetic forms Bazin had described. Comolli and Narboni's 1969 *Cahiers du cinéma* editorial, which was to shape dramatically Euro-American research on Hollywood cinema in the 1970s, started from the propostion that since films (like books and magazines) are 'produced and distributed by the capitalist economic system and within the dominant ideology' then they must ask 'which films, books and magazines allow the ideology a free, unhampered passage, transmit it with crystal clarity, serve as its chosen language? And which attempt to make it turn back and reflect itself, intercept it, make it visible by revealing its mechanisms, by blocking them?' (Comolli and Narboni 1969/1989: 23–4). They are not interested in whether or not cinema is a high or low form: for them, what is important (and what defines specific Hollywood films) is the *class* address of its aesthetic forms.

> **Bazin establishes that narrative coherence and the unity of filmic elements (a kind of classicism in the sense of the French neo-classicism of Racine, for example) define the best in Hollywood cinema.**

Comolli and Narboni claim that, while ideology says that 'cinema "reproduces" reality', in fact this idea of reality is 'nothing but an expression of the prevailing ideology'. Here they challenge Bazin's classical notion that the camera 'is an impartial instrument which grasps, or rather is impregnated by, the world in its "concrete reality"' (25). They proceed to distinguish five basically different types of film considered in relation to prevailing ideology. The types range from those completely complicit with prevailing ideology; to those which can be read on two levels, one of which

Touch of Evil (1958)—Orson Welles as a corrupt detective checks out Janet Leigh, pawn in the struggle between Welles and Leigh's husband, Charlton Heston

critiques prevailing ideology; to those which take politics as their subject-matter but do not challenge governing cinematic codes; to, finally, those which 'point out the gap produced between film and ideology by the way the films work, and show how they work' (28).

It was this famous formulation that resulted in the pervasive 1970s binary of a 'classical realist' and a 'counter' cinema perhaps most clearly articulated in Peter Wollen's essay on Godard's *Vent d'est* (1982). This in a way combined Bazin's notion of classicism from classical drama and novel and the ideological schematics of Comolli and Narboni. The ordering and coherence devices of classical Hollywood realism are seen to cover over ideological contradictions and to position the spectator through editing practices within dominant ideology.

Christian Metz's bold attempt to establish an over-arching 'language of film' with his semiotic model of classical Hollywood (he called it 'la grande syntagmatique') was an important attempt to make a science out of filmic narrative patterns (Metz 1974). His in-depth analysis of *Adieu Philippine* (1962) provided a model that others—such as Stephen Heath (1975) in his brilliant study of Welles's *Touch of Evil* (1958)—strove to follow. In doing so, he revealed how diverse and multifaceted these narratives were. While Metz failed to develop a set of codes that would apply to all films, his schema has been useful in determining how far a film fits, or departs from, classical narrative modes. His work helped in understanding film as a 'discourse', and the multiple ways time and space could be ordered in film. But, even within the 'classical' group, fitting a film into Metz's language of film—into the codes he had defined—exposed segments that could not be labelled according to the choices which Metz had described. It was also not always clear how charting the film's narrative segments helped in understanding its meanings (but see Stam *et al.* 1992: 37–56 for positive claims).

Metz's (1975) later psychoanalytically based research on the 'Imaginary Signifier' was influential in introducing *subjectivity* into theories seeking to establish fixed systems on which Hollywood worked. Metz combined Lacan's linguistic extensions of Freud's psychoanalytic theories and his distinction between an 'Imaginary' and a 'Symbolic' psychic arena with Metz's own semiotics to produce an important application of psychoanalytic theories to film and its reception. His most important contributions here were finding a correspondence between Lacan's mirror phase and the spectator's identification with the screen; and his distinction of two main kinds of cinematic identification, which he called 'primary' and 'secondary'.

In Britain and then the United States, the scholar who took up and developed Comolli and Narboni's ideas in the 1970s was Noël Burch. Burch's research developed their notions of five kinds of cinema ranging out from the classical to the avant-garde. This had a great impact on the *Screen* group as well as on the United States' burgeoning cinema studies. However, these scholars, coming as many did out of literary training, returned to Bazin's implicit linking of cinema with the classical *novel* instead of with the popular melodrama, and to the centrality of realism to the form.

Colin MacCabe's (1974) essay 'Realism and Cinema: Notes on Some Brechtian Theses' is a case in point. The essay succinctly summarized and furthered many of the *Cahiers* ideas, only now with specific reference to the classical novel, to Brechtian theatre, and Rossellini films. MacCabe shares with Bazin the idea that classical Hollywood cinema relies on realism, but he is concerned to show that this is only one construction of a 'real', not *the* reality that Bazin claimed cinema could capture. For MacCabe, 'The detour through literature is necessary because, in many ways, the structure is much more obvious there and also because of the historical dominance of the classic realist novel over much film production' (1974: 8). MacCabe argues that classical realism is characterized by a hierarchy of discourses 'defined in terms of an empirical notion of truth', which means that the 'metalanguage is not regarded as material: it is dematerialised to achieve perfect representation—to let the identity of things shine through the window of words' (8). As will be clear

below, the conception of 'classical cinema' produced from this analogy was ultimately insufficient to account for the complex traditions on which 'classical' cinema actually relied.

Noël Burch's 1979 film *Correction, Please!* provided an amusing and informative demonstration of how Hollywood's classical narrative style was historically produced as a method for engaging the spectator's identification and permitting the evolution of a profitable film production *system* not that different from factory modes of production. His film cleverly satirized Hollywood realism and suggested strategies for reversing and revealing its ideological codes.

It is important that this post-Bazin notion of the classical cinema was primarily ideological. It was designed to show how the Hollywood system worked to produce its formidable realist illusionism with its individualist, materialist, and inherently capitalist ideology, repeated from genre to genre through the repetition of similar cinematic codes and conventions.

> **This post-Bazin notion of the classical cinema was primarily ideological. It was designed to show how the Hollywood system worked to produce its formidable realist illusionism with its individualist, materialist, and inherently capitalist ideology, repeated from genre to genre through the repetition of similar cinematic codes and conventions.**

While the broad outlines of the first conception of classical cinema as an *ideological* institution that serves specific class needs and whose values never stray far from mainstream US perspectives still seems valid, clearly there were problems with the rigidity of some formulations and with the absence of empirical research to back up broad claims about the ideological construction of the classical cinema. In much of the discussion, 'Hollywood' is both essentialized and homogenized and analysed with insufficient historical specificity.

It is precisely such lacks that David Bordwell, Janet Staiger, and Kristin Thompson began (and continue) to address, attacking certain broad claims made by ideologial scholars of cinema through the accumulation of data on Hollywood and other films from the silent era onwards (Bordwell *et al*. 1985). Like Metz's 'language of cinema', what has become known as 'the Wisconsin project' aims to return cinema analysis to 'science' and away from thematic modes, although their method differs from that of Metz. They refuse the psychoanalytic argument about an ideological appeal to an unconscious and pursue a cognitive psychology approach. Viewers are seen as predisposed to look for the cues a film's narrative provides, and then to organize the sensory data into patterns for processing information already available to the viewers. The method was first worked out in relation to early Soviet directors and Carl Dreyer's films, as well as with Japanese cinema. A 'hypothetical entity', the viewer 'executes operations based on inferences and assumptions to generate the *fabula* from the *syuzhet*, which provides cues as to the order, frequency, and duration of events' (Nichols 1992: 59). For Bordwell, 'the classical Hollywood film . . . presents psychologically defined individuals as its principal causal agents, struggling to solve a clear-cut problem or to attain specific goals, the story ending either with a resolution of the problem, or a clear achievement or non-achievement of the goals. Causality revolving around character provides the prime unifying principle, while spatial configurations are motivated by realism as well as compositional necessity' (Stam *et al*. 1992: 189). Bill Nichols notes the many strengths of Bordwell's analysis of narrational process, including 'its supple blend of theory, criticism and, to a more limited extent, history' (Nichols 1992: 55).

But ironically the structure of Bordwell's overall system is not so dissimilar from that of the ideological notion of classical cinema: Bordwell's formalism results in a highly condensed and somewhat mechanical theory in which he isolates in all texts a 'dominant' to which all other elements are subordinated (Altman 1992). However, for Bordwell, this structure emerged for reasons of narrative coherence rather than (as with MacCabe) to impose as 'truth' a limited and class-based concept of reality. Bordwell, Staiger, and Thompson (1985) offer empirical studies to support claims *vis-à-vis* how film narrative evolved historically, and show that things were in fact more varied and less ideologically driven by bourgeois economic motives than the French-influenced proponents of classical cinema had argued.

I do not here aim to debate in depth the relative merits of these two broad positions on classical cinema—positions that remain pretty much in circulation and that, as indicated, strangely mimic each other in their would-be scientism and would-be 'objectivity'. While I value the empirical research of scholars like Bordwell, I am not convinced by the substitution of a 'formalist poetics' for a governing system of ideology (see *Film Criticism* 1993, esp. Kaplan 1993, Wood 1993). Bordwell's poetics usefully involves close attention to the surface of a film, which means giving perception a bigger role and attending carefully to any one film's unique functions and effects. Important also is the detailed attention to historical development in analysing film narrative. But this begs the question of what Bordwell, Staiger, and Thompson mean by 'history' just as the question was begged by the ideological group. As Nichols points out, Bordwell's notion of history is very limited, not including reference to television, the other arts, or to non-Western films. Further, while Bordwell claims that feminist analyses and concern with minority discourse in film are simply new ideological orientations, telling us nothing about a film *per se*, I would note that there cannot be a 'poetics of film' which is not already deeply implicated in Western issues of race and gender. Bordwell's 'science' excludes feminist theory and also, as Nichols notes, 'regards the viewer as a sexless, genderless, classless, stateless "hypothetical entity"' (Nichols 1992: 64). Only cyborgs—that is, imaginary entities that combine human and machine—Nichols ironically concludes, fit the kind of decoder of cues, or executer of operations that Bordwell's poetics requires.

Thus, we have the irony of a similarity between Bordwell's position and that of Comolli and Narboni. Both claim to outline a specific classical *system*, but their concerns with the system are quite opposite: the French position focuses on cinema's ideological inscription, Bordwell's on the way it functions cognitively to transfer meaning regarding narrative codes and plots. He is not interested in any film's ideology; the French are not interested in any film's 'poetics'. And neither can deal with historically positioned subjects for whom much is at stake in cinematic identification.

Both these conceptions of the 'classical' minimize, if they do not ignore, the other powerful influences—those of popular stage melodrama and consumer culture—feeding the developments in Hollywood and producing the film industry as a site of tension and contradictions. In regard to the melodramatic aspects of sensationalism and the spectacle, the invention of film at the turn of the century was part of a crucial change taking place in the late nineteenth century with the advent of modern consumer culture and advertising. As Allon White has argued, this change 'involved the displacement of pleasure into the realm of the signifier (form, style, association) and its dissociation from the "real" world of work and dreary production'. White notes that this 'dissociation was a necessary correlative to the unfettering of commodity-centered, consumer capitalism' and that 'the creaming off of the signifier from the signified marked a new phase in the production of Western subjectivity in its long march from Feudalism to a bureaucratic society of controlled consumption' (White 1983).

Consumer culture hooks onto the subject's inevitable desiring mode, re-enforcing and exploiting it by constant stimulation. Beginning with the department store and the stage melodrama, the culture of the spectacle is fully inscribed in society with the development of the cinema as an apparatus. Film becomes the form that replaces the popular theatre melodrama in the way it addresses desires invoked by the new consumer culture and, while the popular stage melodrama continues, it is also affected by the culture of the spectacle. The popular novel begins to use description in a self-consciously 'cinematic' style, while some theatre leaves spectacle to the cinema and becomes minimalist.

Film's mode as spectacle dovetails with modes of consumer culture in a circular fashion. That is, film emerges at a certain stage of consumer culture, its modes increasing consumerism and encouraging upward class-striving through accumulation of consumer products. Cinema stimulates new desires and signifying of status through objects. With the invention of cinema, a new self-consciousness is built into the subject's constitution. If Lacan's mirror phase had always been a necessary part of the subject's entry into the Symbolic, it now becomes an inherent part of cultural experience. The other self offered by the mirror becomes part of society's cultural mechanisms, transforming the subject's ways of perceiving and desiring.

Many of the theories of classical cinema I have outlined tended to omit these aspects of sensationalism and spectacle, along with attention to the subject in general, let alone the subject as gendered. Paradoxically, the new culture of the spectacle (mainly used to reinscribe oppressive female modes) as it emerged in women's melodrama could be used to *destabilize* and

subvert the unifying and ordering aspects of classicism, especially *vis-à-vis* the female subject, the female spectator.

> Paradoxically, the new culture of the spectacle (mainly used to reinscribe oppressive female modes) as it emerged in women's melodrama could be used to *destabilize* and subvert the unifying and ordering aspects of classicism, especially *vis-à-vis* the female subject, the female spectator.

Male theorists of classical cinema basically had in mind a male spectator and male unconscious processes. While still working within the limits of French male theory of the classical cinema (and not yet theorizing women's melodrama), Laura Mulvey's well-known 1975 essay 'Visual Pleasure and Narrative Cinema' set up the terms for the first round of feminist discussion of classical cinema in illuminating how that cinema basically was constructed for the male spectator which theorists had assumed without question. Constructing a model of the cinematic gaze as it embodied Freud's twin mechanisms of voyeurism and fetishism, Mulvey showed how, in classical cinema, woman was situated as bearer of meaning rather than maker of meaning. This insight about the main classical male genres led Mulvey to claim that Hollywood could not offer anything to women, and that women must free the camera from its realist oppressions.

Melodrama

It was in response to Mulvey's essay and in an effort to see what Hollywood might offer women that feminist film theorists turned to study the melodrama form that explicitly addresses woman, that is, to what has been called 'the weepie' or 'the woman's film'. The most constructive and challenging work on the classical cinema, then, emerged almost by default in this new attention to the women's melodrama form. The 1970s concept of classical cinema is qualified in this research, or repositioned in different ways depending on theorists' concerns. In critiquing the male bias of classical film theory, feminist film theorists (perhaps unintentionally) opened classical film up to far different perspectives, issues, and concerns.

Earlier (largely male) historians and literary theorists had been concerned to chart the history of melodrama as a specific theatre and film genre. Peter Brooks (1972) and Thomas Elsaesser (1972) expanded the concept of melodrama beyond the confines of a specific theatrical genre to focus on a generalized type of aesthetic experience that produces specific emotional effects in the spectator. Brooks's main thesis is that melodrama is a response to the 'loss of tragic vision' exacerbated by the Industrial Revolution and the creation of a society deprived of an organic and hierarchical order. The ensuing solidification of the bourgeois class, with its specific form of nuclear family, was accompanied by an ethical vacuum in the public sphere. Melodrama, then, is a type of sense-making characterized by 'indulgence of strong emotionalism; moral polarization and schematization; extreme states of being, situations, actions; overt villainy, persecution of the good and final reward of virtue; inflated and extravagant expression; dark plottings, suspense, breathtaking peripety' (Brooks 1976: 4).

If one accepts Peter Brooks's general definition of the melodramatic, then all the main Hollywood genres are melodrama in attempting an ethical recentring, a 'search for a new plenitude in reaction to the decentering of modern consciousness' (Brooks 1976). This produces some confusion in relation to theories of the classical cinema which originally did not per se include the term 'melodrama', nor distinguish amongst the main forms of Hollywood genres within an overall category of 'melodrama'.

A further distinction needs to be made between the melodrama form (including those addressed to male spectators) and the Bazinian and Bordwellian concepts of the 'classical'. For, as Brooks and Elsaesser had already pointed out, melodrama conventions often disrupt or work against the ordering and unifying tendencies which the concept of the 'classical' implies. In Rick Altman's words, melodrama permits excess not to be positioned outside the system but to have a system of its own—a system that complicates and puts pressure on the dominant (Altman 1992: 34). But the early male critics engaged in this work focused more on broadly defined bourgeois ideology about the family in general than on the films' specifically *female* address.

But it was feminist film critics who discovered a need to distinguish the films specifically geared for female audiences (women's melodramas) from those aimed at both male and female spectators generally. Films focused on in this research include the series of films made from the notorious stage melodrama *East Lynne* (see Kaplan 1992); King Vidor's *Stella Dallas* (1937); the two versions of *Imitation of Life* (Jonathan Stahl, 1934, Douglas Sirk, 1959); and Dorothy Arzner's films. The focus on women's melodrama—as against the implicit category of melodrama for all Hollywood films—included giving attention to film and television melodrama forms seen as explicitly addressing female spectators, and as dealing with issues pertinent to women. There is, then, a 'politics' of melodrama structures that feminist theorists exposed and (sometimes building on work by Stephen Heath) linked to the psychoanalytic processes at work in melodrama. The fact that melodrama is the genre which, in its recent form, arises with modernization—that is, at the intersection of absolutist (or premodern) social forms and later specifically capitalist forms—makes it particularly pertinent to the study of maternal (and other) images in the modern period (Kaplan 1992: 21–6). For feminists, melodramas open space prohibited by the so-called classical realist film text, which is restricted to oppressive patriarchal norms.

> For feminists, melodramas open space prohibited by the so-called classical realist film text, which is restricted to oppressive patriarchal norms.

In remedying the gap in male discussion of melodrama, feminist critics brought renewed interest in melodrama, and asked new questions of the form while building on Brooks's and Elsaesser's theories. In a first wave of work, critics like Laura Mulvey (who saw the possibilities of the woman's film) and Mary Ann Doane (to take two important examples) began to explore the important difference between films addressed to a male and to a female spectator. Mulvey, writing in 1977, defined the family melodrama as explicitly a form with female address, one that deliberately functioned to counter-balance the dominant male genres. For her, 'a dramatic rendering of women's frustrations, publicly acting out an adjustment of balance

Duel in the Sun (1946)—
Gregory Peck and Jennifer
Jones in a combination of
classical western and
melodrama

in the male ego is socially and ideologically beneficial' (1977/1989: 40). But she goes on to assume that the melodrama involves 'reaffirmation of the Oedipus complex'. That is, although in the family melodrama '[t]he phallocentric, castration-based, more misogynist fantasies of patriarchal culture' are 'sacrificed in the interest of civilization', Mulvey reads 'civilization' in terms of how man comes to be man. Adapting Freud and Kristeva, for Mulvey 'civilization' is produced through male rejection of the mother, and the insistence on the mother's serving patriarchy. Nevertheless.

Mulvey finds something important for women in these films about female victims. First, the mother may try to keep her son with her, down in the Imaginary and in this way resist the mother's position as a patriarchal function. As Mulvey puts it: 'In the absence of any coherent culture of oppression, the simple fact of recognition has aesthetic importance: there is a dizzy satisfaction in witnessing the way that sexual difference under patriarchy is fraught, explosive, and erupts dramatically into violence within its own stomping ground, the family' (39).

Building on this work, Mary Ann Doane has shown that most women's films construct a heroine who is a victim, entailing a masochistic identification for the female viewer. These repeated masochistic scenarios effectively immobilize the female spectator, refusing her the imaginary identification which in the male forms produces a sense of mastery and control.

Mary Ann Doane's work has been central in theorizing the female spectator in the woman's film. In a 1984 essay, she uses Freud's work on femininity to build on Mulvey's essay, arguing that woman is constructed differently in relation to the processes of looking (Doane 1984). Doane goes to French feminist theory to show how woman cannot assume the fetishistic position because 'the lack of distance between seeing and understanding, the mode of judging "in a flash" (a reference to Freud's theory of the girl's sudden reaction to seeing the penis for the first time) is conducive to what might be termed as "over identification" with the image' (69).

Doane views this over-identification with the image as necessarily entailing a passive, masochistic position because of the position woman is assigned in cinematic narrative. On the other hand, woman may also identify with the active hero, in which case, as Mulvey had already argued, woman took up a masculine spectator position. Doane moves from here to discussion of woman's more natural transvestism resulting from her apparently greater inherent bisexuality. As Juliet Mitchell has noted (in contrast to some recent feminist Freudian revisionists), male sexual identity is more sure than feminine identity because of the greater compulsion (via the castration complex) to turn away from the first feminine identification with the mother. While the girl also must reject this early feminine identification (as Mitchell put it, the shadow of the phallus falls over the girl's ego as also over the boy's, creating a masculine 'I' born out of the baby's desiring what the mother desires), this identification, albeit much reduced, nevertheless remains. The girl is then more naturally bisexual than the boy, slipping easily over into masculine identification.

But for Doane this transvestism is not recuperable, and woman is left with only two alternatives: the masochism of over-identification or the narcissism entailed in becoming one's own object of desire' (Doane 1987: 18–22). A third possibility, that of the masquerade (i.e. exaggerating the accoutrements of the patriarchal feminine in order to create a distance from the image, to reveal femininity as precisely a mask covering a non-

identity and thus to disrupt patriarchal systems), is not really a solution. But in this later work, Doane sees possibilities of dislocating the position assigned woman through understanding the various spectatorship places (176–83).

Doane's formulation tends to generalize the mechanisms she explores to the entire genre of the woman's film, including its subgroupings. Elsewhere, I have differentiated those films addressing women that involve such despecularization of the female spectator from others which function to allow the female spectator certain kinds of pleasure in the struggle to resist patriarchal definitions and positionings (Kaplan 1992).

Another problem with psychoanalytic film theory in general, pointed out by Teresa de Lauretis, is the focus on the gaze—on woman as spectacle, to the detriment of considering types of identification other than with the camera. De Lauretis (1985) argues that narrative identificationn and closure are equally important and may afford the female spectator more space. These arguments gain force through linking the woman's melodrama to the nineteenth-century popular woman's novel, since obviously issues of the gaze are less central in fiction.

In a second wave of work on the family melodrama, critics like Linda Williams (1984) and Tania Modleski (1983) (to take again just two examples) have used spectatorship theory to argue that women are not merely offered identification with victims in these films. Referring to *Stella Dallas*, for example, Williams showed that female victims are situated in relation to other female figures with whom the female spectator identifies as well and that, out of this multiple and shifting series of identifications, the spectator learns about victimization, about woman's deprivations, and glimpses other female ways of being (Williams 1984), while Modleski's (1993) study of Hitchcock argued that they included female address. Stimulating debates followed these interventions (Kaplan 1985a, b, 1986).

Conclusion

Mulvey's early work exposed the oppressive aspects of the classical cinema outlined for women, but did not critique the theory *per se*. It offered an understanding of the sexist bias of classical cinema without questioning its premises. But the study of melodrama and the address of the genre of the woman's film as summarized above did implicitly begin to critique the male assumptions and obsessions of prior formulations of classical cinema. Feminist film criticism of women's melodramas thus opened up new avenues of discussion *vis-à-vis* classical cinema. It complicated the rigid totalizing tendencies in both conceptions of classical cinema with which I began. It allowed for multiple identifications, not just a blind adherence to a proposed 'dominant' (Bordwell *et al.* 1985: 41–84) or a capitalist bourgeois ideology (Burch 1969; Comolli and Narboni 1989).

Certainly, the overall values that Hollywood cinema still promotes are those of individualism, materialism, heterosexuality (despite the increasing interest in gay and lesbian couples and issues), and the nuclear family. And it promotes these values through a specific set of cinematic codes, prime among which is illusory realism. Hollywood illusionism masks the actual operations of power and patriarchal hierarchies. As long as it does this, it is an ideological cinema whose strategies promote unconscious identification with protagonists through appeals to erotic aims.

Yet the breakdown of the Hollywood studio system has allowed variations of the classical cinema to become more mainstream. Arguably, since 1960 the large Hollywood studios that provided the institutional basis for the cinema that film theorists named 'classical' have become less monolithic and, in the course of this process, the distribution and exhibition systems have changed significantly. If the needs of the American middle classes continue to find expression in Hollywood film even today, it is in a form modified to fit existing social formations.

BIBLIOGRAPHY

***Altman, Rick** (1992), 'Dickens, Griffith, and Film Theory Today', in Jane Gaines (ed.), *Classical Hollywood Narrative: The Paradigm Wars* (Durham, NC: Duke University Press).

Bazin, André (1967/1971), *What is Cinema?*, 2 vols., trans. Hugh Gray (Berkeley: University of California Press).

***Bordwell, David, Janet Staiger,** and **Kristin Thompson** (1985), *The Classical Hollywood Cinema: Film Style and Mode of Production to 1960* (New York: Columbia University Press).

Brooks, Peter (1976), *The Melodramatic Imagination* (New Haven: Yale University Press).

Burch, Noël (1969), *Theory of Film Practice* (Princeton, NJ: Princeton University Press).

Comolli, Jean-Louis, and **Jean Narboni** (1969/1989), 'Cinema/Ideology/Criticism', in Bill Nichols (ed.), *Movies and Methods*, 2 vols., i (Berkeley: University of California Press).

de Lauretis, Teresa (1985), 'Oedipus Interruptus', *Wide Angle*, 7/1–2: 34–40.

Doane, Mary Ann (1981), 'Film and the Masquerade: Filming the Female Body', *October*, 17 (Summer), 25–32.

—— (1984), 'The Woman's Film: Possession and Address', in *Re-Vision: Essays in Feminist Criticism* (Frederick, Md.: University Publications of America, with the American Film Institute).

—— (1987), *The Desire to Desire* (Bloomington: Indiana University Press).

Elsaesser, Thomas (1972), 'Tales of Sound and Fury: Observations on the Family Melodrama', *Monogram*, 4: 2–15.

Film Criticism (1993), 17/2–3 (Winter–Spring), Special Issue: *Interpretation Inc.: Issues in Contemporary Film Studies*.

Heath, Stephen (1975), 'Film and System: Terms of Analysis, Part I', *Screen*, 16/1 (Spring), 7–77.

Kaplan, E. Ann (1985a), 'Dialogue: Ann Kaplan Replies to Linda Williams' "Something else besides a Mother": *Stella Dallas* and the Maternal Melodrama', *Cinema Journal*, 24/2: 40–3.

—— (1985b), 'Dialogue: E. Ann Kaplan Replies to Petro and Flinn' (continuing *Stella Dallas* debate), *Cinema Journal*, 25/1: 51–4.

—— (1986), 'Dialogue: Thoughts on Melodrama': Reply to Christine Gledhill' (continuing *Stella Dallas* debate), *Cinema Journal*, 25/4: 49–53.

—— (1992), *Motherhood and Representation: The Mother in Popular Culture and Melodrama* (New York: Routledge).

—— (1993), 'Disorderly Disciplines', *Film Criticism*, 17/2–3 (Winter–Spring), Special Issue: *Interpretation Inc.: Issues in Contemporary Film Studies*, 48–52.

MacCabe, Colin (1974), 'Realism and Cinema: Notes on Some Brechtian Theses', *Screen*, 15/2 (Autumn), 7–32.

Metz, Christian (1974), *Film Language: A Semiotics of the Cinema* (New York: Oxford University Press).

—— (1975), 'The Imaginary Signifier', *Screen*, 16/2 (Summer), 14–76.

Mitchell, Juliet (1975), *Psychoanalysis and Feminism* (New York: Vintage Books).

Modleski, Tania (1983), 'The Rhythms of Reception: Daytime Television and Women's Work', in E. Ann Kaplan (ed.), *Regarding Television. Critical Approaches: An Anthology* (Frederick, Md.: University Publications of America).

Mulvey, Laura (1975/1989), 'Visual Pleasure and Narrative Cinema', in *Visual and Other Pleasures* (London: Macmillan).

—— (1977/1989), 'Notes on Sirk and Melodrama', in *Visual and Other Pleasures* (London: Macmillan).

Nichols, Bill (1992), 'Form Wars: The Political Unconscious of Formalist Theory', in Jane Gaines (ed.), *Classical Hollywood Narrative: The Paradigm Wars* (Durham, NC: Duke University Press).

Nowell-Smith, Geoffrey (1977), 'Minnelli and Melodrama', *Screen*, 18/2: 113–18.

Rosen, Philip (ed.) (1986), *Narrative, Apparatus, Ideology: A Film Theory Reader* (New York: Columbia University Press).

Stam, Robert, Robert Burgoyne, and **Sandy Flitterman-Lewis** (1992), *New Vocabularies in Film Semiotics: Structuralism, Post-Structuralism and Beyond* (New York: Routledge).

White, Allon (1983), 'Why did the Signifiers Come out to Play?', MS.

Williams, Linda (1984), '"Something else besides a Mother": *Stella Dallas* and the Maternal Melodrama', *Cinema Journal*, 24/1: 2–27.

Wollen, Peter (1982), *Readings and Writings: Semiotics and Counter-Strategies* (London: Verso).

Wood, Robin (1993), 'Critical Positions and the End of Civilization; or, A Refusal to Join the Club', *Film Criticism*, 17/2–3 (Winter–Spring), Special Issue: *Interpretation Inc.: Issues in Contemporary Film Studies*, 79–92.

Casablanca

Richard Maltby from Richard Maltby, *Harmless Entertainment: Hollywood and the Ideology of Consensus*
(Metuchen, NJ: Scarecrow Press, 1983)

The primary fiction that the Hollywood cinema of the consensus—to whose aesthetic strategies *The Green Berets* (1968) and *Guess who's Coming to Dinner* (1967) both adhere—requires its audience to accept is that they should think of the story a film is telling them as if it were a real event. That is not to say that they are intended to regard, say, the story of *The Wizard of Oz* (1939) as having actually taken place in front of a fortuitously placed camera. But they are expected to operate a particular suspension of disbelief in which the mimesis of the photographic image reinforces the circumstantial and psychological 'realism' of the events those images contain, so that they can presume upon those normative rules of spatial perception, human behaviour, and causality which govern their conduct in the world outside the cinema. Thus they may respond to the characters as if they were real people, and regard the story that is told through the characters as if it were unfolding before them without the mediation of cameras or narrative devices.

Hollywood's realism operated at two levels. Perfect reproduction effaced the techniques by which it produced a seamless flow, and concentrated the audience's attention on the contents of that flow, the narrative. The spatial construction of narrative placed the spectator in the film, while the ordering of events attached the spectator emotionally to its characters as benevolent sources of meaning and significance. Despite the opportunism of its techniques, the cinema of the consensus was committed absolutely to the maintenance of continuity as the primary ingredient of its realism. As a result it was firmly attached to the articulation of a coherent narrative structure.

The narrative of *Casablanca* (Michael Curtiz, 1943)—which may indisputably be regarded as a 'classic Hollywood text' of the consensus—is constructed to support and clarify the story of the film, aiming at a coherence in the revelation of the plot in order to concentrate attention on the story as it is revealed. The audience is attached to the film by the process of the revealing of the story, not by the facts of the story's revelations. One example among many is the introduction of Ingrid Bergman, and the establishment of her previous relationship with Bogart. Up to this point the film has concentrated on establishing its locale, Bogart's cynical isolationism ('I stick my neck out for nobody'), and the apparent major plot device of the theft of the letters of transit and the arrival of Resistance leader Victor Laszlo (Paul Henreid). Henreid and Bergman first appear entering Rick's Café in a long medium tracking shot, which takes them past Sam (Dooley Wilson) at the piano. Wilson and Bergman

seem to recognize each other, and Wilson looks worried and shakes his head. A signal to the audience's attention has been provided, but it is not immediately pursued. Henreid and Bergman are joined first by Berger (John Qualen), a member of the Resistance, and then by Captain Renault (Claude Rains), in conversations about Henreid's situation. Bergman asks Rains about Wilson—'somewhere I've seen him'—a remark whose significance is signalled by its delivery in extreme close-up. Rains supplies an enigmatic description of Bogart, and its impact on Bergman is again shown in close-up when the group is joined by Major Strasser (Conrad Veidt). However, the subject is not pursued and conversation returns to Henreid's politics and future. But the disruptive influence of Bogart's presence is registered by the repetition of close shots of Bergman, detaching her from the men's conversation. When Rains and Veidt return to their table, a female guitarist begins a song, during which Bergman and Wilson exchange looks of recognition, and Wilson repeats his concerned expression. Once more, the cue is left hanging while Henreid joins Qualen at the bar. Bergman calls Wilson over to her table. Wilson tries to convince her Bogart has another girl, but she tells him 'You used to be a much better liar, Sam.' He replies, 'Leave him alone, Miss Ilsa, you're bad luck to him. In its ordering, her next line encapsulates in microcosm the mechanism of the narrative: 'Play it once, Sam, for old times' sake . . . play it, Sam, play, "As Time Goes By".' The audience are inveigled into a process of revelation, without discovering, until the end, what the object of that revelation is. The spectator is cued to anticipate an event, the content and meaning of which has not been disclosed. Wilson's playing of a song whose significance is never explained is made important by its presentation over an extreme, melancholic, close-up of Bergman that lasts for twenty seconds, much longer than any previous shot. The song brings Bogart to the table, and the existence of a mutual bond is again established by the intercutting of extreme close-ups of their faces (the first close-up of Bogart in the film), reinforced by the sudden introduction of violins on the soundtrack. At this point, with the nature of their involvement completely unstated by the same means that it has been declared central to the narrative, Rains and Henreid appear once again to change the subject, and the couple spend the rest of the scene exchanging looks and reminiscences of their last meeting ('The Germans wore grey, you wore blue') which provide the spectator with no more explicit information.

The process of revelation is continued, at a broader level, thoughout the narrative. The audience witness Bogart's

Casablanca continued

The classical narrative text 'speaking with two voices'—*Casablanca* (1942)

Casablanca continued

remembering his time with Bergman in Paris, while her marriage to Henreid, her intention to leave Henreid for Bogart, and Bogart's final decision to send her to America with Henreid are all revealed by similar constructions to that of her introduction. The plot is presented as a linear causal chain, each event located by a relationship of cause and effect to those which precede and follow it, but it only functions if it is correctly placed in the chain. Bogart's memory of Paris is, obviously, chronologically misplaced—it happened before all the other events of the film. But it is, more importantly, placed at the point in the plot when its partial vision of events (Bergman's explanations will qualify it later) is most emotionally affective.

The linear causal chain of the plot leads inevitably to a point of resolution, but because the spectator is engaged in the process by which the story is revealed, he or she can ignore the determinist causality of such a structure and the restrictions it places on possible interpretations of an event. There is, inevitably, a tension between the plot's determinist pressure towards a resolution of events, and the 'realist' objections to an idealist simplicity in the tidy end-stopping of events at the film's conclusion. This structurally insoluble tension in narrative realism (the force that draws realism towards melodrama) is dissipated by the consensus cinema's mode of construction. Guided through the plot by the revelatory narrative, the audience is encouraged to feel unconcerned about the conflict between determinism and normative, unresolved reality by the coherence of what they see and hear. Their acceptance of the story comes not from what they are told, but from the way it is told to them. They can accommodate the contradictions of realist narrative by seeing the events of the film as amounting to a crisis which determines the course of the lives of the characters in it. The typical film of the consensus ends at the point at which another film might begin: in *Casablanca*, for example, Bogart's adventures with the Free French in Tangiers, or Bergman and Henreid in America.

What holds for narrative structure also holds for scene construction. Because the coherent narrative locates an individual scene at one point in its causal chain, an element of the scene must be reserved for the elucidation and justification of that process of causal linkage. Each scene in *Casablanca* advances the plot by confirming the knowledge the audience have derived from previous scenes, and adding further information to it. The process of confirmation is enacted through the consistency with which the scenes are presented, a consistency which can be regarded as a form of psychological and circumstantial realism. Consistency of character motivation projects a believable psychology: when Bogart rejects Bergman on her first night-time visit to the

café the audience recognize that his drinking has exposed the sentimentality beneath the cynical exterior. When he meets her in the market the next morning and asks for the explanation he turned down the night before, the audience understand that the cynicism ('after all, I got stuck with a railway ticket, I think I'm entitled to know') is only a defensive veneer. Bogart's psychology, along with that of the other characters, is being gradually revealed to the audience, who have to construct it from the information the film provides. Circumstantial realism, similarly, is provided by the consistency with which the film describes and relates its locations and the creation of the seamless illusion hinges, at a level more basic than psychological characterization, on the two fundamental areas of perception most immediately available to cinematic manipulation: the depiction of time and space.

A cinematic narrative is temporally composed of a set of ellipses; it is a distillation of a series of significant events. The presentation of time within a narrative is more immediately apparent than the presentation of space, since the periods not included in the narrative are evident by their omission. We may, for example, see a man getting into his car and driving off, and then cut to his arriving at his destination. The coherent narrative, however, attempts to disguise the elliptical nature of its temporal construction by subordinating both the actual time of a depicted event and the real time experienced by the spectator in the cinema to the artificial, perceived time presented by the narrative. For this purpose, it uses a number of devices to create continuity in perception of two narratively linked discontinuous events. The most simple device is a passage of 'linking' music, which, by its rhythmic or patterned management of the passage of time, provides a suitable vehicle for the presentation of the narrative's temporal continuum. Appropriately enough, the opening bars of 'As Time Goes By' have this function in *Casablanca*. The same purpose, the subordination of external time to the narrative continuum, may be served by the use of 'linking' shots, the content of which is unimportant save for their function of relating two consecutive scenes by an association of ideas. For example, one scene may end up with a tilt up off the characters onto blue sky, followed by a cut, perhaps imperceptible, to blue sky, which tilts down to the same characters in a different location, different characters, or whatever. The plane to Lisbon serves this purpose on more than one occasion in *Casablanca*, transferring attention from one group of people looking at it to another, or to the scene of its arrival. The same effect can be achieved by the use of fades or dissolves, which have their own connotations as accounts of elapsed time, or, in the extreme assertion of narrative control over plot events, by a montage sequence. In each case the linkage device

Casablanca continued

establishes a chain of causality which is stylistically asserted by the film, subordinating other perceptions of time to that of the narrative. The arbitrariness of all these devices is contained by their conventionality. The attribution of a distinctive connotation to each of them (a fade implies a longer ellipsis than a dissolve, while a wipe suggests spatial rather than temporal alteration) covers their presence as techniques by emphasizing their function as meaning. The coherent narrative cinema requires that the scene-to-scene linkage should be as unobtrusive as possible, since the main intention is to persuade the audience to assume the connections of linear causality, in order that they focus their attention on the plot or theme. The technical devices of the cinema of coherence aim to divert the spectator's attention away from themselves as mechanisms of the illusion, and to concentrate it more on the illusion they create—that is, to divert the spectator's attention away from the film as object to the subject of the film.

A similar argument may be advanced in relation to the depiction of space within the scene. A coherent narrative aims to present space in terms which are immediately recognizable to its audience. This requirement encourages the construction of images which do not distort conventional perspective relations, implying that most images will be recorded by lenses in a relativey narrow range of focal lengths. Equally, it encourages the development of

conventional patterns for the juxtaposition of shots: the pattern of establishing long shot, medium shot, close-up is one example; angle–reverse angle cutting is another. When these conventions of the image are disrupted, the audience is being signalled: for example, the close-up of Bogart when he first sees Bergman not only takes the camera closer to him than it has been before, breaking a convention of distance, but is also shot with a wider-angle lens than is used for other close-ups, and taken from an angle above, rather than level with, Bogart's eyeline. All this communicates surprise and discomfort without articulating them explicitly, or markedly disrupting the image stream. Unless aiming for a particular extraordinary effect such as shock, the coherent narrative requires the audience to understand the way the space in a scene works (e.g. the area in which a character can move), in the same way that it aims for an unconscious awareness of the temporal ellipses in the narrative. They share the same purpose of convincing the audience of the film's stylistic benevolence in presenting the most readily comprehensible depiction of events. We understand by a simple time ellipsis that nothing important has happened in it, and this process is made easier by a stylistic device that is self-effacing and allows us to ignore it. The normal perception of spatial relationships similarly allows us to take them for granted as comprehensible. Thus it is possible for us to divert our energies towards comprehending the events of the plot, rather than the manner of their presentation.

Casablanca

Rick Altman 'Dickens, Griffith and Film Theory Today' in Jane Gaines (ed.), *Classical Hollywood Narrative: The Paradigm Wars* (Durham, NC: Duke University Press, 1992)

For years the classical text was seen as opposed to the modernism of the Brechtian, the reflexive, and the dialogic. Then, in the wake of Barthes's *S/Z*, study after study attempted to champion this or that novel or style of filmmaking by demonstrating its relative modernity. Perhaps we now have reached the point where we acknowledge the short-sightedness of both enterprises. If so many apparently classical texts have modernist leanings, then maybe the classical text is not as unitary as was once thought. It operates as a dialogic text precisely because its single-focus linearity presupposes an embedded dual-focus context. With one foot in history and the other still in myth, the classical narrative text must always speak with two voices, each using its own logic.

Take the case of the quintessential Hollywood, Warner's 1942 *Casablanca*. The film's linear narrative stretches from Rick and Ilsa's idyll in Paris, through their reunion in Casablanca, to Rick's final heroic decision to send Ilsa off with her husband, while he and the French captain Renault walk off into the distance towards a career in the Resistance. Like *Le Père Goriot*, however, *Casablanca* does not owe its longevity to this familiar linear story. If *Casablanca* continues to enjoy success, it is not so much because of the ability of Bogie and Bergman to express the changing state of their emotions (in fact, in this film they are better at hiding emotions than expressing them), but because of the stakes for which they are playing. The secret of this film lies in its apocalyptic intensity. With the stereotypically sinister German major Strasser and the archetypically pure Resistance hero Victor Laszlo embodying the values of Good and Evil, as represented by the Nazis and their victims, the atmosphere of *Casablanca* provides a melodramatic backdrop to the personal actions that capture our more immediate attention.

While character psychology appears to advance the film through a chain of cause-and-effect relationships, the major moments are either coincidental or only minimally motivated. What brings Ilsa to the very café run by the man she jilted in Paris? (Little more than coincidence.) How does Rick gain possession of the visas apparently needed to liberate Ilsa and her husband? (Through the minimally motivated activities of the Peter Lorre character Ugarte, who is killed off as soon as the function has been fulfilled.) What motivates Rick's decision to send Ilsa off to freedom with her husband? (The overall melodramatic set-up much more than any clearly developed line of psychological reasoning.) How do Ilsa and her husband actually escape from Casablanca? (Not through the use of the much-touted visas which turn out

to be nothing more than a plot-unifying Macguffin, but by an armed confrontation between the Nazi commander and his liberty-loving American opponent.) What leads Captain Renault, ever the self-serving neutral womanizer, to break his bottle of Vichy water and march towards a life of bravery and moral rectitude? (Congenial hatred of the Hun? Embodiment of audience desires? No explanation is offered except to recognize that Renault is making the right decision within the film's melodramatic framework, even if the decision is not clearly motivated by the film's psychological progression.)

Nearly every character, every glance, serves to heighten the air of impending doom—or freedom. With the exception of *Casablanca*'s profiteers (and even profiteering has long been recognized as a common symptom of apocalyptic intensity), every character is directly defined by the conflict between national allegiance and personal independence. An aroused soldier, a sad woman, an expectant old man—all embody the hope and freedom represented by the United States in opposition to the cruelty and imprisonment threatened by the Nazis. Even the paradigms of money, clothing, and linguistic accent contribute to this opposition. Indeed, this effect has been heightened by the fact that one of the film's descriptive terms—concentration camp—has since taken on such strong connotations of inhuman cruelty.

We should not conclude, though, that the entire power of the film's melodrama is spent of the local and historical. By its very nature melodrama carries eternal mythic qualities, like those that make Major Strasser embody not just Nazism, but Evil itself, and those that make Bogie and Bergman an archetypal couple. The film's theme song further reinforces this sense that we are witnessing more than just an episode in the life of some guy named Rick.

Whenever the film moves towards psychology and time it is wrenched back towards myth and eternity. It is the very conflict between the two that leads to the bitter-sweet conclusion.

Why does *Casablanca* continue to enchant audiences around the world? Because of its linear causality? Yes, without a doubt. The film's suspense and expectation are carefully used to focus our attention on the future. As we dutifully fill all the plot's little gaps, we settle comfortably into the spectator position allotted to us. Because of the film's melodramatic underpinnings? Yes again. *Casablanca* is a film about human allegiance to things of eternal beauty and value. The one pushes us towards a temporal solution, the

Casablanca continued

union of Bogie and Bergman, the beautiful couple, while the other pulls us towards the eternal apotheosis of Good. That the melodramatic reasoning holds sway in the end does not mean that we should accept mythic causality as the film's dominant, overwhelming classical narrative causality. Instead we should retain from this analysis the importance of reading the text—even at this schematic level—as an amalgam of deformed, embedded melodramatic material and carefully elaborated narrative classicism. To the personal identification that pushes us forward along a suspenseful linear hermeneutic corresponds a process of cultural identification that keeps us ever-mindful of a broader set of oppositions compared to which the problems of three people don't amount to a hill of beans.

6 Post-classical Hollywood

Peter Kramer

Since the 1980s critical debates within film studies and related disciplines such as cultural studies have increasingly been concerned with the identification, description, explanation, and evaluation of epochal shifts. The proliferation of the prefix 'post' is the most visible sign of this widespread concern with a set of fundamental transformations in the socio-economic organization and forms of cultural expression prevalent in the United States and Western Europe. Post-feminism and postmodernism have featured prominently in discussions of contemporary American cinema (Modleski 1991; Denzin 1991; Corrigan 1991). In recent years 'post-classicism' has emerged as a closely linked third term signalling an epochal shift in Hollywood cinema (Jenkins 1995; Rowe 1995; Neale and Smith, 1998). At the most basic level, this critical term is used to mark the end of the classical period in American film history, that is the disintegration or displacement of classical narration and of the studio system as the dominant forms of aesthetic and institutional organization within mainstream American cinema. Post-classicism does not refer to a complete break in American film history; rather the term is meant to highlight the fact that, despite overriding stylistic and institutional continuities, Hollywood has undergone a set of fundamental changes which deserve critical attention. In contrast to the relative aesthetic and institutional homogeneity and stability of classical Hollywood which has been described most authoritatively by

David Bordwell, Janet Staiger, and Kristin Thompson (1985) and Thomas Schatz (1988), the post-classical period is seen to be characterized by differing and frequently changing approaches to the unchanging main objective of the American film industry, which is to make money by telling entertaining stories to paying audiences (Jenkins 1995).

This basic description of post-classicism raises a number of important questions. When does the classical period end and the post-classical era begin? What are the most important stylistic and thematic innovations introduced during the post-classical period? What is their relationship to changes in the organization of the film industry? And why did these changes occur in the first place? By necessity, the concept of post-classicism also gives rise to concerns about the notion of classical Hollywood cinema. What are the characteristic features and the historical boundaries of this dominant mode of film practice? The critical debate about most of these issues is still in its early stages, as the concept of post-classicism is not yet established as an obligatory reference-point in discussions of contemporary American cinema. However, some of these questions about the conceptualization of historical developments in American cinema have been discussed extensively with reference to other periodizing terms, such as 'postmodernism' (Corrigan 1991; Denzin 1991), New Hollywood (Tasker 1996; Schatz 1983, 1993; Hillier 1993; Neale 1976), and, most generally, the era following the Second World War. In fact, while the 1960s are usually regarded as the decade which saw the rise of the New Hollywood and the beginning of post-classicism, most accounts of these developments explain them with reference to a series of crucial events in the immediate post-war period (between 1946 and 1953) such as the antitrust action against the major Hollywood studios, the decline of cinema attendances, and the rise of television. Furthermore, it was during this same period that the concept of classicism was first introduced into film criticism in a sustained and rigorous fashion. Arguably, the very act of identifying Hollywood classicism already implied a certain historical distance from it, a vantage-point from which classicism could be seen as a stage in the development of American cinema. The first decade after the end of the Second World War, then, provides an appropriate starting-point for a historical investigation of the various attempts which film critics and film scholars have made to conceptualize the history of Hollywood beyond its classical period.

André Bazin, classicism, and changes in the Hollywood aesthetic

Schatz (1988: 8) and Bordwell, Staiger, and Thompson (1985: 3) point to André Bazin as the most important source for the basic assumptions underpinning their respective projects: that the Hollywood aesthetic can be understood as a form of 'classicism', and that this classical film aesthetic is in turn dependent on a particular 'system' of production. Bazin developed this approach to American cinema between 1945 and 1958, in the context of a massive influx of Hollywood films into France and of new trends in European filmmaking, most notably neo-realism (Andrew 1978, chs. 4–7). Bazin's use of the term 'classical' was double-edged. On the one hand, it derived from his enthusiasm for American cinema, which contrasted sharply with the disdain for Hollywood shown by many of his contemporaries amongst established French critics. By labelling Hollywood cinema a 'classical art', he elevated it, setting it up as an artistic practice worthy of serious consideration. On the other hand, right from the start, Bazin rejected the limitations that the rules of classicism imposed on filmmaking, in particular on the more 'realistic' practices that he championed, such as long takes, deep-focus cinematography, and staging

in depth. Both his admiration and his critique of classical Hollywood are brought into sharp focus in an oft-quoted passage from his 1957 essay 'On the *politique des auteurs*': 'Paradoxically, the supporters of the *politique des auteurs* admire the American cinema, where the restrictions of production are heavier than anywhere else. . . . The American cinema is a classical art, but why not then admire in it what is most admirable, i.e. not only the talent of this or that film-maker, but the genius of the system, the richness of its ever-vigorous tradition, and its fertility when it comes into contact with new elements' (Bazin 1985: 257–8).

A closer look at Bazin's writing reveals that the classicism of American cinema provided him with a backdrop against which he could define and promote the qualities of a new kind of realist cinema which was emerging in Europe and in the United States in the 1940s, exemplified most strikingly by *Paisa* (Italy, 1946) and *Citizen Kane* (USA, 1941). 'The Evolution of the Language of Cinema' is arguably Bazin's most famous and influential essay, an early version of which appeared in the first issue of *Cahiers du cinéma* in April 1951. In this essay, Bazin proposed a periodization of the history of cinema. Despite the gap between silent cinema and talking film, the years from 1920 to 1939 constituted a unified period characterized by the world-wide diffusion of 'a common form of cinematic language . . . originating largely in the United States' and based on the principles of continuity editing (1967: 28–31). By 1939 this cinema 'had reached a level of classical perfection' in Hollywood and elsewhere, yet it was also on the verge of a 'revolution in the language of the screen' (30, 37). In Hollywood, directors such as Orson Welles and William Wyler participated in the international 'regeneration of realism in storytelling' which insisted on 'bringing together real time, in which things exist, along with the duration of the action, for which classical editing had insidiously substituted mental and abstract time' (39). This would seem to suggest that Hollywood's classicism of the 1930s was superseded, or at least partially displaced, by a new aesthetic in the 1940s, which could be called 'post-classical'.

In the essay 'The Evolution of the Western' Bazin discussed this epochal shift with respect to what he had called 'the American film par excellence' (1971: 140). Again the years 1939–40 marked 'a point beyond which some new development seemed inevitable' because with *Stagecoach* (USA, 1939) the western had achieved 'the maturity of a style brought to classi-

In effect, Bazin again presented the outlines of a 'post-classical' American cinema which is described as an impure, less rigorous, highly flexible cinema, characterized by the coexistence of contradictory aesthetic strategies (classical editing, expressionism, realism) rather than a strict and exclusive adherence to the continuity system; by the extension, embellishment, playfulness, and mixing of its genres rather than by generic purity; and by an engagement with topical issues and controversial subject-matter even in its most conventional generic offerings.

cal perfection' (149). Referring to 'the famous law of successive aesthetic periods', which posits the inevitable displacement of classicism by 'the baroque', Bazin observed the emergence of a new kind of western in the 1940s: 'The superwestern is a western that would be ashamed to be just itself, and looks for some additional interest to justify its existence—an aesthetic, sociological, moral, psychological, political, or erotic interest' (150–1). In effect, Bazin again presented the outlines of a 'post-classical' American cinema which is described as an impure, less rigorous, highly flexible cinema, characterized by the coexistence of contradictory aesthetic strategies (classical editing, expressionism, realism) rather than a strict and exclusive adherence to the continuity system; by the extension, embellishment, playfulness, and mixing of its genres rather than by generic purity; and by an engagement with topical issues and controversial subject-matter even in its most conventional generic offerings.

American critical responses to post-war changes in the Hollywood aesthetic and the end of the studio system

Bazin explained changes in the Hollywood aesthetic in the 1940s and 1950s in terms of an internal logic of artistic developments inevitably moving through a series of stages. In his teleological view, the result of such developments in the medium of film was an ever more realistic representation of the world. When American critics considered changes in Hollywood filmmaking in the post-war period, they also addressed questions of realism, yet they were more likely to focus these questions on the issue of Hollywood's 'maturity' or lack thereof, and to draw on a wide range of social, cultural, and industrial determinants to explain the complex developments they observed. While the terms 'classical cinema' and 'studio system' were not used, what critics engaged with was in fact the dismantling of the system of production, distribution, and exhibition and of the classical aesthetic which had underpinned Hollywood's operations in preceding decades. In sharp contrast with Bazin's belief in the 'genius' of the Hollywood system, American critics took a largely negative view of American film culture, and responded to its fundamental transformation in the late 1940s and the 1950s with more scepticism than hope.

In the aftermath of the Second World War critics looked for signs of Hollywood's social and artistic maturation. In his bi-weekly column in *The Nation*, James Agee identified and welcomed an important trend towards 'journalistic, semi-documentary, and "social-minded"' films in Hollywood in 1946 and 1947 (1963: 289). Celebrating *The Best Years of our Lives* (USA, 1946) as an outstanding example of this trend, Agee related Hollywood's 'new maturity' to the war experiences of filmmakers such as Wyler and John Huston (237). He also noted the increasing influence of European imports, most notably *Roma, città aperta* (Italy, 1945), which exemplified 'the best general direction movies might take' with its passionate commitment to, and intimate understanding of, a topical and realistic story 'worthy of such knowledge and passion . . . made on relatively little money, as much at least by gifted amateurs as by professionals, in actual rather than imitated places' (236). In 1949 Parker Tyler discussed Hollywood's move, particularly in crime films such as *The Naked City* (USA, 1948), towards 'quasi-documentary', that is the employment of 'documentary devices' such as location shooting and references to a wealth of factual material (1949/1960: 29–35). He also pointed out that Hollywood had produced a series of commercially successful 'problem pictures', most notably *Gentleman's Agreement* (USA, 1947) and *Pinky* (USA, 1949), which dealt with 'such large issues as social prejudices against Negroes and Jews' (107).

However, in the light of Hollywood's commercialism and political conservatism, Agee and Tyler did not expect that these mature trends could make a lasting impact on American film culture.

In 1950 Gilbert Seldes linked the issue of Hollywood's continuing immaturity to the decline of cinema attendances in his comprehensive analysis of mass media in post-war America, *The Great Audience*. Unlike other American critics, Seldes did not object to the profit motive guiding the operations of the film and broadcast industries, but he argued that instead of 'creating genuinely democratic entertainment', they catered only 'to a sizable minority which they pretend is the mass of the people' (1950: 6). Making use of audience statistics, Seldes demonstrated not only that cinema attendance had been declining dramatically since 1946, but also that this decline reinforced Hollywood's tendency to cater primarily to young audiences, most notably adolescents. By the late 1940s it was clear that people over 30 largely stopped going to the cinema, while people in their twenties went regularly but infrequently, so that '[t]he movies live on children from the ages of ten to nineteen, who go steadily and frequently and almost automatically to the pictures' (12). Seldes argued that in the context of recent developments such as the end of block-booking, the divorce of the major producer-distributors from their theatre chains, the temporary closing-off of important foreign markets, and the competition provided by the free domestic entertainment of television, 'the recapture of the adult audience will be an absolute necessity for survival' (22). Unlike European films, however, Hollywood's output had concentrated on 'a small group of myths' concerning heroism, passion, and success that were appropriate for adolescents, especially during courtship, but lost their relevance and appeal when these young people started their working lives, married, and set up their own households (22–4). Seldes urged the film industry to bring its products more in line with mature audiences' everyday experiences by ensuring that story-lines were 'logical', situations and actions 'credible', characters individualized, and their motivations 'understandable' (37).

Seldes warned against a misconception of 'mature' filmmaking which was shared by 'both Hollywood producers and intellectual critics': 'Maturity does not necessarily imply either a tragic sense of life or an excessive sophistication' (36). With reference to the socially conscious films discussed by Agee and Tyler, Seldes demonstrated that Hollywood was able to produce mature films which were entertaining and commercially successful. He expected that the newly fragmented theatrical market and the growing ability of television to deliver 'routine' entertainment free of charge would encourage studios to reduce their output and concentrate on 'making fewer pictures for longer runs', 'attracting fresh audiences' to the movie theatres rather than merely catering for the regulars (41–2). Seldes hoped that studios would take their cue from the rapidly increasing number of so-called 'art theatres', which provided further evidence that there was an audience for mature films (42). The growing number of 'independent producing companies' set up by 'men of talent [who] wished to produce movies without interference from the front office' were particularly suited to deliver such films (48). Despite these possibilities, Seldes's analysis of post-war Hollywood ended on a cautious note. Political pressures, best exemplified by the Hollywood hearings of the House Committee on Un-American Activities, in combination with the rigid Production Code regulating the content of Hollywood's output, prevented studios from producing films which dealt with the realities of contemporary life. In conclusion, Seldes reiterated the social relevance of Hollywood's influence on 'popular emotion' in a 'postwar world [which] has not yet built its foundations' (102).

The remainder of the decade saw a reorientation of critical debates about Hollywood, away from the sense of urgency and the position of high-minded seriousness exemplified by Seldes's study and towards an acknowledgement of the very limited role moviegoing was going to play in American life from then on. With films being ever more explicitly addressed to minority interests rather than to the American public as a whole, the cinema lost its centrality in debates about mass media and American society. Questions of Hollywood's maturity or lack thereof were now discussed with specific reference to the two groups singled out by critics as the most influential target audiences for the post-war film industry—educated people and male youth. Hollywood's attempts to cater to these audiences were received with considerable criticism.

In 1952 Manny Farber launched a sustained critique of the pretensions of the film industry's current output, highlighting in particular its foregrounding of style and message ('overacting, overscoring, overlighting, overmoralizing') and its emphasis on the specialness and artistic merit of individual films (1971: 54–7). Farber contrasted 'smartly tooled art works' such as *Sunset*

Boulevard (USA, 1950) with 'the unspectacular, unpolished "B" (movies)' which 'capture the unworked-over immediacy of life before it has been cooled by "Art"' (55). Drawing on the thematic concerns and stylistic richness of sophisticaed and 'highbrow' works in the American cinema (such as *Citizen Kane*) and, more importantly, in other arts, a number of post-war films departed from the basic objectives of traditional Hollywood filmmaking, which were 'to present some intelligible, structured image of reality . . . to tell a story and to entertain' (72). Instead they presented themselves as symbolic acts of communication between 'a brave, intransigent artist' and a discerning audience, in which story, character, and the reproduction of the sounds and images of reality merely served as vehicles for 'hidden content', and film viewing turned into an act of interpretation (73–5). Farber linked the rise of this kind of 'New Movie' to the emergence of a new generation of filmmakers, such as Elia Kazan (director of *Gentleman's Agreement* and *Pinky*), who had been shaped by the political activism of the Depression years and by their 'higher . . . education' in the New York theatre (82).

By 1957 Farber had broadened his attack by situating a second wave of artistically minded and socially conscious writers and directors, most of whom had previously worked in live television drama and who started to make an impact on the film industry with the release of *Marty* (USA, 1955), in the context of a 'revolution' in American arts (1971: 113–24). In the cinema, music, painting, and literature, Farber saw 'the whole idea of "felt", committed art' under attack from an intellectualized, heavily rhetorical, and excessively technical approach to creative production 'known as advanced, radical, experimental, progressive, or, simply, avant-garde art' (113). The films arising from this movement were characterized by the foregrounding of meaningful detail and a despairing mood, by staginess, unsympathetic characterization, and 'masochistic acting, which is usually in the hands of Strasberg-influenced performers' (118). Farber rejected these films as exercises in self-promotion for their makers appealing to the snobbishness of their educated audiences, and again contrasted the new 'hard-sell cinema' with the transparency of traditional Hollywood entertainment: 'it differs from old-fashioned Hollywood direction in that the style parades in front of the film instead of tunneling under a seminaturalistic surface' (120). Farber argued that the 'male action film', which best exemplified the virtues of tradi-

tional Hollywood entertainment, was rapidly disappearing: 'the action directors are in decline, many of them having abandoned the dry, economic, life-worn movie style that made their observations of the American he-man so rewarding' (12). Directors such as Howard Hawks had flourished in 'a factory of unpretentious picture-making', that is a production system geared towards 'continuous flow of quality' rather than 'momentary novelties' (12–14). With the disappearance of this production system and the closing of action-oriented neighbourhood theatres in the 1950s, these filmmakers and their preferred genres such as the western were pushed towards artistic self-consciousness, thematic seriousness, and big-budget spectacle, creating what Bazin had called the 'super-western'.

At the same time, Hollywood abandoned the traditional image of the American male as mature, active, efficient, graceful, and stoic, and instead concentrated on a new type of masculinity, represented by Montgomery Clift, Marlon Brando, and James Dean. Writing in the mid-1950s, both Parker Tyler (1960: 127–8) and Pauline Kael (1966b: 44–62) linked the rise of these new male stars to a generational shift in post-war American culture. Dissatisfied with the political and material achievements of the parent generation, young people, who clearly dominated the cinema audience in the 1950s, began to question traditional values and lifestyles and through their actions gave rise to 'the social problem of juvenile delinquency', which was quickly taken up by Hollywood, with Brando and Dean being 'selected to illustrate the neurotic types that make up rebellion in the young' (Tyler 1960: 127). In sharp contrast to traditional images of masculinity, Tyler described these stars as 'naturally infantile types', intuitive, undisciplined, and heavily reliant on their 'babyish' good looks (128). Kael noted their ability to provoke 'violent audience reactions' in movie theatres and described the new character type as 'a complete negation of previous conceptions of heroism: the hero is not responsible for his actions—the crazy, mixed-up kid becomes a romantic hero by being treated on an infantile level' (1966b: 57, 60).

While Hollywood's new heroes were targeted specifically at a young male audience, and its artistic 'New Movies' appealed primarily to educated audiences, the film industry also continued to pursue an undifferentiated mass audience with big-budget widescreen spectacles. These films attempted to redefine and revitalize the cinematic experience itself by turning it into an innovative and unique technological and cultural event for a mass audience which had grown out of the moviegoing habit and had transferred its habitual consumption of audiovisual entertainment to television. Reviewing a wide range of widescreen and 3-D processes (typically supported by stereophonic sound and colour), Tyler argued in 1953 that the film industry was effectively relaunching the cinema itself by foregrounding its technological basis and its ability to transform the audience's experience of themselves and their surroundings: 'Television is centripetal in relation to its spectator, drawing the world into his domestic space, while 3-D movies are centrifugal in relation to their spectator's axis, drawing him out, collectively, into the world's space' (1960: 121).

In his second study of mass media in post-war America, Gilbert Seldes described the widescreen revolution in equally epochal terms, referring to the temptation 'to write a second obituary for the movies' in 1952–3, so as to register the death of a certain kind of 'flat' cinema in the same way that twenty-five years earlier 'silent' cinema had died with the coming of sound (1956: 17). Seldes was considerably more optimistic than in his earlier book about the possibility that American cinema might be revitalized: 'we have the exciting prospect of experiencing, for the third time in our lives, a new art of the movies' (60). This new art would combine the power of widescreen technologies to envelop, overwhelm, astonish, and unsettle the cinema audience with Hollywood's traditional storylines and characterization and its careful guiding of viewer attention through shot composition and continuity editing. In contrast to his earlier condemnation of Hollywood's immaturity, Seldes now argued that, despite the cinema's 'appeal to our most infantile desires' and its avoidance of 'the realities of existence', the formal and stylistic rigour and elegance of filmic storytelling constituted 'a separate gratification, as legitimate in its essence as that of any other art' (13). Seldes was willing to accept the mythical structure of Hollywood movies precisely because movies had been displaced from the centre of American culture by television's provision of entertainment as 'a free and continuous and integrated part of the daily home life of an entire nation' (1).

Also writing in 1956, Pauline Kael judged Hollywood's increasing reliance on 'big' pictures much more negatively (1966a). She argued that the inflated budgets, epic length, and wide screens of Hollywood's big pictures allowed them to become a massive 'compendium' of exotic locations, stock situations, realistic details, recognizable characters, and spectacular views that were not fused into a coherent whole but served mainly to celebrate the 'glamour' and 'magic' of 'bloated production methods' and thus of Hollywood's apparently limitless resources (52, 54). Kael predicted that this approach to filmmaking, which displaced the delineation of story events with the attempt to turn the production and release of the film into a major event, would soon lose its appeal and Hollywood would thus again lose favour with the general public: 'Spectacles will cease to be events, and audiences can be more comfortably bored at home' (64).

Building on these critical interventions in the 1950s, the early 1960s saw the appearance of book-length studies offering a broad historical evaluation of the fundamental changes in Hollywood's theatrical market and its production strategies in the immediate post-war period. In 1961 Ezra Goodman announced 'the end of Hollywood' (1961: 438). With television now serving as the primary outlet for audiovisual entertainment, the major studios' traditional concern with the production of films for the theatrical market was no longer economically viable. The major studios sold off their back catalogues of movies to television and their real estate to development companies, they transferred the efficiency and tight control characteristic of traditional studio operations to telefilm production, or they merged with television companies. The studios' reduced output of theatrical films had to compete with 'the good Hollywood movies, mostly those made up to the latish Thirties', which were available to audiences free of charge on the domestic television screen (447). Thus, theatrical production had effectively become an anachronism: 'Today, in the television ice age, the motion picture has already taken on an archaeological tinge' (p. x).

Richard Dyer MacCann saw the future of American cinema more optimistically, as is indicated by the title of his 1962 study *Hollywood in Transition*. MacCann argued that, far from being obsolete, films made for theatrical release had been given 'a new position' (p. x). Liberated from the 'tyranny' of self-censored, studio-controlled, assembly-line-like film production (p. xii), the production of a major theatrical feature had turned into a complex, infinitely variable, and highly volatile enterprise, a time-consuming, labour- and capital-intensive high-risk business venture whose only certainty was 'sudden change' and whose main aim was to create 'a special event' (3, 108). Apart from encouraging technological innovation, adaptations of Broadway hits and bestselling novels, and sensationalist films dealing with taboo subject-matter, this new situation also created opportunities for innovative, realistic, and socially conscious filmmaking. MacCann suggested that a new generation of filmmakers might be able to realize this potential, and that an increased emphasis on the preservation, study, and revival of the classics of American cinema, and on the training and promotion of young creative personnel and executives, would provide a good basis for the regeneration of American film culture. The model for such a more 'intellectual' approach to filmmaking could be found in France, where 'thirty or forty new young directors . . . have been fortified by a decade of talk and criticism [and] . . . fed with motion picture history at the film showings of the Cinémathèque in Paris', resulting in an explosion of cinematic creativity (64).

Thus, between the late 1940s and early 1960s critics debated the disappearance of many of the certainties of American film culture of preceding decades. The stability and continuity of the studio system, the undifferentiated mass audience, the dominance of traditional storytelling and transparent entertainment, and the centrality of cinema in American life were all things of the past. Critics agreed that in the 1950s American cinema in its traditional form had come to an end, and the widescreen revolution and Hollywood's big pictures had failed to restore the movies to their previous key position in American popular culture. It was not clear what shape Hollywood might take in the future, nor was there a lot of confidence that an improvement on the old studio system could be expected. It was understood, however, that European film culture would have an important influence on the 'new' Hollywood that was eventually going to emerge from this period of transition.

New waves, new schools of Anglo-American film criticism, and the New Hollywood

In the early 1960s it became a critical commonplace to celebrate an artistic renaissance in world cinema, which was said to have begun in 1956 and to include the work of individual directors such as Michelangelo Antonioni and of movements and schools such as the French Nouvelle Vague (Houston 1963: 182–95).

Anglo-American critics tended to agree that Hollywood's contribution to this renaissance was minimal. Hollis Alpert declared in 1960 that in sharp contrast with the traditional 'belief that Americans were pre-eminent in the motion picture field', Hollywood was now 'losing such world-wide respect as it once had' (1960/1971a: 253), and in 1966 Dwight MacDonald stated categorically: 'None of the important postwar schools or directors have been American' (1969: 38). In this critical climate, 'newness' became an important category in discussions of American cinema. At the low-budget and experimental end of American film production, critics engaged with a self-declared 'New American Cinema' exemplified by the work of writers and directors such as Jonas Mekas, Kenneth Anger, and John Cassavetes, certain aspects of which constituted, according to David Bordwell, a conscious 'modernist' break with Hollywood classicism (Houston 1963: 185–8; MacDonald 1969: 39; Bordwell 1989: 54–8). Even at the centre of Hollywood production, a group of former television directors including Sidney Lumet and Arthur Penn, who had been much vilified by Manny Farber in the 1950s, could now be celebrated as a 'new breed', combining 'greater interest in social questions' with stylistic experimentation and improvisation, thus arguably constituting 'America's "new wave"' (Hart 1965; Jenkins 1995: 115).

However, this concern with, and positive evaluation of, newness was not characteristic of the bulk of Hollywood criticism in the 1960s, which concentrated on the systematic critical re-evaluation and close analysis of the work of a small group of Hollywood directors, most of whom had received their training and directed many of their important films during the studio era of the 1930s and 1940s, working mainly in well-established genres such as the western. Following on from Manny Farber's celebration of Hawks and the 'male action film' and from the *politique des auteurs* of *Cahiers du cinéma* with its similar emphasis on Hollywood directors such as Hawks and Alfred Hitchcock, Anglo-American 'auteurist' criticism in the 1960s elevated the films of certain genre directors to the status of art (Bordwell 1989: 42–53; Caughie 1981: 9–67). These critics rejected the self-consciously artistic and socially relevant films of the new generation of theatre- and television-trained directors joining Hollywood in the 1950s, and engaged with contemporary cinema mostly in terms of the latest works of old masters (Gillet 1959/1971; Sarris 1963/1968).

The general critical shift towards a re-evaluation of

the studio era provided the context for one of the earliest uses of the term 'new Hollywood'. In a 1959 *Esquire* article entitled 'Elegy for Wonderland' veteran screenwriter Ben Hecht wrote that while 'the good old Hollywood' in which writers had been used and abused by powerful producers was 'dead', the 'new Hollywood . . . has in a measure solved the writer problem . . . [by] making movies so full of horses, bonfires, collapsing temples, Indian uprisings, wild beasts and uncovered breasts . . . that a writer would actually be in the way' (1971: 356, 362). Unlike his outright condemnation of contemporary Hollywood, Hecht's attitude towards the 'old' Hollywood was a mixture of contempt and nostalgia, a grudging acknowledgement that an industrial system inimical to art could nevertheless produce 'beauty and fine drama': 'The great Hollywood factories were interested only in turning out a standard product for mass consumption. But talent, brought to heel, did speak in this mass product' (363).

In Andrew Sarris's polemical reformulation of these ideas, the very restrictions imposed on directors working in Hollywood studios, especially in the 1930s and 1940s, were a pre-condition for the kind of qualities auteurist critics looked for: 'The auteur theory values the personality of a director precisely because of the barriers to its expression' (1963/1968: 31). The 'modern' cinema of the post-war period, mainly in Europe but also in the United States, tended to elevate the director, giving him more control over the production process, valuing his personal experience and originality, and thus encouraging him to depart from traditional modes of filmic communication and indulge his idiosyncrasies: 'Paradoxically, however, the personalities of modern directors are often more obscure than those of classical directors who were encumbered with all sorts of narrative and dramatic machinery' (32). In Sarris's view, the art of cinema was based on the precarious balance of, on the one hand, commercial imperatives, collaborative work procedures, and stylistic and generic conventions, and, on the other hand, the unique vision and powerful personality of a director, capable of 'a sublimity of expression almost miraculously extracted from his money-oriented environment' (37). Idiosyncratic self-expression was thus kept in check by the overriding objective to tell meaningful and entertaining stories to a mass audience: 'The classical cinema was more functional than the modern cinema. It knew its audience and their expectations' (32).

Although Pauline Kael attacked Sarris and other auteurist critics for what she perceived as their logical inconsistencies, their 'narcissistic male fantasies', and their critical elevation of 'trash' films to the status of 'true film art' (1966b: 319), she shared their concern with coherent storytelling as the basis for successful filmmaking. In her 1964 survey of contemporary filmmaking, she stated that 'processes of structural disintegration are at work in all types of movies', ranging from the experimental works of the New American Cinema and recent art-house favourites such as *Last Year at Marienbad* (France, 1961) to Hollywood's big pictures such as *Cleopatra* (USA, 1963) which included 'incomprehensible sections' or were simply 'incoherent' (1966b: 8–9, 14). Echoing Manny Farber's critical outbursts in the 1950s, Kael saw the disintegration of filmic narrative as a symptom of the disintegration of traditional film culture in general. She lamented the rejection of 'craftsmanship as well as meaning' and 'critical standards' in the films and manifestos of the New American Cinema (18–19). Similarly, an emphasis on 'technique', 'purely visual content', and the possibility of open-ended 'elaborate interpretations' meant that '[t]he art-house audience accepts lack of clarity as complexity, accepts clumsiness and confusion as "ambiguity" and as style' (15, 20–1). While experimental filmmaking and art cinema were thus transforming film into an élitist and excessively intellectual cultural form, Kael was equally critical of the experiences facilitated by Hollywood's mainstream releases. The lack of concern for coherent storytelling on the part of producers and directors in charge of the volatile and overblown process of filmmaking was matched by the audience's enthusiastic response to spectacular attractions and shock effects, irrespective of their degree of narrative motivation.

Kael tentatively explained the change in audience expectations with reference to 'modern life and the sense of urgency it produces', which was exemplified by television: 'It's possible that television viewing, with all its breaks and cuts, and the inattention, except for action, and spinning the dial to find some action, is partly responsible for the destruction of narrative sense . . . it may be that audiences don't have much more than a TV span of attention left' (9–10). Kael contrasted this set of expectations with the audience response characteristic of an earlier period (the 'classical cinema' in Sarris's terminology): 'audiences used to have an almost rational passion for getting the story straight . . . A movie had to tell some kind of story that held together: a plot to parse' (9). On the basis of this plot, traditional Hollywood films could develop the simple qualities that Kael, much like Farber and Sarris, was holding up as the foundation of a truly popular American cinema, now that this cinema largely seemed to have disappeared: 'energy', 'excitement', 'honest vulgarity', 'vitality' (24, 26).

For Kael and other critics, Hollywood's long-awaited renaissance finally occurred when the traditional qualities of American filmmaking were combined with the intellectual sophistication and stylistic innovations of the new directors and new waves of European cinema in films addressing contemporary and specifically American subject-matter. It is clear, both from critical responses at the time and from later retrospective accounts, that the film which most clearly marked the beginning of this renaissance was *Bonnie and Clyde* (USA, 1967). The film was a substantial hit, establishing the commercial viability of a new kind of Hollywood movie, and it was also the subject of enormous critical controversy (Cawelti 1973). In her review Pauline Kael declared *Bonnie and Clyde* to be 'the most excitingly American American movie' in half a decade, making 'a different kind of contact with an American audience from the kind that is made by European films, however contemporary' (1967/1970: 47). Kael argued that the film, which had originally been developed by scriptwriters Robert Benton and David Newman for François Truffaut and had then been offered to Jean-Luc Godard before it was finally directed by Arthur Penn,

echoed the enthusiasm of French film critics and filmmakers for 'the poetry of crime in American life' and the 'fast action, laconic speech, plain gestures' of traditional Hollywood entertainment (54). In line with the 'romanticism' of the Hollywood tradition, *Bonnie and Clyde* celebrated 'the cynical tough guy's independence', yet it did so in a 'specifically modern' fashion (47–9). It kept an ironic distance from its protagonists and their story and created 'a kind of eager, nervous imbalance' in the spectators, who oscillated between a serious engagement with the events on the screen and comic distanciation from it (49). The film offered neither a 'secure basis for identification' with the protagonists, nor a clear-cut moral framework for judging their behaviour, and it articulated contemporary concerns, especially with the role of violence in American society, through a 'nostalgia for the thirties' (51, 53).

In December 1967 *Time* magazine officially announced a 'renaissance' in American film culture exemplified by *Bonnie and Clyde* (1967/1971: 333). Echoing many of the critical debates of the 1950s and early 1960s, the magazine's cover story outlined a 'new cinema', which had originated in Europe and which 'Hollywood has at long last become part of' (323). This new cinema was characterized by narrative complexity, the foregrounding of cinematic devices, generic hybrids, and taboo subject-matter. According to the article, American audiences had been 'prepared for change and experiment both by life and art', in particular by 'the questioning of moral traditions, the demythologizing of ideals, the pulverizing of esthetic principles' in painting, music, and literature, and also by the familiarity with complex forms of audiovisual communication engendered by television (325). Reversing earlier negative judgements on the influence of television, Hollis Alpert argued that 'the visual training and orientation the young viewers received' through televison had created a cinema audience seeking out 'the visually dynamic film, the more "cinematic" kind of film experience' that was 'principally espoused by younger directors, many of them trained in television' (1968*a*/1971: 337). In the wake of the excitement about *Bonnie and Clyde* and the spectacular box office returns of Mike Nichols's *The Graduate* (USA, 1967), Alpert declared an end to the 'star system', with its emphasis on the personalities of performers on and off the screen (336). Instead of an interest in stars, the response of young movie audiences was more likely to be informed by an intense identification with characters and by a close attention

> For Kael and other critics, Hollywood's long-awaited renaissance finally occurred when the traditional qualities of American filmmaking were combined with the intellectual sophistication and stylistic innovations of the new directors and new waves of European cinema in films addressing contemporary and specifically American subject-matter. It is clear, both from critical responses at the time and from later retrospective accounts, that the film which most clearly marked the beginning of this renaissance was *Bonnie and Clyde* (1967).

The Hollywood renaissance—Warren Beatty and Faye Dunaway in *Bonnie and Clyde* (1967)

to stylistic devices, symbolic messages, and thematic ambiguities in the film: the viewers returning to see *The Graduate* several times 'cultishly attach all sorts of significance to the most minor of details' (1968b/1971: 405). For Steven Farber, the most significant aspect of Hollywood's new youth-oriented films was their frequent display of spectacular violence, which best expressed the films' fundamental 'antagonism toward authority', their 'anti-social bias', and their 'disillusionment with the normal life choices and life styles of American cinema' (1968/1971: 287).

The fundamental reorientation of the American film industry in the late 1960s, which was further solidified by the explicit counter-cultural concerns of popular films such as *Easy Rider* (USA, 1969), led to a more sustained engagement with contemporary Hollywood by auteurist critics. Unlike previous Anglo-American critics publishing books and articles in newspapers and magazines addressed to a general audience, many auteurist writers now addressed themselves to a much more specialized academic readership in film magazines such as *Movie* and *Monogram*, rearticulating key issues and observations in previous debates about Hollywood cinema in increasingly theoretical language (Maltby with Craven 1995: 421–6). *Monogram* writers highlighted the concept of a 'new Hollywood' to describe the transformation of mainstream American cinema in the late 1960s, and they also gave the concept of 'classic' or 'classical' Hollywood a new meaning, which was both broader in its historical application and more specifically tied to a particular type of narrative than earlier usage had suggested (Lloyd 1971; Elsaesser 1971, 1975).

In Bazin's periodization, the year 1939 had been both a high point and a turning-point for Hollywood classicism, marking the beginning of the Hollywood 'baroque' in the 1940s. Anglo-American critics from Seldes to Sarris had used the studio era of the 1930s and 1940s (which Sarris was mainly referring to when he used the label 'classical') as the main reference-point in their discussions of American film history, characterizing the following decades as a period of transition. For *Monogram* writers Thomas Elsaesser and Peter Lloyd, however, Hollywood's classical period lasted from the 1910s to the mid-1960s. During this period 'the filmic language evolved by Griffith, Stroheim and Murnau . . . retained its validity as the syntactical basis, whatever its modifications in terms of sound-effects, montage and camera-movements' (Elsaesser 1971: 5), and the long careers of key directors such as John Ford and Raoul Walsh produced 'the component parts of this essential classicism' (Lloyd 1971: 11). Although both writers acknowledged substantial changes in Hollywood's mode of production and in the cinema's status in American culture during this period, in their view classical Hollywood was unified by a fairly stable system of genre conventions, by the centrality of a basic narrative formula focusing on goal-oriented characters who had to learn to balance individual desire and communal values, and by a particular stylistic approach to filmic storytelling characterized by 'efficiency, formal elegance and lucid simplicity' (Elsaesser 1971: 8).

In the late 1960s television-trained directors, '[o]wing perhaps to the harmful influence of the auteur theory', increasingly departed from these fundamental qualities of classicism to 'indulge in a kind of baroque and ornate elaboration of basically simple plots, without there being so much as a shred of dramatic or thematic necessity for their stylistic grand-guignol' (Elsaesser 1971: 8). The single most important 'aesthetic feature' marking the difference between classical and modern American cinema was 'the increasingly dislocated emotional identity of the central protagonist, and the almost total absence of the central drive and its dramatic mechanisms' (10). Without clearly defined goals and 'clearly identifiable moral and social objectives', the actions of the heroes of modern cinema frequently revolved around 'outbursts of unmotivated and wholly irrational violence' (10). Modern films thus signalled 'the gradual collapse of the efficacy of the heroic individual', and, instead of hinging on decisive action which brought about clear results, the films tended to move towards an 'ambiguous, open-ended situation' (Lloyd 1971: 12).

By 1975 the modern trend in Hollywood cinema had produced a substantial body of work by a group of high-profile directors which Elsaesser referred to as 'the new Hollywood of Altman, Pollack, Boorman, of Rafelson, Hellman, Spielberg or Ashby' (1975: 13). While classical Hollywood cinema expressed 'a fundamentally affirmative attitude to the world it depicts', key films of the new Hollywood had a 'liberal outlook' which led them to 'reject affirmation' and instead to project 'a radical scepticism . . . about the American virtues of ambition, vision, drive' (14–15). This shift had partly been caused by the changing status of cinema and the changing composition of its audiences. While television now catered for the mass audience previously served by classical Hollywood cinema, the new Hollywood had to address itself to 'ideologically less representative' segments of the population, and it did so by reflecting 'stances of dissent typical among minority groups' (14). The 'liberal' response to this challenge, which had become the focus of discussions of the new Hollywood, was exemplified by road movies. These combined 'the unmotivated hero and the motif of the journey', which largely functioned as an end in itself rather than getting the hero anywhere, thus expressing his disillusionment or cynicism (13). However, there was also a 'conservative' response exemplified by the 'cop thriller', which featured 'over-determined heroes' and 'moralized violence' (15). Further responses included the disaster movie, the critical examination of classical genres in the form of 'pastiche' and 'parody', and the celebration of 'an affirmative, innocent past' in the 'nostalgia movie' (14, 18). Elsaesser noted that even the most radical formal and ideological departures from classical storytelling in the liberal films of the new Hollywood, which reflected the 'fading confidence in being able to tell a story' so characteristic of the work of leading European directors, nevertheless remained true to the basic objective of Hollywood cinema to engage audiences emotionally in its stories (13). Unlike many recent European films, the new Hollywood 'remains an audience-oriented cinema that permits no explicitly intellectual narrative construction' and operates by 'shifting and modifying traditional genres and themes, while never quite shedding their support' (18).

Also in 1975 *Movie* published a discussion amongst its main contributors about contemporary Hollywood which confirmed many of the observations and insights put forward by Elsaesser and Lloyd, although, in more traditional auteurist fashion, the magazine judged recent developments in Hollywood much more negatively (Cameron *et al.* 1975). In response to the persistent claims made by these and other publications (Madsen 1975) about a fundamental shift in Hollywood cinema, in 1976 the leading scholarly film magazine *Screen* finally took note of what was now officially known as the 'New Hollywood Cinema'. Steve Neale listed a variety of 'formal and thematic changes' which had been identified by auteurist critics. These ranged from '[t]he use of devices such as the zoom and telephoto lenses, slow-motion and split-screen [which] destroyed the dramatic and spatio-temporal unity that founded classical mise-en-scène with its economy, density and "subtlety" of signification', to the breakdown of genre conventions (1976: 117–18). Neale also

reviewed the various 'socio-cultural factors which have been seen to some extent as determinants' for the above changes, including 'the breakdown of censorship codes' (which had been finalized when the Production Code was replaced with a ratings system in 1968) and 'the breakdown of confidence in traditional American values' (118). Echoing Elsaesser's argument, Neale argued that in the 1950s television had taken over cinema's role as 'the main vector of ideology in the mass media', being able to fulfil it much more effectively due to its 'presence in the home, continuous transmission, (and) relative cheapness' (118). This allowed cinema 'to diversify its appeal and, therefore, its product', responding in particular to 'the rise of the youth movement and the struggles for liberation of both blacks and women: the growth of counter-cultures and ideologies generally, some of which could be sought and appealed to as a potential audience which was not catered for by television' (119). For Neale, Hollywood here acted as a safety-valve, giving in to ideological pressure only to recuperate oppositional stances. Despite changes in its mode of production and in its narrative strategies, Hollywood continued to operate successfully as a capitalist enterprise and did not disrupt the fundamental operations of the 'classical text' with its 'ordering meta-discourse' aimed at eliminating ideological contradictions and thus creating an imaginary 'unity of position' for the spectator (120–1). In Neale's view, contemporary Hollywood continued the hegemonic project of classical cinema.

The theoretically sophisticated discussions of the 1970s about recent developments in Hollywood cinema had two major results. On the one hand, 'New Hollywood' became firmly established as an important concept in critical debates, referring to American mainstream cinema since 1967 and, more specifically, to the stylistic, narrative, and thematic innovations characteristic of the films of certain directors and of certain 'liberal' cycles. On the other hand, the concept of 'classical Hollywood' was applied to a dramatically extended period in American film history which lasted from the 1910s to the 1960s, and the notion of a 'classical text' went even further by also incorporating the films of the New Hollywood. In this way, academic discourse effectively erased previous critical debates about complex changes in the Hollywood aesthetic and about the multiplicity of social, cultural, and industrial factors shaping these changes that had been conducted between the late 1940s and the mid-1960s. Hollywood's 'transitional' post-war period was of interest only in so far as it paved the way for the emergence of the New Hollywood from 1967 onwards.

Critical responses to developments in the New Hollywood: movie brats, neo-classicism, and post-modernism

When 'New Hollywood' became firmly established as a critical term in film studies in the mid-1970s, Hollywood itself was in the midst of an aesthetic, cultural, and industrial reorientation, which was signalled most dramatically by the unprecedented box-office successes of *Jaws* (USA, 1975) and *Star Wars* (USA,

1977). In subsequent years critics described Hollywood's reorientation in the second half of the 1970s in terms of the films' increasing emphasis on special effects and cinematic spectacle (Neale 1980), their return to a psychologically and politically regressive outlook (Wood 1985, 1986, ch. 8; Britton 1986) and the film industry's increasingly narrow focus on 'blockbusters', that is heavily promoted big-budget films (Monaco 1979, chs. 1–3). In retrospect, the original New Hollywood of the years 1967–75 came to be seen as a brief and exceptional period in American film history in which artistically ambitious and politically progressive filmmaking had been commercially viable, competing successfully for a while with conservative film cycles (Maltby 1983, ch. 10; Ray 1985, chs. 8–9; Ryan and Kellner 1988, chs. 1–3). Auteurist critics have

An unprecedented box-office success—*Star Wars* **(1977)**

Spielberg's first blockbuster, *Jaws* (1975)

continued to explore and evaluate the achievements of the small group of directors who had been at the centre of Hollywood's short-lived artistic renaissance (Pye and Myles 1979; Kolker 1980, 1988). Other critics, however, have concentrated on a general outline and critique of the aesthetic and commercial logic underpinning Hollywood's operations since the 1960s, best exemplified by *Jaws* and subsequent films by George Lucas and Steven Spielberg (Monaco 1979; Thompson 1981; Biskind 1990; Schatz 1993; Wyatt 1994). These critics emphasize the incorporation of Hollywood studios into giant industrial conglomerates since the mid-

1960s, the proliferation of delivery systems for films gaining momentum with the successful introduction of pay-cable and home video in the mid-1970s, and the multi-media marketing of movies, which connects their theatrical release with the launching of a whole product line of popular cultural artefacts (ranging from pop songs to computer games), while also using a film's theatrical exposure as the key to ancillary markets such as video and pay-cable, where the bulk of film revenues have been generated since the mid-1980s. Confusingly, this second group of critics frequently employs the term 'New Hollywood' to refer to the much longer

period they are dealing with, and, in particular, to the years after 1975. Thus, in different critical contexts 'New Hollywood' may refer to the period 1967–75 as well as to the post-1975 period, to the aesthetic and political progressivism of the liberal cycles of the earlier period as well as to the regressiveness of the blockbusters of the later period (Tasker 1996).

As if that was not confusing enough, critical discourses about the New Hollywood often revolve around the very same issues that concerned critics writing about Hollywood's transitional period between the late 1940s and the mid-1960s. For example, European influences, stylistic innovations, taboo subject-matter, new cinematic conceptions of heroism and masculinity, and critical awareness of social realities had already been hotly debated with respect to key Hollywood films and cycles of the late 1940s and the 1950s, long before they became identified with the Hollywood renaissance after 1967. Juvenilization, the technological renewal of the cinematic experience, the trend towards big event pictures, and the displacement of narrative by spectacle had all been the subject of critical debates in the 1950s, long before the new breed of blockbusters in the 1970s and 1980s provoked strong critical reactions along these lines. Such continuities in critical debates and in Hollywood's aesthetic and commercial logic often go unacknowledged. Consequently, recent critical discourses about the New Hollywood (in both its restricted and its general meaning) have tended to exaggerate its newness, instead of situating the New Hollywood in relation to long-term trends in the post-war period.

To complicate matters further, since the 1980s critics have made concerted efforts to apply the concepts of modernism and postmodernism to developments in post-war American cinema. These concepts are used both to demarcate historical periods and to characterize particular film cycles. They may be used primarily with reference to aesthetic issues, or more generally with reference to the totality of a cultural formation, comprising cultural artefacts as well as media industries, forms of social organization, and ideologies. In the light of the wide-ranging and varying applications of these concepts in film criticism, it is difficult to map them onto the established periodizations of post-war Hollywood which take the concept of classicism as their starting-point. For example, studies of the emergence and development of postmodern culture in the United States tend to refer broadly to the post-war period, identifying the 1960s as a decade of crucial

cultural transformations in the arts, yet locating the key examples of postmodern cinema such as *Blade Runner* (USA, 1982), *Blue Velvet* (USA, 1984), and *Batman* (USA, 1989) in more recent years (Denzin 1991; Jameson 1991; Corrigan 1991). In this view, then, despite the late appearance of exemplary postmodern films, the whole period since the Second World War is overshadowed by postmodernism. In sharp contrast, an analysis using a narrow Bazinian definition of Hollywood classicism, which sees the year 1939 as a crucial historical turning-point, would identify *Citizen Kane* as the beginning of a modernist trend in American cinema which gained momentum with the self-consciously artistic New Movie of the 1950s and the experiments of the New American Cinema in the early 1960s, and culminated in the artistic renaissance of the New Hollywood between 1967 and 1975. Alternatively, using *Monogram*'s definition of classicism as the dominant Hollywood aesthetic betwen the 1910s and the mid-1960s, only the sustained attack on the fundamental principles of Hollywood storytelling in the liberal cycles of the New Hollywood qualifies as a genuinely modernist intervention into mainstream American cinema. In both cases, the post-1975 period may be characterized either as a turn towards postmodernism or as a return to the principles of classicism.

These periodizations intersect with the standard auteurist account of developments in Hollywood since the late 1960s, which concentrates on the impact of the so-called 'film school generation' or 'movie-brats' (Belton 1994, ch. 14; Hillier 1993). In their highly influential 1979 book *The Movie Brats*, Michael Pye and Lynda Myles discussed the work of a closely knit group of filmmakers born in the 1940s (with the exception of Francis Ford Coppola, who was born in 1939). The group, consisting of Coppola, Scorsese, George Lucas, Brian De Palma, John Milius, and Steven Spielberg and also including some of their frequent collaborators such as Gary Kurtz, represented 'a ciné-literate generation of filmmakers' (1979, p: vii). They had become thoroughly familiar with Hollywood's history through television broadcasts of old movies, had learnt about European film movements in art-houses, and had had the opportunity (which many of them took) to learn their profession at film school and to gain practical experience in the exploitation sector, most notably with Roger Corman's New World Pictures, before they moved into regular feature production from the late 1960s onwards, writing scripts and acting as producers as well as working as directors, and

AMERICAN CINEMA: CRITICAL APPROACHES

often giving support to, or working with, each other. According to Pye and Myles, this new generation of filmmakers was detached from, and often critical of, the Hollywood establishment, and approached mainstream filmmaking in an analytical and self-conscious fashion, producing a new kind of movie which combined the powerful storytelling of classical Hollywood with the transgressive subject-matter of exploitation cinema and the stylistic innovations of European new waves.

> **According to Pye and Myles, this new generation of filmmakers was detached from, and often critical of, the Hollywood establishment, and approached mainstream filmmaking in an analytical and self-conscious fashion, producing a new kind of movie which combined the powerful storytelling of classical Hollywood with the transgressive subject-matter of exploitation cinema and the stylistic innovations of European new waves.**

Pye and Myles's account of Hollywood cinema since the late 1960s identified a crucial generational shift in the film industry, although it largely ignored the parallels to, and connections with, earlier waves of Hollywood outsiders making a strong impact on the industry (such as the theatre- and television-trained writers and directors of the 1950s and 1960s). Their account emphasized the transformation of the 1960s outsiders into the Hollywood establishment of the 1970s. Due to a string of box-office hits, from Coppola's *The Godfather* (USA, 1972) to Spielberg's *Close Encounters of the Third Kind* (USA, 1977), the six key filmmakers and their associates 'at the end of 1977, stood unchallenged as the powers within a new Hollywood. They inherited the power of the moguls to make films for a mass audience' (7). Thus, in effect Pye and Myles argued that, following three decades of aesthetic and economic crisis and flux, the late 1970s saw a return to the stability, popularity, and high standards of the studio era. In this neo-classical Hollywood, auteurs had taken over the executive role of the moguls.

Robert Phillip Kolker approached the crucial shift in late 1970s Hollywood with reference to the concepts of modernism and postmodernism. In his 1980 study *A Cinema of Loneliness*, Kolker explored 'the growth of modernism' in mainstream American cinema of the 1960s and 1970s (1980: 16), grouping older directors such as Arthur Penn, Robert Altman, and Stanley Kubrick together with movie brats Coppola and Scorsese. In Kolker's view, the work of these filmmakers balanced entertainment values with a critical investigation of 'the nature of their medium, its history, its methods and effects' (p. viii). Their self-conscious approach to filmic storytelling, '*refusing* the classical American approach to film, which is to make the formal structure of a work erase itself as it creates its content', demanded an equally self-conscious spectator: 'These directors delight in making us aware of the fact that it is film we are watching, an artifice, something made in special ways, to be perceived in special ways' (9). In the revised edition of his book, Kolker declares that, as far as mainstream American cinema is concerned, '[t]he modernist project . . . is over', with '[p]ostmodern American film . . . returning with a vengeance to a linear illusionist style' (1988, p. xi). Kolker dates this transition in the second half of the 1970s, and sees Steven Spielberg as its key figure, who best exemplifies contemporary Hollywood's 'increased ability . . . to use images and narratives to manipulate response' and to subject the viewer to 'great imaginary structures of displaced yearning, misplaced heroism, and forced amelioration' (p. xi). Schatz gives a similar account, discussing *Annie Hall* (USA, 1977) as an exemplary modernist film, and situating it in the context of a commercial cinema still 'dominated by classical narratives that are technically more proficient . . . than products of the Old Hollywood but otherwise rely on the same principles of construction and methods of viewer engagement' (1983: 223). He goes as far as saying that in particular the films of Lucas and Spielberg 'are even "more classical" than traditional Hollywood movies because of the narrative and technical expertise of their creators' (223).

Noel Carroll (1982) argues that both Hollywood's modernism and its (postmodern or neo-classical) revisionism participate in a culture of allusion. In the 1970s the outlook of large segments of the cinema audience as well as many directors had been shaped by the comprehensive education in film history they had received through television, art-houses, college courses, film societies, film criticism, and film schools while growing up in the 1950s and 1960s. Film history became an important reference-point in the artistic communcation between filmmakers and their audiences. By alluding to the cinema's past in their films, directors created complex texts which engaged and thus rewarded the audience's film-historical knowledge. Instead of distancing spectators from the textual operations of their films, directors employed allusions as 'expressive devices: they are a means for projecting and reinforcing the themes and the emotive and aesthetic qualities of the new films' (Carroll 1982: 53). The culture of allusion embraced a wide variety of practices, 'including quotations, the memorialization of past genres, the reworking of past genres, homages, and the recreation of "classic" scenes, shots, plot motifs, lines of dialogue, themes, gestures, and so forth from film history' (52). While allusions might be used critically by filmmakers such as Robert Altman in a challenge to the ideas and values underpinning traditional genres and the contemporary social order, they were equally in evidence in the revisionist genre films that gained dominance in the second half of the 1970s, addressing themselves both to an older film-educated audience and to a much less knowledgeable 'adolescent clientele' (56). Filmmakers developed 'a two-tiered system of communication which sends an action/drama/fantasy-packed message to one segment of the audience and an additional hermetic, camouflaged, and recondite one to another' (56).

Since the mid-1970s, then, critical debates about the New Hollywood have been characterized by a confusing proliferation of contradictory and shifting definitions of the term, and by different attempts to conceptualize the development of mainstream American cinema in the post-war era with reference to modernism and postmodernism. Yvonne Tasker's (1996) review of these debates indicates that, while there is still no agreement about proper definitions and mappings, there is perhaps a general direction in which these definitions and mappings develop. The original association of the term 'New Hollywood' with the artistic renaissance of the late 1960s and early 1970s has largely been displaced by its identification with the post-1975 period. Furthermore, the critical analysis of the stylistic and thematic innovations introduced by a new generation of auteurs has given way to a concern with the corporate strategies of media conglomerates, with blockbusters and multi-media marketing, and with new forms of film consumption. Indeed, Tasker suggests that changes in the wider cultural and media

landscape may be the best way to separate New Hollywood from classical American cinema and to situate it in relation to postmodernism: 'The newness of the new Hollywood stems from the rapidly changing entertainment world in which it exists. In this context an analysis of film style in the new Hollywood might be most usefully approached through an awareness of the interaction between film and other media and the proliferation of cultural commodities, rather than exclusively in terms of a relationship to the cinematic past' (1996: 226–7). Hence, New Hollywood may be defined not so much in terms of stylistic and thematic changes in filmmaking, clearly separating the contemporary period from a previous modernist moment in American film history as well as from Hollywood's classicism, but in terms of a postmodern multi-media world which undermines the very notion of 'film as a distinct medium' (Tasker 1996: 226). Postmodern New Hollywood, then, is American filmmaking in the age of a fully integrated multi-media culture which originated in the 1960s and consolidated itself in the 1970s and 1980s.

> Hence, New Hollywood may be defined not so much in terms of stylistic and thematic changes in filmmaking, clearly separating the contemporary period from a previous modernist moment in American film history as well as from Hollywood's classicism, but in terms of a postmodern multi-media world which undermines the very notion of 'film as a distinct medium'. Postmodern New Hollywood, then, is American filmmaking in the age of a fully integrated multi-media culture which originated in the 1960s and consolidated itself in the 1970s and 1980s.

The historical poetics of classicism and post-classicism

In her discussion of the New Hollywood, Yvonne Tasker employs the term 'post-classical' to refer primarily and specifically to stylistic changes in mainstream American filmmaking since the 1960s (1996: 220–1). She refers to Bordwell, Staiger, and Thompson's monumental study *The Classical Hollywood Cinema* (1985) as the most comprehensive account of the normative stylistic system, which the innovations of post-classicism need to be defined against. In doing so, Tasker follows the model of other recent critics such as Justin Wyatt (1994: 7–8, 15–16, 60–4), Henry Jenkins (1995: 113–17), and Richard Maltby and Ian Craven (1995: 217–21), all of whom have identified significant departures from classical storytelling, as described in *The Classical Hollywood Cinema*, in certain film cycles since 1960, although they acknowledge that the majority of American films stay firmly within the classical tradition. While the term 'post-classical' may also be used more loosely to refer to other aspects of contemporary American cinema (Rowe 1995; Neale and Smith, 1998), its value as a critical tool would seem to depend on its precise application to the form of stylistic analysis exemplified by Bordwell, Staiger, and Thompson's study.

Bordwell has called this form of analysis 'historical poetics of the cinema', and defined it as 'the study of how, in determinate circumstances, films are put together, serve specific functions, and achieve specific effects' (1989: 266–7). While historical poetics proceeds from the stylistic analysis of individual films and sees any film as 'the result of deliberate and founding choices' made by filmmakers, '[t]he poetician aims to analyze the conceptual and empirical factors—norms, traditions, habits—that govern a practice and its products' (269). To establish the norms and traditions governing a mode of film practice such as classical Hollywood, it is necessary to analyse a large number of films and to ensure that these films constitute a representative sample of the vast corpus they are meant to exemplify. The idiosyncrasies of individual films are thus discussed systematically in relation to the norms embodied in a larger body of texts. Similarly, the use of particular devices in any given film is analysed in relation to the stylistic system of the film as a whole. Furthermore, film analysis is typically complemented by an investigation into the concrete work procedures of filmmaking and the system of production which organizes them. This investigation can make use of a variety of sources ranging from written codifications of rules and norms (e.g. manuals) to interviews with participants. Finally, historical poetics aims to identify stylistic developments within particular film practices, by tracing the diffusion of new stylistic devices such as, for example, zooms, split screens, and freeze frames across the overall corpus of films, and by identifying changes in the normative stylistic system which, in any given film, assigns individual devices a particular function, in Hollywood usually for the purpose of storytelling.

An example of a systemic stylistic change in classical Hollywood filmmaking would be the introduction of aimless protagonists, the loosening of causal connections between narrative events, the foregrounding of stylistic devices in their own right, which serves to demonstrate the filmmakers' artistic presence and intentions, and the refusal of unambiguous narrative closure, which invites audiences to speculate about the film's significance. According to Bordwell, these are some of the key narrational strategies of European art cinema that were absorbed by the filmmakers of the New Hollywood in the late 1960s. While *Monogram* had argued that this absorption constituted a decisive break in the development of mainstream American filmmaking, Bordwell writes: 'these new films do not constitute a sharply distinct style, but can better be explained by that process of stylistic assimilation we have seen at work throughout Hollywood's history' (Bordwell, Staiger, and Thompson 1985: 373). Bordwell uses the penultimate chapter of *The Classical Hollywood Cinema*, entitled 'Since 1960: The Persistence of a Mode of Film Practice', to argue, in effect, that all stylistic innovations in American filmmaking in recent decades 'remain within classical boundaries' (377), and that the date 1960 is a fairly arbitrary cut-off point for their study, which is by no means meant to indicate the end of the classical epoch. By analysing narrational strategies in a sample of recent Hollywood films and their codification in contemporary scriptwriting manuals in comparison with practices in early American feature filmmaking in the mid-1910s, Kristin Thompson (1998) has also argued forcefully for the overall continuity of the classical Hollywood up to the present.

Bordwell, Staiger, and Thompson's work has been criticized (much like *Screen*'s concept of the classical text) for its tendency to play down or erase the differences between individual Hollywood films and between particular œuvres, cycles, and periods, and to describe the basic tenets of classical Hollywood style in such general terms that any form of mainstream filmmaking would appear to fit into this model (Britton 1988–9; Williams 1994). Henry Jenkins (1995), however, argues that *The Classical Hollywood Cinema* and its underlying methodology allow for a more dynamic account of stylistic differences and developments than they are sometimes given credit for. At the centre of Bordwell, Staiger, and Thompson's study and of the project of historical poetics in general are, after all, processes of stylistic change, brought about, for example, by the introduction of new technologies such as synchronized sound or by the encounter with alternative stylistic systems such as European art cinema. Jenkins finds the description and explanation of such stylistic changes offered by Bordwell, Staiger, and Thompson 'essentially correct', although he would prefer to shift the critical focus of the investigation from the ultimate assimilation of new stylistic elements into the established system, to the early stages of that process, that is the 'periods of transition and experimentation before the system can fully stabilize itself around these changes' (1995: 114, 104). During these usually very brief periods, new stylistic elements are perceived by filmmakers and audiences alike as a disruption of the normative stylistic system or as a welcome novelty. The force of this perception is easily underestimated when such innovations are analysed in retrospect from a position which has already witnessed their complete assimilation.

While numerous examples of the process of defamiliarization and assimilation can be found in Hollywood between the 1910s and the 1940s, Jenkins suggests that the post-war period is characterized by the dramatic intensification of stylistic change: 'Since the breakdown of the studio system, Hollywood has entered a period of prolonged and consistent formal experimentation and institutional flux with a media-savvy audience demanding . . . aesthetic novelty and difference. As a result, stylistic changes which might have unfolded over several decades under the studio system have occurred in a matter of a few years in contemporary Hollywood' (114). It is this increased speed and intensity of stylistic change which the concept of post-classicism is meant to describe. While Jenkins's examples are mainly from the 1960s, 1970s, and 1980s (the movie brats, 'high-concept' films, MTV aesthetics), his analysis would also seem to apply to the immediate post-war period, during which critics, and presumably American filmmakers and audiences as well, responded very strongly to a wide variety of stylistic developments which included: the increasing use of long takes, deep-focus cinematography and staging in depth; the move towards quasi-documentary; the

self-conscious artistry of the New Movie; the widescreen revolution; and the big picture.

Some of these developments in the post-war period have been covered in *The Classical Hollywood Cinema*. Yet, in general, critical debates about developments in post-war American cinema have dealt with stylistic change only in a cursory, abstract, and unspecific fashion, quickly moving from observations about individual film examples to claims about fundamental shifts in the overall aesthetic and industrial system. In this situation, the conceptual debate about Old Hollywood and New Hollywood, modernism and postmodernism, classicism and post-classicism, is perhaps less urgent and productive than the kind of careful, systematic, and complex stylistic analysis which historical poetics demands.

BIBLIOGRAPHY

Agee, James (1963), *Agee on Film* (London: Peter Owen).
Alpert, Hollis (1960/1971*a*), 'Are Foreign Films Better?: Show of Strength Abroad', in Arthur F. McClure (ed.), *The Movies: An American Idiom* (Rutherford: Fairleigh Dickinson University Press).
—— (1968*a*/1971*b*), 'The Falling Stars', in Arthur F. McClure (ed.), *The Movies: An American Idiom* (Rutherford: Fairleigh Dickinson University Press).
—— (1968*b*/1971*c*), 'The Graduate Makes Out', in Arthur F. McClure (ed.), *The Movies: An American Idiom* (Rutherford: Fairleigh Dickinson University Press).
Andrew, Dudley (1978), *André Bazin* (New York: Oxford University Press).
Bazin, André (1951/1967), 'The Evolution of the Language of Cinema', trans. Hugh Gray, in *What is Cinema?*, 2 vols., i (Berkeley: University of California Press).
—— (1957/1985), 'On the *politique des auteurs*', trans. Peter Graham in Jim Hillier (ed.), *Cahiers du Cinéma*, i: *The 1950s: Neo-Realism, Hollywood, New Wave* (London: Routledge & Kegan Paul).
—— (1971), 'The Evolution of the Western', trans. Hugh Gray, in *What is Cinema?* 2 vols., ii (Berkeley: University of California Press).
Belton, John (1994), *American Cinema/American Culture* (New York: McGraw-Hill).
Biskind, Peter (1990), 'Blockbuster: The Last Crusade', in Mark Crispin Miller (ed.), *Seeing through Movies* (New York: Pantheon).
Bordwell, David (1989), *Making Meaning: Inference and Rhetoric in the Interpretation of Cinema* (Cambridge, Mass.: Harvard University Press).
—— **Janet Staiger**, and **Kristin Thompson** (1985), *The*

Classical Hollywood Cinema: Film Style and Mode of Production to 1960 (London: Routledge & Kegan Paul).

Britton, Andrew (1986), 'Blissing Out: The Politics of Reaganite Entertainment', *Movie*, 31–2: 1–42.

—— (1988–9), 'The Philosophy of the Pigeonhole: Wisconsin Formalism and "The Classical Style"', *CineAction*, 15: 47–63.

Cameron, Ian *et al.* (1975), 'The Return of Movie', *Movie*, 20: 1–25.

*Carroll, Noel (1982), 'The Future of Allusion: Hollywood in the Seventies (and Beyond)', *October*, 20: 51–81.

Caughie, John (ed.) (1981), *Theories of Authorship* (London: Routledge & Kegan Paul).

Cawelti, John G. (ed.) (1973), *Focus on 'Bonnie and Clyde'* (Englewood Cliffs, NJ: Prentice Hall).

Corrigan, Timothy (1991), *A Cinema without Walls: Movies and Culture after Vietnam* (London: Routledge).

Denzin, Norman K. (1991), *Images of Postmodern Society: Social Theory and Contemporary Cinema* (London: Sage).

Elsaesser, Thomas (1971), 'The American Cinema: Why Hollywood?', *Monogram*, 1: 4–10.

*—— (1975), 'The Pathos of Failure. American Films in the 1970s: Notes on the Unmotivated Hero', *Monogram*, 6: 13–19.

Farber, Manny (1952/1971), *Negative Space: Manny Farber on the Movies* (London: Studio Vista).

Farber, Steven (1968/1971), 'The Outlaws', in Arthur F. McClure (ed.), *The Movies: An American Idiom* (Rutherford: Fairleigh Dickinson University Press).

Gillet, John (1959/1971), 'The Survivors', in Arthur F. McClure (ed.), *The Movies: An American Idiom* (Rutherford: Fairleigh Dickinson University Press).

Goodman, Ezra (1961), *The Fifty-Year Decline and Fall of Hollywood* (New York: Simon & Schuster).

Hart, Peter (1965), 'New Breed Scans New Horizons', *New York Times*, 10 Jan. 1965.

Hecht, Ben (1959/1971), 'Elegy for Wonderland', in Arthur F. McClure (ed.), *The Movies: An American Idiom* (Rutherford: Fairleigh Dickinson University Press).

*Hillier, Jim (1993), *The New Hollywood* (London: Studio Vista).

Houston, Penelope (1963), *The Contemporary Cinema* (Harmondsworth: Penguin).

Jameson, Fredric (1991), *Postmodernism; or, The Cultural Logic of Late Capitalism* (Durham, NC: Duke University Press).

Jenkins, Henry (1995), 'Historical Poetics', in Joanne Hollows and Mark Jancovich (eds.), *Approaches to Popular Film* (Manchester: Manchester University Press).

Kael, Pauline (1956/1966a), 'Movies, the Desperate Art', in Daniel Talbot (ed.), *Film: An Anthology* (Berkeley: University of California Press).

—— (1966b), *I Lost it at the Movies* (London: Jonathan Cape).

—— (1967/1970), *Kiss Kiss Bang Bang* (London: Calder & Boyars).

Kolker, Robert Phillip (1980), *A Cinema of Loneliness: Penn, Kubrick, Coppola, Scorsese, Altman* (New York: Oxford University Press).

*—— (1988), *A Cinema of Loneliness: Penn, Kubrick, Scorsese, Spielberg, Altman*, 2nd edn. (New York: Oxford University Press).

Lloyd, Peter (1971), 'The American Cinema: An Outlook', *Monogram* 1: 11–13.

MacCann, Richard Dyer (1962), *Hollywood in Transition* (Boston: Houghton Mifflin).

MacDonald, Dwight (1966/1969), *Dwight MacDonald on Movies* (Englewood Cliffs: Prentice Hall).

Madsen, Axel (1975), *The New Hollywood: American Movies in the 1970s* (New York: Thomas Y. Crowell).

Maltby, Richard (1983), *Harmless Entertainment: Hollywood and the Ideology of Consensus* (Metuchen, NJ: Scarecrow).

—— with Ian Craven (1995), *Hollywood Cinema: An Introduction* (Oxford: Blackwell).

Modleski, Tania (1991), *Feminism without Women: Culture and Criticism in a Postfeminist Age* (London: Routledge).

Monaco, James (1979), *American Film Now: The People, the Power, the Money, the Movies* (New York: Plume).

Neale, Steve (1976), 'New Hollywood Cinema', *Screen* 17/2: 117–22.

—— (1980), 'Hollywood Strikes Back: Special Effects in Recent American Cinema', *Screen*, 21/3: 101–5.

—— and Murray Smith (eds.) (1998), *Contemporary Hollywood Cinema* (London: Routledge).

Pye, Michael, and Lynda Myles (1979), *The Movie Brats: How the Film Generation Took over Hollywood* (New York: Holt, Rinehart, & Winston).

Ray, Robert B. (1985), *A Certain Tendency of the Hollywood Cinema 1930–1980* (Princeton: Princeton University Press).

Rowe, Kathleen (1995), 'Melodrama and Men in Post-Classical Romantic Comedy', in Pat Kirkham and Janet Thumim (eds.), *Me Jane: Masculinity, Movies and Women* (London: Lawrence & Wishart).

Ryan, Michael, and Douglas Kellner (1988), *Camera Politica: The Politics and Ideology of Contemporary Hollywood Film* (Bloomington: Indiana University Press).

Sarris, Andrew (1963/1968), 'The American Cinema', *Film Culture*, 28; repr. rev. as 'Toward a Theory of Film History', in *The American Cinema: Directors and Directions 1929–1968* (New York: Dutton).

*Schatz, Thomas (1983), *Old Hollywood/New Hollywood: Ritual, Art, Industry* (Ann Arbor, Mich.: UMI Research Press).

—— (1988), *The Genius of the System* (New York: Pantheon).

—— (1993), 'The New Hollywood', in Jim Collins, Hilary Radner, and Ava Preacher Collins (eds.), *Film Theory Goes to the Movies* (New York: Routledge).

Seldes, Gilbert (1950), *The Great Audience* (New York: Viking).

—— (1956), *The Public Arts* (New York: Simon & Schuster).

*Tasker, Yvonne (1996), 'Approaches to the New Hollywood', in James Curran, David Morley, and Valerie Walkerdine (eds.), *Cultural Studies and Communications* (London: Arnold).

Thompson, Kristin (1998), 'Narrative Structure in Early Classical Cinema', in John Fullerton (ed.), *Celebrating 1895: The Centenary of Cinema* (London: John Libbey).

Thomson, David (1981), *Overexposures: The Crisis in American Filmmaking* (New York: William Morrow).

Time (1967/1971), 'The Shock of Freedom in Films', in Arthur F. McClure (ed.), *The Movies: An American Idiom* (Rutherford: Fairleigh Dickinson University Press).

Tyler, Parker (1960), *The Three Faces of the Film* (New York: Thomas Yoseloff).

Williams, Christopher (1994), 'After the Classic, the Classical and Ideology: The Differences of Realism', *Screen*, 35/3: 275–92.

Wood, Robin (1985), '1980s Hollywood: Dominant Tendencies', *CineAction*, 1: 1–5.

*—— (1986), *Hollywood from Vietnam to Reagan* (New York: Columbia University Press).

Wyatt, Justin (1994), *High Concept: Movies and Marketing in Hollywood* (Austin: University of Texas Press).

Critical concepts

7

Authorship and Hollywood

Stephen Crofts

Authorship is by far the best-known 'theory' of cinema, and Hollywood much the best-known national cinema. Many conceptions of authorship have arisen in relation to Hollywood—and other national cinemas—over the last seven decades, and proper consideration of these varied notions requires contextualization in terms of the institutions which support them. For, unlike most other ways of making sense of cinema, discourses of authorship have emerged across the whole gamut of cinematic institutions from film production and circulation through film reviewing, criticism and analysis, and film education, to film history and theory. In doing so, discourses of authorship assert the central significance of individual creativity within the cinema, and usually locate this in the director.

The attachment of authorial discourses to Hollywood warrants some comment. Authorial discourses, after all, find stronger empirical connection to the more artisanal modes of filmmaking practice which characterize art and avant-garde cinemas. Both these modes of filmmaking exhibit greater degrees of individual creativity than were possible within the industrial modes of production characteristic of Hollywood in what David Bordwell, Janet Staiger, and Kristin Thompson (1985) identify as the classical period to 1960, and often subsequently. Classical Hollywood had little use for a discourse of authorship and few outside Walt Disney, Alfred Hitchcock, and Charlie Chaplin attained name status (1985: 96–112, 78), this is not at all to deny the *differentiation* and *innovation* which Bordwell, Staiger, and Thompson note as accompanying the standardization of Hollywood. In the context of its successful marketing of films by star and genre, directorial power could be greater in practice than was acknowledged in promotion: 'Narrative coherence and clarity supported the movement of star personalities to the foreground and their directors toward the top of the pyramid . . . the movement from the 1930s has been increasingly in the direction of assuming that one individual . . . producer, director, writer . . . ought to control almost all aspects of filming so that that individual's personal vision can be created' (Bordwell *et al.* 1985: 335–6). Whereas the mobilization of authorial discourses was crucial to the substantial emergence and circulation of art cinemas in the 1950s, it was not until some while later—and, indeed, partly in response to competition from art cinemas—that Hollywood, under the package-unit system, came to accept the frequent attachment of authorial discourses to its films. Authorship has therefore recently added the promise of certain spectatorial pleasures, the cachet of cultural respectability, or cult status to the labels which traditionally typified classical Hollywood's promotion of its films—genre and star.

Film critics and reviewers have used the principle of authorship to argue for the artistic respectability of cinema and to attribute the status of creative artist to those working within the industrial system of Hollywood. As a polemical principle of film criticism and reviewing, authorship has had massive success and has placed many Hollywood directors in the international pantheon. It has been used to force the cultural and educational recognition of film and is now institutionalized into most Western film reviewing and criticism, film books, film festivals world-wide, and film studies syllabuses. The fact that the discourse of authorship arose in European rather than American critical institutions testifies to the strength of the former's aesthetic discourses. As early as 1959 Jean-Luc Godard could proclaim the success of the principle of authorship in 'having it acknowledged that a film by Hitchcock, for example, is as important as a book by Aragon. Film authors, thanks to us, have finally entered the history of art' (Godard 1959/1972: 147). For Andrew Sarris, transplanting the principle to the less congenial soil of the United States in 1962, authorship was 'primarily a critical device for recording the history of American cinema, the only cinema in the world worth exploring in depth beneath the frosting of a few great directors at the top' (Sarris 1962/1971: 130). The principle attained broad acceptance in Anglo-American reviewing and criticism in the 1970s and 1980s.

Its critical success, however, belies its theoretical bankruptcy. Firstly, Sarris muddied the issue enormously by mistranslating 'la politique des auteurs'—

correctly 'the principle of/polemic for authors'—as 'the auteur theory' (124). Furthermore, many commentators have noted the failure of the principle's proponents to theorize or even logically justify their chosen critical tool and it remained less a clearly defined concept than a critical construct which arbitrarily attributed significance to the work of some directors rather than others.

Both the critical success and the theoretical limits of the principle stem from the embedded cultural force of the key Western concept underpinning it: the human individual. But once we recognize with Foucault that 'man is an invention of recent date . . . [a]nd perhaps nearing its end' (1966/1973: 387), it becomes easier to theorize the principle and to analyse the discourses which traverse and constitute it within its various institutional locations. This account seeks to examine the historical development of what I shall abbreviate as Authorship: the critical discourse of authorship on film. It thus acknowledges how some significant recent shifts in Western theories of subjectivity have informed Authorship.

The history of the varying conceptualizations of authorship follows broadly the three principal emphases in Western critical and theoretical writing on film since the 1950s:

1. the aesthetically focused textual analysis characterizing most work until the 1970s;

2. the theoretical turn of the mid-1970s associated with *Screen*'s challenge to the impressionism and empiricism of most previous writing on film; and

3. the move dating from the mid-1980s towards film histories encompassing institutions of production and circulation, and sometimes the cultures and societies in which film texts are produced.

Textual analysis

Four modes of Authorship can be associated with the emphasis on textual analysis: forerunners of auteurism, auterism, auteur-structuralism and the author or instance of politics and/or pleasure.

The key relation attended to is that between text and reader. With the exception of the politicized criticism of the fourth mode, questions of social provenance, not to mention industrial production, are bracketed off, usually in the service of an avowedly or implicitly aesthetic critical undertaking. This critical activity routinely disengages certain thematic and stylistic properties from the text(s) concerned and attributes to them the coherence associated with the name of an author—who, as Foucault notes (1969/1979: 18), is a discursive construction independent of any empirical director. Often an evaluative exercise, such criticism uses author-names to mark out film texts by given directors as being aesthetically—or, occasionally, politically—superior to others.

The first two modes treated here are overtly aesthetic in conception, and occur principally within institutions of film reviewing, criticism, and sometimes history. Their guiding assumptions, if not polemic, are of cinema as 'art', and their conceptions of subjectivity are very much those of a transcendental individualism and Romantic sensibility. The last two modes, introducing structuralism, historical materialism, and psychoanalysis, are more analytical in aim, and operate largely in the fields of film criticism and analysis. Their polemic is sometimes political, and partly theoretical, testing the productivity of theoretical discourses in the analysis of film texts. They largely dissent from auteurism's Romantic notions of individual expressivity, and anticipate and bleed over into the two notions of authorship discussed in Modes 5 and 6.

Mode 1: proto-auteurism

This forerunner of auteurism emerges sporadically in European film reviewing and criticism from the 1920s onwards. Not only does it lack the later systematic, polemic thrust of auteurism proper but, more significantly, it restricts itself to directors who empirically possessed more creative freedom than most within Hollywood. This meant a canon centring on Chaplin, D. W. Griffith, Erich von Stroheim, King Vidor, Orson Welles, and John Ford, alongside such European directors as Sergei Eisenstein, Vsevolod Pudovkin, Abel Gance, and Marcel Carné. In general, this was a common-sense transfer of the discourse of authorship from other artistic practices, epitomized in Alexandre Astruc's famous proclamation of the 'camera-pen' (1948).

Proto-auteurism constituted a readily identifiable critical currency in France, the Soviet Union, and Britain from the 1920s until the present. It was made possible in these countries by the substantial art film production and/or exhibition sectors and their often powerful aesthetic discourses. This contrasted with the entertainment imperative of Hollywood, whose central producer and producer-unit modes of production operative between the 1930s and mid-1950s militated against public acknowledgement of directorial creativity.

Four instances from the early 1920s to 1950 plainly demonstrate that auteurism—and indeed some later developments in the history of Authorship—did not emerge unheralded:

1. Among the first authorial criticism on film may well be Louis Delluc's (1922–3) analyses of Griffith, Thomas Ince, Maurice Tourneur, Marcel L'Herbier, and Chaplin (see Tariol 1965: 104–9). In their clear interest in recognizable constants of style and world-view across the works of the directors concerned, these accounts foreshadow auteurism in the style of the *Cahiers du cinéma* of the 1950s.

2. Similarly, Lindsay Anderson's (1950) treatment of Ford adumbrates auteur-structuralism in his argument that *They were Expendable* (1945) 'illuminate[s Ford] films which came before it and reveal[s] qualities in them which may up to now have gone unremarked. In this light recognisable patterns emerge from the rather baffling diversity of Ford's films' (1950: 1).

3. Writing in 1930, Paul Rotha applies authorial principles selectively to Hollywood in order to suggest that certain artists are capable of transcending the anonymous machine:

despite these conditions of manufacture, the mass production, the obstinate committees, the uncreative producers, the horrors of the star system and the corrugated iron environment, there are occasions when a single film, the creation of one man's mind, makes its appearance. There are, in Hollywood, fortunately, men whose very personality overrides the machinery. With wisdom and discretion they use to full advantage the organisation of Hollywood and its excellent technical resources. (1930: 141)

4. Countering this vision of Romantic expressivity in and against Hollywood, a sound empirical recognition of directorial creativity where production circumstances licensed it may also be discovered. The following appeared in 1943 in a French student newspaper: 'The problem of film authorship is not resolved and cannot be so, a priori. The facts of production are just too vari-

able from work to work, for one to be able to accept the director as invariably the unique creator. The cinema is a team art. Each film requires of the critic an individual judgment concerning its authorship' (quoted in Crisp 1993: 238). Written by André Bazin, this prefigures not only his later moderation of the excesses of *Cahiers*' 1950s application of auteurism, but also the empirical approach to authorship in film production taken up by 1980s film historians.

Mode 2: auteurism

This ungainly portmanteau word is the term which regularly describes the best-known conception of authorship. In the early 1950s critics in *La Revue du cinéma* in its second series and *La Gazette du cinéma*, consolidated in their successor, *Cahiers du cinéma*, and in *Positif*, the already established principle of proto-auteurism as a *polemic*, which was strenuously advocatory, evaluative, and canonic. The context in which these critics worked included the huge influx of Hollywood films after the fall of the Vichy government and the thriving ciné-club movement which facilitated 'an unmatched perception of the historical dimensions of Hollywood and the careers of individual directors' (Wollen 1969/1972: 75–7). In the context of contemporaneously available forms of entertainment, these critics adopted a Romantic discourse of creativity as a means of cultural assertion for film as art in the age of the rise of television (Crisp 1993: 73).

Concerned not just with reviewing but also with historicizing cinema, the highly influential *Cahiers* polemicized against the 1950s script-based French cinema of psychological realism; for such French directors as Jean Cocteau, Jean Renoir, Robert Bresson, and Gance; and for Hollywood directors such as Howard Hawks, Hitchcock, Fritz Lang, Douglas Sirk, and Nicholas Ray. This Hollywood canon extended beyond those directors praised by proto-auteurists to embrace many (e.g. Sam Fuller, Vincente Minnelli) whose celebration scandalized some contemporary critics, and others (Don Weis, Edgar G. Ulmer) to whom later, less passionate commentators have been strikingly less kind. Apart from Bazin, Astruc, and Amédée Ayfre, the best known of *Cahiers*'s reviewers in the phase of establishing auteurism as a critical orthodoxy were the so-called 'young Turks'—Jacques Rivette, Godard, Claude Chabrol, François Truffaut, and Rohmer (often under

his real name, Maurice Schérer)—who were later to be central to the world's first film movement led by directors aware of film history, the Nouvelle Vague. Most stridently auteurist, perhaps, was Truffaut, whose article 'Une certaine tendance du cinéma français' (1954) was soon mythologized as inventing auteurism and giving the journal a sense of direction it previously lacked. Bazin consistently served as internal moderator and distanced himself from the excesses of the younger guard (Bazin 1957). The consolidation of auteurism is marked in Éditions Universitaires' starting its film-book series in 1954 with monographs on individual directors.

Given *Cahiers*' extension of the canon to directors who had limited influence over scripts, stylistic criteria of evaluation usually took explicit precedence over thematic ones. Style, 'mise-en'scène, through which everything on the screen is expressed' (Hoveyda 1960: 42), distinguished the 'auteur' from the mere 'metteur-en-scène', the mere manufacturer, whose use of mise-en-scène, it was deemed, did not transform the script material into an original work. Witness Bazin in 1953: 'Huston has no truly personal style. The author of *I Confess* [Hitchcock, 1952] has a personal style. He is the inventor of original cinematic forms, and in this his superiority to Huston is incontestable' (1953: 53). Bordwell, Staiger, and Thompson invaluably clarify how the narrating instance of Hitchcock's films supplies textual evidence supporting such views: 'Hitchcock's authorial persona oscillates between being modest and uncommunicative (i.e. presenting a single character's point of view) and flaunting its omniscience by suppressing crucial information' (1985: 79).

In the auteurist critical enterprise, the author is impressionistically read off from thematic and/or stylistic properties in the film(s). In Foucault's analysis, the purpose of this process is 'to construct the rational entity we call an author. Undoubtedly this construction is assigned a "realistic" dimension as we speak of an individual's "profundity" or "creative" power . . . Nevertheless, these aspects of the individual . . . which comprise an individual as author . . . are projections . . . of our way of handling texts: in the comparisons we make, the traits we extract as pertinent, the continuities we assign, or the exclusions we practise' (1969/1979: 21). Critics thus read certain textual characteristics as signifiers of a particular signified, called the director. Much interpretative latitude is possible here, not least on account of the third-person mode of narration adopted by conventional fictional cinema, or, in Émile Benveniste's terms, its holding of *discours* onto *histoire*

(1975: 237–50). So vertical overhead camera angles may signify Lang, Hitchcock, or Chabrol, tilt frames Hitchcock, eye-level camera Hawks, and simultaneous track and zoom Robert Altman. In thematic terms, male camaraderie marks Hawks, the overreaching hero Anthony Mann, and so on. The shortcomings of such simple ascriptions are evident enough. Can these same features not be found in many different directors' films? By what criteria does the reader select certain features as pertinent? Why do readers routinely construct authors on the basis of continuities, not discontinuities, from work to work? Why is thematic consistency a guarantee of good films (witness Andrew MacLaglen)? What ideological values are masked in the critical promotion of certain authors at the expense of others?

A striking comment on this last issue, of canon formation, is made in Hoveyda's (1960) retrospect on the previous six years of *Cahiers*' polemic for directors such as Hitchcock, Roberto Rossellini, and Lang: 'The evidence was undeniable: our favourite authors, when it came down to it, were all talking about the same things. The "constants" of their particular universes belonged to everybody: solitude, violence, the absurdity of existence, sin, redemption, love and so on. Each epoch has its own themes, which serve as a backdrop against which individuals, artists or not, act out their lives' (1960: 41). As John Hess (1974) has noted, a Catholic metaphysic, tinged with existentialism, structures a film aesthetic. Auteurism, it should be remembered, was polemical and evaluative before it was analytical.

Cahiers debated vigorously with *Positif* about canons. The difference between the two was at bottom political. *Cahiers* favoured directors whose optimism and spirituality drew on contemporary strains of cultural conservatism, an ostrich-like reaction against the Resistance-based left progressivism of the post-war period. *Positif*, conversely, was leftist, Surrealist, and anti-Catholic, favouring, amongst Hollywood directors, liberals like Elia Kazan, Sidney Lumet, and Fred Zinneman, and the less than uplifting world-views of Stanley Kubrick and William Wellman, along with Richard Brooks, Frank Tashlin, and John Huston.

With less polemical thrust as time has proceeded, auteurist criticism remains the dominant mode of Authorship, widely circulated as it now is throughout Western film reviewing and criticism. Hollywood was the prime concern of the Anglo-American criticism which transplanted auteurism, to Britain in 1962 via *Movie*, and to the United States in the same year via *Film Culture* (Sarris 1962/1971). For *Movie*, the principle was mobilized in the service of polemics for Hollywood, and against what was perceived as the uncreative torpor of British cinema. Culturally, *Movie* was reacting against the élitism of Bloomsbury and Leavisite assumptions, and film-culturally, against the dilettantish strain of *Sight and Sound* and its high-cultural protocols. One of the lasting benefits of *Movie*, especially Victor Perkins's work, has been its rich mise-en-scène analyses of Hollywood films, analyses which were remarkably precise given the then non-availability of video (and rarely even Steenbeck editing-tables) for close analysis.

Sarris's cultural context in the United States was scarcely more favourable than that of *Movie*. His concern was to redeem Hollywood from the high-cultural critical dismissal which denigrated it in favour of European art cinema, and from sociological readings which denied its aesthetic values. Hence both the boldly polemic assertiveness of his nine-rank pantheon of Hollywood directors published in *The American Cinema* (1968) and his preparedness to 'wrench . . . directors . . . from their historical environments', a practice common to almost all auteurism, but rarely made so explicit (1962/1971: 128). Distinguishing himself from *Cahiers*' young Turks, he avers that 'the critic can never assume that a bad director will always make a bad film', and acknowledges changes through directors' careers and 'the constant flux' of his pantheon of auteurs (Sarris 1962/1971: 132, 134). Pauline Kael (1963) merits a proverbial footnote for her vigorous, if ill-focused, attack on Sarris, advancing an empiricist suspicion of systematized criticism and a robust faith in the critic's common sense. More substantially, Jonathan Rosenbaum notes not only Sarris's omision of 'two important blacklisted directors' Cy Endfield and Jules Berry, but also how auteurist celebrations of Welles's 'genius' have long obscured his involvement with left politics (1991: 42–3).

Auteurism was to become a major element of a very significant feedback loop from the French Nouvelle Vague to Hollywood with the emergence in the late 1960s of the New Hollywood associated with such names as Altman, Arthur Penn, Martin Scorsese, and Woody Allen (see Kramer, Part 2, Chapter 6). Three factors were laying the groundwork for this: European art-film imports to the United States were beginning to present positive evidence to American critical taste of production practices which were overtly supportive of directors; a growing recognition of auteurist critical practices urged more director-centred practices and promotions; and these were more readily accommodated after Hollywood's 1950s adoption of the package-unit system and its 1960s production crises.

Auteurism habitually maps the critical activity of reading textual characteristics as traces of a director onto the empirical entity who on set calls 'Cut!', the director of the film. For all that this figure sometimes fools obsequious interviewers about his or her 'real intentions', the figure is usually characterized as an individual expressing her- or himself untrammelled by cultural determinants and transcending industrial interference. Against this assumption, as Wollen argues, it is vital to distinguish the structure of 'Ford' from Ford the person (1969/1972: 168). What is elided in the process of mapping auteurism onto the empirical individual is consideration of any potential difference in assumptions between that individual and the reader's construction of an author from the film texts. Readings which ignore the distinction between empirical author and author-name makes a wild leap of faith from the moment of reading to the moment of production. Not only do they disregard a whole semiosis; they also re-create the world in their own ideological image, whether the homogenization is transcultural or transhistorical or both.

Auteurism differently

An immediately obvious variant on this pattern is the assertion that authorial functions other than direction are involved in the collaborative work of most filmmaking. Cases have been made for the producer as author (e.g. Val Lewton, Arthur Freed), performer as author (e.g. the Marx brothers, Clint Eastwood as actor, Mae West), and scriptwriter as author (e.g. Jules Furthman, Ben Hecht, Frank Nugent). It is from the scriptwriters' standpoint that directorial auteurism has been most forcefully debated. Richard Corliss argues for a *politique des collaborateurs*, that scripts have to be considered alongside, if not before, direction, and valuably adumbrates, for instance, the significance of the contributions to Ford's films of Nunally Johnson, Dudley Nichols, and Nugent (Corliss 1972: 20–3; 1974/1975). Such argument has, however, barely troubled the status of the director as author.

With the partial exception of *Cahiers*' category E, described below, all the following modes of Authorship variously challenge the communication model underpinning auteurism, with its assumptions of a transcendental subject in full control of the meanings she or he somehow directly 'communicates' to the reader.

Mode 3: auteur-structuralism

Auteur-structuralism is a kind of shotgun marriage very much of its moment. It grew out of the intellectual left in London in the late 1960s, which was then increasingly receptive to European theoretical discourses, and out of the film-cultural work of the British Film Institute's Education Department, which was urging serious analytical attention to film, and was soon to advance film studies into universities. The speed of development of film study, historically telescoping an array of intellectual influences, may account for the simultaneous circulation of authorial discourses, with their Romantic aesthetics, and ideas of applying to film analysis the structuralist methodology of Lévi-Strauss, belonging to a markedly less individualist paradigm, and promising a rigorously scientific basis from which to counter the predominant impressionism of film reviewing and criticism. Besides drawing on different paradigms, these discourses also inhabited different institutional locations: film reviewing on the one hand, and film criticism and analysis on the other, the latter fast growing with, for instance, the establishment in 1967 of both the Cinema One and Movie paperbacks series of film books.

Auteur-structuralism employed a theoretical sophistication and analytical substance lacking in auteurism. With its emphasis on the importance of systematically analysing a body of texts, auteur-structuralism conceives of the author as a set of structures identifiable within a director's films. In the words of Nowell-Smith, whose book on Luchino Visconti was virtually the first instance of auteur-structuralism, 'The purpose of criticism becomes therefore to uncover behind the superficial contrasts of subject and treatment a structural hard core of basic and often recondite motifs. The pattern formed by these motifs, which may be stylistic or thematic, is what gives an author's work its particular structure, both defining it internally and distinguishing one body of work from another' (1967: 10).

Auteur-structuralism crystallized most famously and influentially in Wollen's *Signs and Meaning in the Cinema* (1969/1972). His structuralist analysis contrasts the relative simplicity of the crazy comedies' inversion of the macho adventure dramas in Hawks's œuvre with 'the richness of the shifting relations between antinomies in Ford's work that makes him a great artist, beyond being simply an undoubted auteur' (1969/1972: 102). Marshalled under the cardinal antinomy of nature–culture are overlapping pairs of binary oppositions, with some pairs of binaries in different films 'foregrounded, discarded or even inverted, whereas others remain stable and constant'—garden–wilderness; plough share–sabre; settler–nomad; European–American Indian; civilized–savage; book–gun; married–unmarried; East–West (with this last open to further disaggregation as Boston–Washington); and, in *The Last Hurrah* (1958), Irish immigrants–Plymouth Club; Celtic–Anglo-Saxon; and so on (1969: 104, 94). This structuralist analysis also invaluably illuminates such oddball Ford films as *Donovan's Reef* (1963) and *Wings of Eagles* (1957).

Many regarded such heuristic yields as adequate justification for auteur-structuralism. But there was robust theoretical debate. This arose not just from auteur-structuralism's strange yoking-together of the pre-structuralist with the structuralist, but also from its appearance at a time when post-structuralist theoretical discourses were, in the anglophone world, just beginning to destabilize the empiricist and idealist securities of structuralism. Theoretical problems arising from the auteur–structuralism conjunction include the following. Firstly, the trans-individual origination and currency of myths, the focus of Lévi-Strauss's structuralism, render them less than compatible with a body of works predicated on the individualism of an auteur. Thus in Wollen's assessment of Ford quoted above, there is a clear desire to hold on to the evaluative passion endemic in much auteur criticism, with little sense of embarrassment about retaining the 'great artist' while uncovering the structure. Confusingly, the conclusion to the 1972 edition insists that the auteur be an 'unconscious catalyst', not that 'he has played the role of artist, expressing himself or his vision in the film, but because it is through the force of his preoccupations that an unconscious, unintended meaning can be decoded in the film' (1972: 167–8). After encountering semiotics, such directorial structures became the authorial subcode (Brewster 1973: 41) or the author as a textual system constructed, and susceptible to appropriation, by the critic (Nowell-Smith 1976: 29–30). A second critique of auteur-structuralism points out that many of the structures disentangled by the analysis have a wider than individual currency, such as the garden–wilderness binary which is found in almost all westerns, as well as in most Ford films. In other words, this auteur seems to have the capacity to subsume broadly cultural as well as film-industrial determinants of meaning. Thirdly, this begs the question of the pertinence of the films made by a given director as the criterion of sample selection. Why not all films from a given genre in a given year? Or even all films, as Wollen himself suggests, made by given directors with or without a given producer?

Auteur-structuralism was also debated from the standpoint of post-structuralist ideas, notably those of the later Barthes, which underpin the later, theoretical deconstruction of authorial principles examined below. One question concerns, in Brian Henderson's words, the auteur-structuralists' 'failure to found their criticism theoretically, the absence of an auteur-structuralist epistemology' (1973: 27). Another critique advanced by Henderson is that structuralism 'is an empiricism' which assumes the object as given, as already fully constituted, and posited as other and unchanged in the process of reading (33). Other charges levelled against auteur-structuralism include the reduction of films to structures alone, and the privileging of themes above all else.

Read symptomatically, almost all of the logical contortions and rhetorical slippages evident in auteur-structuralism in general, and in Wollen's two accounts in particular, find their explanation in the convergence of imported theoretical discourses, vitalizing the empiricist traditions of British philosophy, with the polemical desire to intellectualize film studies. As Rob Lapsley and Mike Westlake argue, Wollen's 1972 conclusion is better read not 'as a resolution of the problem of synthesising auteurism and structuralism, but as transitional text from a pre-structuralist concept of the author as creator of meaning to a post-structuralist concept of the author as a construct of the reader' (1988: 111).

Mode 4: author as instance of politics and/ or pleasure

The demise of the May 1968 'revolution' bequeathed a legacy of intellectual speculation on the reasons for its failure to unseat French capitalism. It gave urgency to work on ideology analysed as a means of assisting dominant groups to retain political power. The renowned political typology of Jean-Louis Comolli and Jean Narboni (1969) categorized films in terms of their perceived political effectivity in circulating or challenging dominant ideologies. Although New Left politics here displaced aesthetic achievements as the criterion of evaluation and canon formation, the aesthetic pleasures associated with some author-names

The complex notion of authorship—John Ford's *Young Mr Lincoln* (1939)

rather surreptitiously reappeared in the typology's then fashionable category E.

This embraces

films which at first sight seem to be under the sway of the dominant ideology, but in which . . . there is a disjunction, a dislocation, a distortion between the starting point and the end product. The ideology is not intentionally transmitted by the author . . . but encounters obstacles in the film which throw it off course . . . with the result that it is both exposed and denounced by the filmic structure which seizes the ideology and *plays it back against itself*, allowing its limits to be seen at the same time as transgressing them. . . . An oblique, symptomatic reading will reveal, beyond the film's apparent formal coherence, cracks and faultlines which an ideologically anodyne film does not have. (Comolli and Narboni 1969: 13–14)

Poised like auteur-structuralism between contending paradigms, this category could, perhaps conveni-

ently, combine left political credentials with a reinstatement of the auteurist vision of the (preferably left-wing) artist critiquing, even if only momentarily, the conventions of Hollywood, as in the ostensibly disruptive characteristics of certain favoured directors: the fauvist lighting of the climax of *Some Came Running* (Minnelli, 1959) or the insistently obtrusive grilles, blinds, and paintings of *Imitation of Life* (Sirk, 1959).

The most famous film analysis associated with category E is that of *Young Mr Lincoln* (Ford, 1939) by the editors of *Cahiers du cinéma* (1970). It is more concerned with historical and ideological factors than are most representatives of category E, and in its albeit mechanistic materialism—reading the film in terms of the perceived ideological needs of the Republican Party—anticipates the next section ('Historical Emphases') articulations of the author with culture. It also sets up somewhat anomalous roles for the author. As Lapsley and Westlake note, Lincoln's contradictory positions of both having and being the phallus are not allowed by *Cahiers* to offer multiple reading positions—as in the fantasy model—but are reined in to a limiting auteurist reading such that the 'incompatible functions in the figure of Lincoln . . . set . . . up tensions within the text "which oppose the order of Ford's world"' (1988: 122; *Cahiers du cinéma* 1970/1976: 46). This contradicts *Cahiers*' expressed desire to 'force the text, even to rewrite it' (1970/1976: 44). Such a tension between authorial intentionality and textual productivity recalls Wollen's 1972 conclusion to *Signs and Meaning in the Cinema*, which is similarly positioned on the cusp between pre- and post-structuralist paradigms.

Caughie's (1981) concept of 'the author in the text' extends and reworks *Cahiers*' category E. It dynamizes the reader–text relationship in terms of 'a theory of the subject of enunciation in film which involves an understanding of the shifting relation between enunciating subject and spectating subject' (1981: 201). Caughie distinguishes the author here as a subject position constructed and shifting in the film's performance whereby the reader, identified by means of classical cinema's third-person narration with the film's diegesis and thus finding no first-person authorial source in the text, can nevertheless, at certain points, be pulled back from identification, shifted from the register of *histoire*, in Benveniste's (1975) terms, to that of *discours*, to appreciate 'a moment of pure delight, of visual delight, of an excess of style' (Caughie 1981: 203). Pleasurably dislodged from identification with the fiction by these moments, the viewer constructs 'the figure of the author . . . to fill the subject position of the film's performance. The appearance of this new subject establishes me outside the fiction, but still within the textual space, still within a certain possession of the film (the performance is for me) . . . In those films where the director does not operate as a recognisable figure, the "performer" is as likely to be identified as the actor, the designer, or simply the film itself' (1981: 204–5). While Caughie's examples remain strikingly close to those of category E—Sirk, Minnelli, Max Ophuls, Josef von Sternberg—the instances can be extended to less critically respectable films: James Bond movies, for instance, the bulk of which persistently joke about their implausibilities, or the manifest implausibilities of adventure films like *Raiders of the Lost Ark* (Steven Spielberg, 1981) which the narrative drive delightedly

recuperates, or any number of postmodern 'spoof' films.

Theoretically, then, this model advances considerably *Cahier's* category E. It constructs the author as a figure of discourse and takes cognizance of the interaction between subject and text underlined by poststructuralism. Yet its definition of the author potentially embracing actors, cameraperson, set designer, and so on is somewhat promiscuous. And in opening up 'questions of subjects other than the purely textual subject—social subjects, sexual subjects, historical subjects' (1981: 206), Caughie's essay sets up a number of theoretical and historical questions of textual positions and spectator identifications which have not been elaborated until quite recently (Crofts 1993: 68–88; Stacey 1994).

Theoretical emphases

Whereas the conceptions of authorship described above largely see the author as constitutive of the text, the two versions considered here separate empirical author and text, and largely discount the former from consideration. Underlying earlier versions of authorship had been a communication model of language, which Saussure's structural linguistics radically challenged, emphasizing the non-natural, but merely linguistically differential, relationship of signifier and signified, and arguing that meaning was generated within systems of signification, and with no necessary reference to outside phenomena. In these theoretically concerned constructions of authorship, language or discourse therefore take over the role formerly ascribed to authors, and refuse to be instrumentalized by an author. In opposition to the expressive humanism of auteurism, the theories of subjectivity informing this work can be broadly characterized as anti-humanist. The theoretical turn of the mid-1970s built on the poststructuralist ideas mentioned in connection with auteur-structuralism above. It polemicized for theory, against empiricism and impressionism, especially in terms of the (originally British) intellectual and academic discourses and institutions in which it operated.

Mode 5: author as effect of the text

This conception of the author is indissolubly linked with the name of Roland Barthes, whose writings were translated and imported into anglophone film theory by Stephen Heath. Inverting the norm, Barthes pronounces the birth of the reader at the expense of the death of the author (1968). It follows from Saussurean linguistics' focus on the purely differential nature of signifier and signified that meaning arises in the act of reading rather than being author-ized in and by the mind of a creative individual: 'language . . . ceaselessly calls into question all origins . . . a text is [intertextually] made of multiple writings, drawn from many cultures and entering into mutual relations of dialogue, parody, contestation, but there is one place where this multiplicity is focused and that place is in the reader and not . . . the author. The reader is . . . simply that *someone* who holds together in a single field all the traces by which the written text is constituted' (Barthes 1968/ 1977: 146, 148). For Heath, the old-fashioned 'author is constituted *at the expense of* language, of the orders of discourse (he is what the texts can be stripped away to reveal)' (1973: 88–9). This notion of the author is fundamentally incompatible with the anti-humanism of Althusser's conception of the subject—favoured by Heath—which refused to see subjects as given, unified beings but rather as constructed and positioned by ideology. Therefore authorship becomes an irredeemably ideological construction that forecloses thinking about theories of the subject in ideology. In the face of the text's ceaseless productivity, any author exterior and prior to it appears unthinkable. The author becomes merely an effect of the text, 'a *fiction*, figure—fan of elements—of a certain pleasure which begins to turn the film, or series of films, the ones over the others, into a plurality, a play of assemblage and dispersion' (1973: 91).

Some problems arise from this stance regarding authorship. For all the justified post-structuralist stress on how, in the reading process, the reader enters 'into a process of dispersal and inter-mixture with the film' (Nowell-Smith 1976: 31), the reader does not have to dissolve in the process. Moreover, the author is no more a mere effect of a structure than he or she is a punctual source of meaning. To fly from one old-fashioned, humanist pole to the opposite, anti-humanist pole may be to indulge in extremism. Bordwell critiques a widespread academic consequence of this move: '"Theory" justifies the object of study, while concentration on the object can be attacked as naïve empiricism' (Bordwell 1989: 97). Later critiques of Althusser, particularly by Hindess and Hirst (1975), allow greater agency to the subject; and such conceptions of subjectivity underpin the first grouping of

historically oriented ideas of authorship examined below.

Mode 6: author as author-name

While sharing Barthes's desire to displace notions of originating subjects, Foucault rejects his relish for the ecstasy of the free-floating signifiers of 'écriture', 'the negative where all identity is lost' (1968/1977: 142). Foucault's attention to the relations between discourse, power, and subjects directs him rather to a concern with the conditions of existence of discourses, including those of authorship (1969/1979: 28). He theorizes the author as a function of the circulation of texts. Institutions of authorship allow an author-name, which labels a given body of texts, to be disengaged from any author as expressive individual. The very existence of pseudonyms epitomizes this separability.

The author-name is one way of regulating the circulation of texts. It serves as a means of distinction of certain texts from unauthored ones. Many texts are unsigned, including many journalistic texts prior to the rise of personality journalism. Among authored texts the author-name serves to classify and evaluate texts differentially: a Campion film, for example, as against a Tarantino film. The history constructed in this chapter already indicates how, even within its relatively brief account of film criticisms, the author-function 'does not operate in a uniform manner in all discourses, at all times, and in any given culture'; and the 'precise and complex procedures' by which texts are attributed to creators include those instanced above with reference to auteurism (Foucault 1969/ 1979: 23). These principles will be further applied in the historical analysis of author-names in Mode 10 below.

Historical emphases

If the preceding focuses on textual analysis and theory can be characterized as involving theories of subjectivity which are respectively constituting and constituted, most of the historically oriented approaches to authorship see the author as both constituting *and* constituted, in other words, as both agent and effect. The historical emphasis emerges after the theoretical concerns which had preoccupied film studies in the 1970s—which had justifiably critiqued most existing film histories as auteurist and empiricist—were themselves running aground on their own theoretical purism. These 1980s historical emphases broadly sought to remedy the aestheticism and theoreticism observed respectively in the two previous tendencies of Authorship. This historical work is found mainly in academic and intellectual institutions. A first grouping of historically oriented approaches to authorship conceives the director variously in relation to three instances: culture and society, film industry, and film texts. This grouping focuses largely on the moment of production of the texts, treating the empirical author. The second analyses consumption or reading, treating the textual author. Drawing on Foucault, it anlyses historically author-names in critical and/or commercial circulation.

Mode 7: author as social subject

This stress on the social subjectivity of the author, usually seen in its inscription in the film text, constitutes a crucial qualification of auteurism's transcendental subject. As long as it was saddled with such assumptions, Authorship, in Nowell-Smith's words, 'continued to ascribe to the author as subject whole sets of categories, concepts, relations, structures, ideological formations and God knows what, enough to blow to pieces any mind that had to contain them' (1973: 96). John Tulloch's genetic structuralism, it might be noted, would assimilate the author's social subjectivity into auteur-structuralism (1977: 553–84).

In recent years (Crofts 1983: 19) it has become easier to see John Ford ('My name's John Ford. I make Westerns') as being *not* wholly responsible (an inference Wollen once permitted) for the western genre, for its transformation of desert into garden, and so on (Wollen 1969: 94). The films labelled by Ford's name can be seen instead to inflect conventions of genre and narrative structure. Auteurist readings of Ford overload his individual psyche when charting the marked shift in attitude towards Indians evinced by *The Searchers* (1956) and *Cheyenne Autumn* (1964). The first represents Indians as subhuman, bestial and vicious, deserving a fair deal of what a vengeful Wayne–Ethan can give them; in the second, harried by the cavalry, they figure as sympathetic, honourable human beings. To ascribe such changes to the 'mellowing' of the ageing individual is a typical auteurist move (e.g. Bogdanovich 1967; Sarris 1976: 161). To see this change as related—by a characteristic generic displacement—to contemporary civil rights movements is to de-centre the author, to conceive of the film credited to Ford as being

historically and culturally shaped. Ford no longer stars as the films' 'onlie begetter'.

Mode 8: author in production institutions

If the preceding mode locates the author in relation to society and culture, this one connects her or him with the production industry. The *locus classicus* of such work is the monumental rewriting of Hollywood by Bordwell, Staiger, and Thompson (1985). Lapsley and Westlake observe rightly that this work

present[s] a model of agents in dialectical interaction with their economic, technological and ideological context. In their version of Hollywood, individuals are not simply bearers of positions, but function in terms of belief, desire and intention. The distinction between, for example, Ford and 'Ford' does not imply the denial of the existence of Ford as an agent in the production process. While the spectator constructs an image of the author on the basis of texts, this in no way rules out the necessity of returning to the concept of the empirical author for an analysis of the film as commodity. Indeed, this was made explicit in the paradigm of Hollywood as a set of norms that the director could choose to follow or, within certain bounds, transgress . . . the authors of the study insisted that the explanation must be in terms of material determinants—economic, technological and ideological . . . The various determinations are irreducible to one another and interact mutually. (1988: 115, 117)

In this broadly historical-materialist conception, the author has of necessity to work within existing industrial and institutional frameworks and dominant aesthetic conventions, and the interrelations between these practices are contingent, not matters of causality *à la* Althusser.

Mode 9: author as gendered

The most influential theoretical discourse affecting film theory in the last two decades, feminism has necessarily impinged on Authorship. It treats the author both in relation to filmmaking institutions and as social subject. As regards access to production, feminist work in film criticism and theory has had more immediate impact on independent cinema production than on Hollywood. Claire Johnston's *The Work of Dorothy Arzner* (1975) represents the first attempt to reconstruct a female and feminist Hollywood, a corrective to Sarris's quaint sneer at Arzner and other Hollywood women directors as 'little more than a ladies' auxiliary' (Sarris 1968: 216). As regards the gendering of representations, feminist work has substantially critiqued the work of male directors (a near-monopoly in Hollywood), with strong emphasis on the patriarchal discourses informing the film director and recirculated by him. Hitchcock's films have understandably been prime candidates for attention (e.g. Mulvey 1975; Modleski 1988).

Mode 10: historical analysis of Authorship

The concept of the author-name opens up the possibility of thinking of authorship in historical and cultural terms. Once the text has left its producer it is substantially subject to the vicissitudes of different markets and of varied critical assumptions. The circulation and meaning of a given author-name is conditioned historically and culturally. The films named as those of Ford do not sell well in the Soviet Union, nor do those ascribed to Ince do the business in the United States that they used to do. What passes for 'Brecht' in Australia is a far cry from the East German version, while 'Freud' meant something very different to those inside and those outside Lacan's École Freudienne. The meaning of 'Ford' which any given reader brings to a film by that name will vary according to his or her cultural, and particularly film-cultural, formation. It may mark a certain spectatorial pleasure; it may connote a reactionary politics; it may signal the 'father' of the western; it may just be meaningless.

In an earlier essay (1983: 20–1), I outlined two examples of the historical construction of the author-name of Ford in the United Kingdom in the late 1960s and early 1970s (Klinger (1994) has analysed Sirk's critical reputation in similar terms). What film-critical assumptions made it possible in 1969 in the UK to ascribe to Ford, as described in Mode 7 above, responsibility for virtually the entire western genre? First, the fast-growing acceptance of Authorship within journals and weeklies. Secondly, this had its corollary in the then merely embryonic state of genre study: witness the collapsing of intentions of genre analysis into auteurism in Kitses' *Horizons West* (1969) and McArthur's *Underworld USA* (1972). Thirdly, the reputation of Ford's films was then riding high, buoyed up especially by Bogdanovich's worshipful interview book (1967).

Prior to its second coming in the United Kingdom in the early 1970s Ford's name was taken up in 1969 in France as an exemplar of *Cahiers'* category E examined above in Mode 4. While the structures of any subversion of a dominant ideology were often shown to be

unconscious, the names of such directors quickly became the marks of certain supposedly disruptive pleasures, especially once transposed to a UK context. Ford's name, especially as 'evidenced' in such films as *Wings of Eagles*, was amongst those hailed in the early 1970s as 'subverting dominant codes'. The clear right-wing politics of many of these films, it seems, were eclipsed by a few ostensibly leftist formal tinkerings. How else, after all—other than via a fetishized author-name—could any self-respecting left-wing intellectual overlook the politics of the average Ford film?

The explanation for this—as for the similar celebration of other author-names detailed in Mode 4—may well lie in the film-cultural formation of the critics concerned. Many of the names honoured in the 1970s for their 'diegetic ruptures' were the same as those earlier promoted by pre-1968 *Cahiers*, by Sarris, and particularly by *Movie* in its passion for Hollywood directors notable for their rich mise-en-scène: Minnelli, Sirk, Nicholas Ray, Hitchcock, Sternberg. 1970s additions to the pantheon included Ford, Sam Fuller, Roger Corman, Tashlin, Ophuls, and Dreyer, several of whom were the subjects of Edinburgh Film Festival retrospectives. The 1970s celebrators of these names and their spectatorial pleasures were mostly of the generation raised on the pre-1968 *Cahiers*–Sarris–*Movie* passion for certain late classical Hollywood films. Of that generation, many, after the post-1968 *Cahiers*–*Cinéthique*–*Screen* critique of the organicist aesthetics of *Movie* and others remained more or less unreconstructed film buffs, while others might be seen to have rationalized their earlier pleasures in new theoretical clothing.

Since the 1970s Authorship's conditions of existence have undergone significant transformations. Building on the success of auteurism and its partial assimilation by Hollywood, Authorship has increasingly become a commercial as well as a critical strategy, installing the author-name as a cult personality in the 1970s. Witness the title *The Film Director as Superstar* (Gelmis 1970); by the decade's end the names of directorial 'movie brats' Spielberg, George Lucas, and Francis Ford Coppola (though very few others) were being used to market films which they *produced* as well as those they directed. Several factors underlie the changes of the last quarter-century. The broader acceptance of Authorship within diverse, interconnecting media institutions has obliged directors to engage with other, wide forms of media coverage, extending to television reviews and frequent interviews, magazine profiles, advertising and sponsorship appearances. Simultaneously, distribution has grown more powerful and more global, and the commodification of culture has accelerated. Author-names have therefore taken on greater significance as marketing labels than previously under the package-unit system, especially as genres have destabilized, and audiences fragmented beyond the entertainment–art split towards a larger number of relatively unco-ordinated subgroups (Andrew 1993: 80).

Such are the conditions of existence of what Corrigan calls the auteur's reappearance 'in the eighties and nineties as a commercial performance of *the business of being an auteur*' (1991: 104). Where Foucault had neglected the empirical author—maybe she or he figured as the hapless victim of what was done to her/his name—Corrigan reinstates this author in adopting a model of social agency to account for directorial engagement in promoting 'the author as a *commercial strategy* . . . as a critical concept bound to distribution and marketing aims that identify and address the potential cult status of an auteur . . . Auteurs have become increasingly situated along an extratextual path in which their commercial status as authors is their chief function as auteurs: the auteur-star is meaningful primarily as a promotion or recovery of a movie or a group of movies, frequently regardless of the filmic text itself' (103–5). While earlier film-buffery, as with Paris's MacMahon cinema in the late 1950s, operated without the knowledge of the director, she or he could now actively work on trying to promote her/his name. Corrigan accordingly examines how three directors have variously interacted with the media in order to construct their auteur personae: 'Coppola's call for "self-creativity" within the technology of agency or [Alexander] Kluge's eliciting of "self-interpretation" across his own mobile persona [or Raúl Ruiz's strategies of] cultural exercise and intellectual game meant to make all notions of self disappear within a hall of mirrors' (123). Corrigan valuably expands the notion of the author-name to account for the post-1970s roles of directors (the difference from Foucault is symptomatic of disciplinary differences: history attends to the dead more often than does film studies). However, Corrigan's claim that 'the commercial conditioning of this figure has successfully evacuated it of most of its expressive power and textual coherence' (136) is somewhat exaggerated. A further worry lies with his seeming promotion of acceptance of the wholesale commodification of culture.

This might be the place to refer to postmodern conceptions of the author. Corrigan deploys such a notion of the author as potentially disappearing behind intertextuality, pastiche, and parody, certainly as being mixed in with a decentred, postmodern condition. Other postmodern accounts of the author (e.g. Andrew 1993) appear to wish to rescue directors (principally French ones) from such an undesirable condition, in moves reminiscent of Rotha (1930) redeeming authors from the popular culture of Hollywood.

The persistence of Authorship

Why does the notion of authorship persist so strongly? While it is not central to the legal and contractual basis of cinematic production and distribution, it still has enormous influence within cultural discourse. Some reasons have been set out above: the author-name has become a central means of marketing and product differentiation; its publicity is widely distributed across many media forms; and it supports the cultural and cult statuses of cinema. Additionally, with the withering away of the socialist alternative to consumer capitalism, individualist discourses enjoy high status globally. Further, the author can serve as a constructed coherence with which the reader identifies (Lapsley and Westlake 1988: 127–8), the more so in the rapid social changes and uncertainties of post-industrial capitalism. Given the entrenchment of Authorship, it is worth recalling its ideological operations. In sum, it perpetuates the divorce between artistic product and any social determination, both at the moment of production (the syndrome of the creative author) and at the moment of reading (the reader who recirculates individualist discourses while pronouncing 'objective' critical judgement on the text).

This chapter clearly points to the necessity of abandoning any theory of authorship based on a communication model of language. Not only the author and the text but, just as importantly, the reading must be seen as historically and culturally shaped. Time and place will, almost always, divide the moment of production from the moment of reading. The 'meaning' of any text will thus vary, as will that of any author-name which may be attached to it.

BIBLIOGRAPHY

Anderson, Lindsay (1950), 'They were Expendable and John Ford', *Sequence*, 11: 1–4.

Andrew, Dudley (1993), 'The Unauthorised Auteur Today', in Jim Collins, Hilary Radner, and Ava Preacher Collins (eds.), *Film Theory Goes to the Movies* (New York: Routledge).

Astruc, Alexandre (1948/1968), 'The Birth of a New Avant-Garde: La Caméra-Stylo', in Peter Graham (ed.), *The New Wave* (London: Secker & Warburg).

Barthes, Roland (1968/1977), 'The Death of the Author', in *Image, Music, Text*, ed. and trans. Stephen Heath (London: Fontana).

Bazin, André (1953), 'De l'ambiguïté', *Cahiers du cinéma*, 27 (Oct.), 137–55.

—— (1957/1968), 'La Politique des auteurs', in Peter Graham (ed.), *The New Wave* (London: Secker & Warburg).

Benveniste, Émile (1975), *Problèmes de linguistique générale* (Paris: Seuil).

Bogdanovich, Peter (1967), *John Ford* (London: Studio Vista).

Bordwell, David (1989), *Making Meaning: Inference and Rhetoric in the Interpretation of Cinema* (Cambridge, Mass.: Harvard University Press).

—— **Janet Staiger**, and **Kristin Thompson** (1985), *The Classical Hollywood Cinema: Film Style and Mode of Production to 1960* (New York: Columbia University Press).

Brewster, Ben (1973), 'Notes on the Text of "John Ford's Young Mr Lincoln" by the Editors of *Cahiers du cinéma*', *Screen*, 14/3 (Autumn), 29–43.

Cahiers du cinéma (1970/72), 'Young Mr Lincoln de John Ford', 223 (July–Aug.), trans. Helen Lackner and Diana Matias as 'John Ford's Young Mr Lincoln', *Screen*, 13/3 (Autumn), 5–44.

*Caughie, John (ed.) (1981), *Theories of Authorship: A Reader* (London: Routledge & Kegan Paul and British Film Institute).

Comolli, Jean-Louis, and **Jean Narboni** (1969), 'Cinéma/idéologie/critique', *Cahiers du cinéma*, 216 (Oct.), 11–15; repr. in Bill Nichols (ed.), *Movies and Methods*, i (Berkeley: University of California Press).

Corliss, Richard (1972), *The Hollywood Screenwriters* (New York: Avon).

—— (1974/1975), *Talking Pictures: Screenwriters in the American Cinema* (New York: Penguin).

*Corrigan, Timothy (1991), *Cinema without Walls: Movies and Culture after Vietnam* (New Brunswick, NJ: Rutgers University Press).

Crisp, Colin (1993), *The Classic French Cinema 1930–1960* (Bloomington: Indiana University Press).

*Crofts, Stephen (1983), 'Authorship and Hollywood', *Wide Angle*, 5/3: 16–22.

—— (1993), *Identification, Gender and Genre in Film: The Case of 'Shame'*, (Melbourne: Australian Film Institute).

Foucault, Michel (1966/1973), *The Order of Things* (New York: Vintage).

*—— (1969/1979), 'What is an Author?', *Screen*, 20/1: 13–29.

Gelmis, Joseph (1970), *The Film Director as Superstar* (Garden City, NY: Doubleday).

Godard, Jean-Luc (1959/1972), 'Debarred Last Year from the Festival, Truffaut will Represent France at Cannes with *Les Quatre Cent Coups*', in *Godard on Godard*, ed. Jean Narboni and Tom Milne, trans. Tom Milne (London: Secker & Warburg).

Heath, Stephen (1973), 'Comment on "The Idea of Authorship"', *Screen*, 14/3 (Autumn), 86–91.

Henderson, Brian (1973), 'Critique of Ciné-Structuralism', part 1, *Film Quarterly*, 27/1 (Fall), 25–34.

Hess, John (1974), 'La Politique des auteurs', part 1, *Jump Cut*, 1 (May–June), 19–22.

Hindess, Barry, and **Paul Q. Hirst** (1975), *Pre-Capitalist Modes of Production* (London: Routledge & Kegan Paul).

Hoveyda, Fereydoun (1960), 'Tâches de Soleil', *Cahiers du cinéma*, 110 (Aug.), 37–43.

Johnston, Claire (1975), *The Work of Dorothy Arzner* (London: British Film Institute).

Kael, Pauline (1963/1966), 'Circles and Squares: Joys and Sarris', in *I Lost it at the Movies* (New York: Bantam).

Kitses, Jim (1969), *Horizons West* (London: Thames & Hudson).

Klinger, Barbara (1994), *Melodrama and Meaning: History, Culture and the Films of Douglas Sirk* (Bloomington: Indiana University Press).

*Lapsley, Rob, and **Mike Westlake** (1988), *Film Theory: An Introduction* (Manchester: Manchester University Press).

McArthur, Colin (1972), *Underworld USA* (London: Secker & Warburg).

Modleski, Tania (1988), *The Women who Knew too Much: Hitchcock and Feminist Theory* (New York: Methuen).

Mulvey, Laura (1975), 'Visual Pleasure and Narrative Cinema', *Screen*, 16/3 (Autumn), 6–18.

Nowell-Smith, Geoffrey (1967), *Visconti* (London: Secker & Warburg).

—— (1973), 'I was a Starstruck Structuralist', *Screen*, 14/3 (Autumn), 92–9.

*—— (1976), 'Six Authors in Pursuit of *The Searchers*', *Screen*, 17/1 (Spring), 26–33.

Rosenbaum, Jonathan (1991), 'Guilty by Omission', *Film Comment*, 27/5 (Sept.–Oct.), 42–5.

Rotha, Paul (1930), *The Film Till Now* (London: Cape).

Sarris, Andrew (1968), *The American Cinema: Directors and Directions 1929–1968* (New York: Dutton).

—— (1962/1971), 'Notes on the Auteur Theory in 1962', in P. Adams Sitney (ed.), *Film Culture Reader* (London: Secker & Warburg).

Sarris, Andrew (1976), *The John Ford Movie Mystery* (London: Secker & Warburg).

Stacey, Jackie (1994), *Star gazing: Hollywood Cinema and Female Spectatorship* (London: Routledge).

Tariol, Jean (1965), *Louis Delluc* (Paris: Seghers).

Truffaut, François (1954/1976), 'Une certaine tendance du cinéma français', *Cahiers du cinéma*, 31 (Jan.), 13–17; trans. as 'A Certain Tendency of the French Cinema', in Bill Nichols (ed.), *Movies and Methods*, i (Berkeley: University of California Press).

Tulloch, John (ed.) (1977), *Conflict and Control in the Cinema* (Melbourne: Macmillan).

Wollen, Peter (1969/1972), *Signs and Meaning in the Cinema* (London: Secker & Warburg).

John Ford

Peter Wollen from Peter Wollen, *Signs and Meaning in the Cinema* (London: Secker & Warburg, 1992).

It is instructive to consider three films of John Ford and compare their heroes: Wyatt Earp in *My Darling Clementine* (1946), Ethan Edwards in *The Searchers* (1956), and Tom Doniphon in *The Man who Shot Liberty Valance* (1962). They all act within the recognizable Ford world, governed by a set of oppositions, but their *loci* within that world are very different. The relevant pairs of opposites overlap; different pairs are foregrounded in different movies. The most relevant are garden versus wilderness, ploughshare versus sabre, settler versus nomad, European versus Indian, civilized versus savage, book versus gun, married versus unmarried, East versus West. These antinomies can often be broken down further. The East, for instance, can be defined either as Boston or Washington and, in *The Last Hurrah* (1948), Boston itself is broken down into the antipodes of Irish immigrants versus Plymouth Club, themselves bundles of such differential elements as Celtic versus Anglo-Saxon, poor versus rich, Catholic versus Protestant, Democrat versus Republican, and so on. At first sight, it might seem that the oppositions listed above overlap to the extent that they become practically synonymous, but this is by no means the case. As we shall see, part of the development of Ford's career has been the shift from an identity between civilized versus savage and European versus Indian to their separation and final reversal, so that in *Cheyenne Autumn* (1964) it is the Europeans who are savage, the victims who are heroes.

The master antinomy in Ford's films is that between the wilderness and the garden. As Henry Nash Smith has demonstrated, in his magisterial book *Virgin Land*, the contrast between the image of America as a desert and as a garden is one which has dominated American thought and literature, recurring in countless novels, tracts, political speeches, and magazine stories. In Ford's films it is crystallized in a number of striking images. *The Man who Shot Liberty Valance*, for instance, contains the image of the cactus rose, which encapsulates the antinomy between desert and garden which pervades the whole film. Compare with this the famous scene in *My Darling Clementine*, after Wyatt Earp has gone to the barber (who civilizes the unkempt), where the scent of honeysuckle is twice remarked upon: an artificial perfume, cultural rather than natural. This moment marks the turning-point in Wyatt Earp's transition from wandering cowboy, nomadic, savage, bent on personal revenge, unmarried, to married man, settled, civilized, the sheriff who administers the law.

Earp, in *My Darling Clementine*, is structurally the most simple of the three protagonists I have mentioned: his progress is an uncomplicated passage from nature to culture, from the wilderness left in the past to the garden anticipated in the future. Ethan Edwards, in *The Searchers*, is more complex. He must be defined not in terms of past versus future or wilderness versus garden compounded in himself, but in relation to two other protagonists: Scar, the Indian chief, and the family of homesteaders. Ethan Edwards, unlike Earp, remains a nomad throughout the film. At the start, he rides in from the desert to enter the log house; at the end, with perfect symmetry, he leaves the house again to return to the desert, to vagrancy. In many respects, he is similar to Scar; he is a wanderer, a savage, outside the law: he scalps his enemy. But, like the homesteaders, of course, he is a European, the mortal foe of the Indian. Thus Edwards is ambiguous; the antinomies invade the personality of the protagonist himself. The oppositions tear Edwards in two; he is a tragic hero. His companion, Martin Pawley, however, is able to resolve the duality; for him, the period of nomadism is only an episode, which has meaning as the restitution of the family, a necessary link between his old home and his new home.

Ethan Edwards's wandering is, like that of many other Ford protagonists, a quest, a search. A number of Ford films are built round the theme of the quest for the Promised Land, an American re-enactment of the Biblical exodus, the journey through the desert to the land of milk and honey, the New Jerusalem. This theme is built on the combination of the two pairs: wilderness versus garden and nomad versus settler; the first pair precedes the second in time. Thus, in *Wagon Master* (1950), the Mormons cross the desert in search of their future home; in *How Green was my Valley* (1941) and *The Informer* (1935), the protagonists want to cross the Atlantic to a future home in the United States. But, during Ford's career, the situation of home is reversed in time. In *Cheyenne Autumn* the Indians journey in search of the home they once had in the past; in *The Quiet Man* (1952), the American Sean Thornton returns to his ancestral home in Ireland. Ethan Edwards's journey is a kind of parody of this theme: his object is not constructive, to found a home, but destructive, to find and scalp Scar. Nevertheless, the weight of the film remains orientated to the future: Scar has burned down the home of the settlers, but it is replaced and we are confident that the homesteader's wife, Mrs Jorgensen, is right when she says: 'Some day this country's going to be a fine place to live.' The wilderness will, in the end, be turned into a garden.

The Man who Shot Liberty Valance has many similarities with *The Searchers*. We may note three: the wilderness becomes a garden—this is made quite explicit, for Senator Stoddart

John Ford continued

....

has wrung from Washington the funds necessary to build a dam which will irrigate the desert and bring real roses, not cactus roses; Tom Doniphon shoots Liberty Valance as Ethan Edwards scalped Scar; a log home is burned to the ground. But the differences are equally clear: the log home is burned after the death of Liberty Valance; it is destroyed by Doniphon himself; it is his own home. The burning marks the realization that he will never enter the Promised Land; that to him it means nothing; that he has doomed himself to be a creature of the past, insignificant in the world of the future. By shooting Liberty Valance he has destroyed the only world in which he himself can exist, the world of the gun rather than the book; it is as though Ethan Edwards had perceived that by scalping Scar, he was in reality committing suicide. It might be mentioned too that, in *The Man who Shot Liberty Valance*, the woman who loves Doniphon marries Senator Stoddart. Doniphon, when he destroys his log house (his last words before doing so are 'Home, sweet home!'), also destroys the possibility of marriage.

The themes of *The Man who Shot Liberty Valance* can be expressed in another way. Ransom Stoddart represents rational-legal authority, Tom Doniphon represents charismatic authority. Doniphon abandons his charisma and cedes it, under what amount to false pretences, to Stoddart. In this way charismatic and rational-legal authority are combined in the person of Stoddart and stability thus assured. In *The Searchers* this transfer does not take place; the two kinds of authority remain separated. In *My Darling Clementine* they are combined naturally in Wyatt Earp, without any transfer being necessary. In many of Ford's late films—*The Quiet Man, Cheyenne Autumn, Donovan's Reef* (1963)—the accent is placed on traditional authority. The island of Ailakaowa in *Donovan's Reef*, a kind of Valhalla for the homeless heroes of *The Man who Shot Liberty Valance*, is actually a monarchy, though complete with the Boston girl,

wooden church, and saloon made familiar by *My Darling Clementine*. In fact, the character of Chihuahua, Doc Holliday's girl in *My Darling Clementine*, is split into two: Miss Lafleur and Lelani, the native princess. One represents the saloon entertainer, the other the non-American in opposition to the respectable Bostonians Amelia Sarah Dedham and Clementine Carter. In a broad sense, this is a part of a general movement which can be detected in Ford's work to equate the Irish, Indians, and Polynesians as traditional communities, set in the past, counterposed to the march forward to the American future, as it has turned out in reality, but assimilating the values of the American future as it was once dreamed.

It would be possible, I have no doubt, to elaborate on Ford's career, as defined by pairs of contrasts and similarities, in very great detail, though—as always with film criticism—the impossibility of quotation is a severe handicap. My own view is that Ford's work is much richer than that of Howard Hawks and that this is revealed by a structural analysis; it is the richness of the shifting relations between antinomies in Ford's work that makes him a great artist, beyond being simply an undoubted auteur. Moreover, the auteur theory enables us to reveal a whole complex of meaning in films such as *Donovan's Reef*, which a recent filmography sums up as just 'a couple of Navy men who have retired to a South Sea island now spend most of their time raising hell'. Similarly, it throws a completely new light on a film like *Wings of Eagles* (1957), which revolves, like *The Searchers*, round the vagrancy versus home antinomy, with the difference that when the hero does come home, after flying round the world, he trips over a child's toy, falls down the stairs, and is completely paralysed so that he cannot move at all, not even his toes. This is the macabre *reductio ad absurdum* of the settled.

8

Genre and Hollywood

Tom Ryall

It is an irony that the critical acceptance of Hollywood cinema was initially achieved through its extensive mapping, by the critics of *Cahiers du cinéma*, in terms of authorial *œuvres* rather than in terms of the genres that, along with the stars, have defined its image for the moviegoing public. For whatever else it is, Hollywood is surely a cinema of genres, a cinema of westerns, gangster films, musicals, melodramas, and thrillers. Indeed, in early reflections on Hollywood cinema, it was this very quality that generated antagonistic criticism, with generic structures being deemed an impediment to artistic achievement. Thus, Paul Rotha, writing in the late 1920s, attacked Hollywood for its standardized pictures made to type (genre). He regarded this as a debasement of cinema inhibiting the creation and development of film art characteristic of European filmmakers from countries such as France and, especially, Germany (Rotha 1930/1967). While his characterization of the American cinema in terms of its standardized generic basis certainly captures one of its significant features, subsequent generations of writers, especially from the late 1960s onwards, have valued such qualities differently. Some have argued that the genre system was a positive quality in Hollywood, providing a useful disciplined framework within which directors worked, ensuring curbs on creative indulgence and guaranteeing that the cinema kept in touch with its mass public (McArthur 1972). At the very least, most writers have seen genre as a necessary concep-

tual tool in relation to American films, and the body of criticism to be discussed here is predominantly concerned with the understanding of genre as a concept and with the definition of individual genres.

The critical literature of genre is both extensive and multifaceted, reflecting influences from a range of disciplines including literary criticism, art history, linguistics and semiotics, and structural anthropology, as well as from the discourses of the film industry itself and from journalistic film criticism and reviewing. But while some agreement may be found about basic terms such as 'convention', 'iconography', 'recurrent patterns', 'audience expectation', and the typology of generic modes (westerns, gangster films, etc.), it is important to note that different models, different sets of assumptions, and different theories underpin the range of accounts that address the generic system of Hollywood and the individual genres in that system, and, at the micro-level, account for the specificities of individual films. As a further complication, 'genre' itself is sometimes replaced by and sometimes situated in relation to a constellation of cognate terms such as 'type', 'mode', 'cycle', 'series', and 'formula'. Although important accounts of genre in cinema can be traced back to at least the 1950s (Bazin 1953/1971; Warshow 1948/1970, 1954/1970; Alloway 1963, 1971), it was not until the late 1960s that something like a corpus of genre criticism emerged in Britain, principally, though not exclusively, from writers working in, or associated in some way with, the Education Department of the British Film Institute (Lovell 1967; Kitses 1969; McArthur 1972; Buscombe 1970; Ryall 1970). Subsequently, the turn to semiotics meant that more attention was paid to underlying systems, to general explanations of communicative phenomena such as genre films, and to attempts to define genre itself as well as defining individual genres. However, some have seen this as an inherently difficult task because of the medley of ways in which individual genres have been identified, with classifications deriving from a varied list of features embracing subject-matter, mode of address, style, audience effects, and so on. David Bordwell has suggested that '[t]heorists have been unsuccessful in producing a coherent map of the system of genres and no strict definition of a single genre has won widespread acceptance' and that 'no strictly deductive set of principles can explain genre groupings' (1989: 147). He cites the Russian Formalist Boris Tomashevsky, whose view was that '[n]o firm logical classification of genres is possible. Their demarcation is always historical, that is to say, it is correct only for a specific moment of history; apart from this they are demarcated by many features at once, and the markers of one genre may be quite different in kind from the markers of another genre and logically they may not exclude one another' (Bordwell 1989: 147).

Problems of definition notwithstanding, for many critics 'genre' seemed more appropriate than traditional approaches for grasping the historical realities of Hollywood with its factory-like production regimes and the organization of production schedules along generic lines. Creative and technical production personnel were hired on long-term contracts which, in some ways, could determine a generic structure. As Edward Buscombe has suggested, 'stars and genre were, particularly at Warners, mutually reinforcing. Because the studio had Bogart, Cagney and the rest under contract they made a lot of gangster pictures; and because they made a lot of gangster pictures they had stars like this under contract' (1974: 59). Elaborate standing sets—the western townscape, the Chicago street—once constructed, the costume collection once established, reinforced generic tendencies; as Rick Altman has put it, 'Hollywood's economic imperative mandates concerted attempts at economy of scale. Only by producing large quantities of similar films [could] studios justify their enormous investment

in real estate, personnel, publicity and technology' (1989: 328). Films were marketed and advertised in ways which highlighted their generic specificity and, in addition to this, the trade press used generic terminology and referred to westerns, gangster pictures, melodramas, and so on in their discussion of Hollywood films. Hollywood studios consciously produced genre cycles, audiences went to see westerns and the like rather than films made by auteurs, and reviewers referred to gangster films and other film types; accordingly, for critics such as Lawrence Alloway (1971), this meant that genre was the pertinent and pre-eminent critical concept for students of the American film.

The auteur approach absorbed cinema into conventional ways of thinking about cultural production and appeared to confer a certain respectability on popular films, permitting their 'creators'—the auteurs—to be discussed as artists along with the poets, painters, composers, and novelists. Genre criticism confronted aspects of popular film—conventionality, formulas, stars, industrial production systems, publicity—which jarred with conventional approaches to artistic production and were often overlooked by auteur critics. It moved against the grain of a criticism dominated both by the individual work valued for its distinctiveness and difference, and by the individual artist valued for the extent to which he or she moved beyond the common to the individual and the personal. The central assumption of genre criticism is that a work of art and communication arises from and is inserted into a specific social context and that its meaning and significance is constrained and limited by this context. Individual artists and filmmakers manipulate signs and meanings, but in contexts which are authorized by communal public consent, and these contexts, in the case of the American cinema, we call genres. The 'rules' of a genre—the body of conventions—specify the ways in which the individual work is to be read and understood, forming the implicit context in which that work acquires significance and meaning. Genres were seen in social terms as institutions implying a bond, or contract, between producers (director, studio) and audience relating to the significance and meaning of what was on the screen. In a different vocabulary, genres constituted systems for the regulation and circulation of meaning which had a public and historical existence and in which the popular American cinema was grounded.

The scope of genre criticism

At the most general of levels, genres have been divided into two kinds—the theoretical and the historical (Todorov 1975: 13–14). Theoretical genres are a priori categories which it is possible to envisage as based upon logical deduction from the basic characteristics of the art form itself rather than the analysis of actual works. For example, the ancient Greeks devised theoretical systems for fictional works which were divided into genres on the basis of mode of delivery, i.e. those in which the narrator speaks, those in which characters speak, and those in which both speak. As can be seen, the intention is exhaustively to predict the gamut of possibilities based upon certain assumptions about the key element of literary activity—in this example, the performance of the speech act (Palmer 1991: 116). In terms of cinema, an equivalent exercise would base itself on the possibilities of cinema in relation to some very general feature such as representation, rather than the familiar divisions of western, gangster film, and musical. Accordingly, films could be divided into the *fictional* (representation of staged events), the *documentary* (representation of actual events), or the *abstract* (non-representational), although even such a broad scheme may have problems with the animated film. Some writers have explicitly proposed theoretical genres for cinema (e.g. Shklovsky 1927; Williams 1984), and others, including V. F. Perkins for example, have implicitly constructed the beginnings of a system of theoretical genres in suggesting that the 'basic genre to inspect is the narrative movie' (*Movie* 1975: 11). Most critical writing, however, has concentrated on historical genres, on groupings of actual films inductively linked on the basis of common themes, styles, and iconography.

In terms of the analysis of historical genres, the scope of genre criticism is broad, and, as a preliminary, it is necessary to distinguish between three levels of analysis to which the concept can refer. The first, and most general, concerns the definition of *generic system*, which relates individual genres to each other in terms of broad shared principles; the second is the analysis of *individual genres*, defining their internal logics and conventions; and the third is the analysis of *individual films* in relation to a genre or genres in the case of the many Hollywood pictures which draw from and relate to more than a single genre. It is also necessary to distinguish between the discussion of generic systems and individual genres as overarching concepts, and the analysis of the individual genre film. Generic systems and genres do not exist in the way in which individual films exist, but rather are abstractions based partly, though not entirely, upon individual films and operating in a different logical universe. Although genre and the individual film are the basic elements of the system, as Fredric Jameson has suggested in relation to literary genres, they

are wholly distinct in nature from each other, the one—the generic system—being a constellation of ideal relationships, but the other—the work itself—being a concrete verbal composition. We must understand the former as constituting something like an environment for the latter, which emerges into a world in which the genres form a given determinate relationship among themselves, and which then seeks to define itself in terms of that relationship. (Jameson 1975: 153)

If 'film' is substituted for 'verbal composition' we have a succinct definition of the circuit in which a genre film is positioned as a historically formed instance of the overarching intertextual entity we refer to as the generic system. From the point of view of the filmmaker, the generic system is the conceptual environment within which the film will be situated, and, from the point of view of the spectator, the conceptual intertextual context, or one of the contexts, within which the individual film makes sense.

There are two further broad dimensions to genre study. The first involves genre history and is concerned with the ways in which genres emerge, develop, and change; the second focuses upon the social and cultural function of genre cinema. Genres change and evolve and, although a western such as *The Searchers* (1956) is recognizably part of a continuum which includes its generic predecessors such as *Stagecoach* (1939) or *The Gunfighter* (1950), the film nevertheless differs from them in certain respects because it was made at a different moment both of the history of the genre itself and, more generally, of the history of the social and political environment. Genres can be studied both in terms of an internal history of forms, themes, and iconography, and in terms of their relationship to broader cultural and social shifts. Thomas Schatz (1981: 38) has proposed an evolutionary model for internal generic development based on a shift from 'straightforward story-telling to self-conscious formalism', from *Gold Diggers of 1933* (1933) to *Singin' in the Rain* (1952) for the musical, from *Stagecoach* to *The*

Searchers for the western. Others, however, have been sceptical about the neatness of such historical patterning and its somewhat segregated view of individual genres. Steve Neale's (1990) brief but suggestive sketch of the historical development of Hollywood's genres, derived from the 'Formalist conception of genre as a historical system of relations', moves away from Schatz's somewhat self-contained account of generic change in favour of a more fluid historical model which links change to a range of factors. Some are internal to cinema such as the state of film technology; some are external and relate film genres to intermedia influences such as vaudeville theatre, popular literature and music, the press and comics, and to changing social patterns of cinema attendance (Neale 1990: 58–62).

Consideration of the social and cultural function of cinema has provided other ways of defining a rationale for the Hollywood genre system (see Kellner, Part 2, Chapter 10). For some, the system is part of the *ideological* network which constrains political perception and regulates attitudes towards social and cultural tensions and conflicts; for others, it is more akin to *mythic* systems of the past, and it has been suggested that 'genre films, television, and literature have to a great extent replaced more formal versions of mythic response to existence such as religion and folk-tale' (Stuart Kaminsky, quoted in Grant 1986: 94). Ideological critiques range from the notion that Hollywood genres are instruments of American capitalist ideology transmitting its beliefs and values in their different ways (Hess Wright 1974) to more nuanced versions which suggest that, while some genres might well be regarded as 'conservative', others, such as horror, film noir, and melodrama, may be seen to question conventional social and political values (Klinger 1984). Writers using the notion of ideology are committed to the idea that the genre system, or, at least, certain genres, impose beliefs and values to some degree; those using notions of myth and ritual posit a more participatory situation in which the audience plays a role in the constitution of the cinema's value systems through box-office acclaim and other interactive mechanisms such as fan magazines and clubs, sneak previews, and so on. Ideological criticism sometimes operates with the model of a passive audience absorbing the appropriate social and political values, and this contrasts with ritual–myth analyses in which the genre system is construed as expressive of deep-seated beliefs and desires 'whose function is the ritualisation of collective ideals, the celebration of temporarily resolved social and cultural conflicts, and the concealment of disturbing cultural conflicts behind the guise of entertainment' (Schatz, in Grant 1986: 97).

Genre systems: some theoretical proposals

A brief examination of the familiar generic categories—westerns, gangster films, musicals, horror films, thrillers, comedies, melodramas, films noirs, women's pictures—indicates the variety of ways in which critics have attempted to define genre systems and individual genres. These range from simple differentiation based on an array of protocols enveloping subject-matter, style, effects, and intended audience; to attention to the ways in which shared elements of subject-matter, theme, or style are handled differently in different genres; to the technical distinctions of semantics and syntactics that can generate a range of combinatory options or genres.

The 'familiar' list above incorporates a variety of differentiating criteria. Understandings of westerns and gangster films derive from the historical subject which is dealt with: the American west and urban America in the 1920s respectively. The musical is recognized in terms of formal qualities such as the presence of musical and dance performance. This can be linked to a range of subject-matters including that of the western—*Seven Brides for Seven Brothers* (1954)— and the gangster film—*Guys and Dolls* (1955). Some genres can be defined in ways which highlight their intended effect on the audience, as in the horror film, the thriller, and the comedy, which elicit fear, suspense, and laughter respectively. Again, these are effects that are realizable across different subject-matters. Melodrama has been defined in terms of a concern with the tensions of domestic life, with intergenerational problems, with heterosexual romance (subject-matter), together with a certain approach to narrative construction and film style and, particularly, an extravagant use of mise-en-scène to embody the emotional highpoints of the drama (formal qualities). In similar fashion, attempts to define the film noir usually range across subject-matter—crime and detection—and the shadow-laden mise-en-scène which is often regarded as the essential generic ingredient. The category of the

A musical with a western setting—*Seven Brides for Seven Brothers* (1954)

women's picture, closely related to the melodrama and sharing its subject-matter to an extent, is based on the nominated target audience of females and their supposed desires and interests.

From the late 1960s onwards there were a number of books and articles which attempted to systematize the varied bases for differentiation, and which sought to construct overall theories of genre, schema for generic definition, and definitions of individual genres (Buscombe 1970; Kitses 1969; McArthur 1972; Ryall 1970). Based primarily on the western and the gangster film, such work isolated two factors in particular. These were, first, the two distinct phases of American history which constituted the basic subject-matter of the two genres, and secondly, the distinctive visual qualities which each possessed. This latter dimension—'iconography', as it was named with a term borrowed from art history—was seen by many critics as the key source of differentiation, providing individual genres with a distinctive evocation of a generic universe by way of a repertoire of established and conventionalized images. In the case of the western, these included the settings (desert and mountain, makeshift townscapes of saloons and gaols); the specificities of costume (the black garb of the hired gun, the tight-bodiced dress of the saloon-girl); the weaponry used by westerners (Colt 45, Bowie knife, bow and arrow); and horses. The gangster genre also lent itself to such analysis with its urban, street-at-night settings, its night-clubs and bootleg liquor factories; the gangster's fedora and well-tailored suit; and the cars and tommy-guns which were the gangster's tools of the trade. However, while this approach appears coherent and plausible when applied to the western and gangster genres, it seems less easy to translate across the generic spectrum. What, for example, would constitute an iconography of the comedy film?

Colin McArthur centred the iconographic description of the gangster film on the physical presence and dress of the leading actors in the genre, thus incorporating the star system into his generic account (McArthur 1972). Such an approach also characterizes Jean-Loup Bourget's account of a particular strand of melodrama variously referred to as 'sentimental melodrama', 'romantic drama', and 'the women's picture' (1971). Such a strand, he suggests, is grounded in the acting presences of an array of female stars including Joan Crawford and Bette Davis, Barbara Stanwyck and Lana Turner. The iconographic approach, couched in terms of stars whose presence shapes and determines the course of the narrative, would be applicable across a range of genres and would at least enable the construction of coherent generic strands (subgenres?) on a consistent basis. Accordingly, James Cagney and Edward G. Robinson may be seen to define a powerful subgenre of the gangster film; John Wayne and Henry Fonda, of the western; Humphrey Bogart and Robert Mitchum, of the film noir; Fred Astaire, Ginger Rogers, and Gene Kelly, of the musical; Chaplin, Keaton, Laurel and Hardy, and the Marx brothers, of the comedy; and so on. In some cases—Cagney and Robinson and the gangster genre, Wayne and the western, Astaire and Kelly and the musical—it can be argued that such stars have defined the generic prototypes which tend to dominate thinking about particular genres. A further point to make is that there are plenty of examples of stars who have worked in particular genres without forging generic identity in the manner of the stars cited above. For example, Gary Cooper and Spencer Tracy both played gangster roles in the early 1930s, but it was Cagney and Robinson whose performances clearly impressed in generic terms. This suggests that other factors play a role in such generic identification and that certain stars are suitable for certain genres rather than others.

The writers cited above differed in their degree of systematicity, but provided models of genre which highlighted certain key dimensions such as iconography and stars which worked as explanations for some genres but not all. This work foregrounded concepts such as 'convention' and 'audience expectation' which are central to any account of genre, and presented persuasive specifications for genres such as the western and the gangster film. However, the work did not provide an easy means of moving from local description of specific genres to general specification of the generic system, and what worked for the gangster film did not necessarily translate easily into an explanation for, say, the musical. This early work on genre emerged from an intellectual climate in Britain which was just beginning to accommodate the structuralist theories that were to have a decisive impact on film studies through the 1970s, and there is a sense in which a number of the issues raised by genre critics were taken up in different ways by the new intellectual-cum-political interests of areas such as semiotics, ideology, psychoanalysis, and feminist theory.

Steve Neale's *Genre* (1980) attempted to redefine genre in the context of such influences and to provide the terms in which the system of genre worked in Hollywood cinema. Previous writers had noted that American genre films belonged 'to the traditions of the American narrative film' (Pye 1975: 31) and, for Neale, this basic shared feature was the foundation of the genre system in Hollywood. Genres, it was suggested, were best considered as variants of 'the traditions of the American narrative film', or 'classical narrative cinema' as it was increasingly called. Its set of broad formal characteristics such as linear narrative progression, closure, symmetry, its balance of narration and spectacle, as well as its 'characteristic semantic fields' (Bordwell 1989: 150–1), defined very broadly a type of narrative film which was different from other models such as the European 'art' film. Neale's work recognized that the Hollywood genre system deployed a limited number of themes in a restricted stylistic context and the factor which differentiated one genre from another was the weight and function of the form and content of the shared general discourse of the system. For example, as many critics have noted, heterosexual romance and desire are present in most, and maybe all, Hollywood films as a key constituent of the 'characteristic semantic field'. However, it is not a uniform presence: whereas romance between the leading characters is an essential feature of the musical, providing the crucial motivation for the progress of the narrative, such relationships are often peripheral to the narrative in the western. The musical *Singin' in the Rain* traces the romance which develops between Don Lockwood (Gene Kelly) and Kathy Selden (Debbie Reynolds) within a story about Hollywood and the arrival of the sound film; the western *My Darling Clementine* (1946) traces a story about the bringing of civilization to the west which has, as an aside, an embryonic romantic encounter between Wyatt Earp (Henry Fonda) and Clementine Carter (Cathy Downs). The certain union of Don and Kathy at the end of the musical is a generic requirement; the rather more tentative finale of the western, in which the hero and heroine part with vague promises of reuniting, is also appropriate in the context of a genre where romance is a secondary concern. The generic system, therefore, is a way of differentially deploying the characteristic discourses of Hollywood films, including romance and other forms of human relationships, violence, social order and disorder, the law, community, work and leisure, current affairs and popular history, and so on. None of these, however, are exclusive to any of the genres. A parallel account is offered for matters of style and narrative address in which the balance between narrative (the advancement of the story) and spectacle (the display of action and performance) varies from genre to genre. Neale summarizes thus: 'part of the very function of genres is precisely to display a variety of the possibilities of the semiotic processes of mainstream narrative cinema while simultaneously containing them as genre' (1980: 31).

Rick Altman, also working in the context of structuralism and semiotics, has suggested that genres can be established from two perspectives:

we can as a whole distinguish between generic definitions which depend on a list of common traits, attitudes, characters, shots, locations, sets and the like—thus stressing the semantic elements which make up the genre—and definitions which play up instead certain constitutive relationships between undesignated and variable placeholders—relationships which might be called the genre's fundamental syntax. The semantic approach stresses the genre's building blocks, while the syntactic view privileges the structures into which they are arranged. (Altman 1989: 95)

The same genre—for example, the western—can be analysed into two distinct, though interrelated, dimensions. First, there is the stock of primary elements embracing themes such as the wilderness, the community, law and order, and icons such as cowboys, Indians, deserts, mountains, and half-built towns. These correspond to the thematic and iconographic elements highlighted by previous writers and constitute a semantic field present in some way in any single instance of the western. Secondly, there are particular structural relationships between such elements established over time to constitute a set of syntactical conventions. Jean Mitry's definition of the western as a genre 'whose action, situated in the American West, is consistent with the atmosphere, the values, and the conditions of existence in the Far West between 1840 and 1900' (quoted in Altman 1984: 10) highlights the broad semantic field underpinning the genre. In contrast, Jim Kitses' (1969) analysis of the genre foregrounds the ways in which particular semantic elements, such as individual and community or savagery and civilization, are placed in opposition to each other, and offers a different way of defining the western in terms of the syntactic or relational structures between the elements specified in the broad semantic field. The semantic perspective offers broad inclusive definitions identifying fixed and recurrent elements which cross all instances of the genre, while the syntac-

tic perspective focuses on narrow, exclusive definitions drawing attention to particular distinctive patterns established between semantic elements in subsets of the semantic genre.

Much of the writing on genre from Bazin and Warshow onwards had built effective categories in a local way, separating off the western from the gangster film in quite clear terms (subject-matter, history, iconography). By contrast, the structuralist-influenced work recognized the somewhat unstable nature of the generic system. Subject-matter, style, narrative address and structure, iconography even, were quite fluid, and elements associated with particular genres often cropped up across a range of genres and operated in a number of different ways, sometimes occupying a central position within a genre, sometimes relegated to a peripheral significance. To take a previously noted example, *Seven Brides for Seven Brothers* clearly operates within the semantic field of the western although its title suggests other concerns. It is set in 'Oregon Territory 1850' (the post-credit title) and the opening sequences show a figure in buckskins (Adam–Howard Keel) driving a wagon into a frontier town. However, the film's credits are accompanied by orchestral versions of two of the main songs from the film—'Bless your Beautiful Hide' and 'Wonderful Day'—and, it might be argued, the musical motifs undercut the 'western' images. Similarly, the opening sequence in the store, in which Adam, a farmer in town to buy winter supplies, adds a wife to the shopping-list, foregrounds the 'romantic courtship' theme usually peripheral to the genre though, in this case, clearly announced by the film's title. When Adam leaves the store and launches into song the generic focus is sharpened and the world of the musical is evoked through one of its central conventions, which permits characters to sing about their thoughts and feelings. From the perspective of structuralist versions of genre, it is the musical conventions that dominate and direct spectator comprehension towards the values and assumptions of that genre rather than those of the western, to which it also clearly relates. This is only a problem if we regard genres as pigeon-holes into which films must fit, rather than elements in a flexible conceptual world—the fluid framework for our reading of individual Hollywood films.

Individual genres: inclusive and exclusive definitions

Another way of recognizing the somewhat fluid nature of generic systems rests on the distinction between inclusive and exclusive definition (Altman 1984: 6–7). Semantic definitions of genre tend to be inclusive, incorporating as many films as possible, while syntactic definitions are exclusive and focused on a small number of films. Inclusive definitions, the characteristic province of the large encyclopaedias of the genre (Buscombe 1988; Hardy 1985), also usually reflect the ways in which the terms are used in everyday common-sense discourse and by the studios themselves. Such definitions envelop a range of films with some degree of intertextual relationship to each other but without laying claim that these relationships are strong or especially significant. These might be regarded as involving a 'weak' or 'neutral' use of the generic term. By contrast, other accounts of the western operate what might be called a 'strong' sense of genre and imply precise and significant interrelationships between individual westerns. André Bazin, for example, identified a small corpus of films as embodying the 'essence' of the western and positioned instances of the genre in relation to this core (Bazin 1971: 149). Accordingly, individual films were located in relation to what Bazin called the 'classic' western, exemplified by films such as *Stagecoach, Virginia City* (1940), and *Western Union* (1941). Bazin also developed contrasting categories such as the 'superwestern' for films from the 1950s like *High Noon* (1952) and *Shane* (1952) that deviated from the classical norms and imported concerns foreign to the genre, and the 'novelistic' western for films such as *Johnny Guitar* (1954) that represent an enrichment of the traditional themes of the genre.

In fact, although exclusive definitions are rarely proclaimed explicitly, they have proved extremely influential, constituting the effective operative contexts for discussion of individual westerns and dominating accounts of the genre. Thus, 'exclusive' accounts of the western normally include *The Great Train Robbery* (1903), *The Covered Wagon* (1923), and *The Iron Horse* (1924) from the silent years, *Stagecoach, Destry Rides Again* (1939), and *Western Union* (1941) from the Bazin classical centre of the late 1930s–early 1940s, and *My Darling Clementine, Red River* (1948), *The Gunfighter* (1950), *Broken Arrow* (1950), *High Noon, Shane, The Searchers, Rio Bravo* (1959), and *Ride the High Country/Guns in the Afternoon* (1962) from later

periods. Together these films constitute a canon and frequently figure as reference-points in discussions of the western, establishing the contours of the genre, exemplifying its basic thematic patterns, and defining its iconographical qualities. However, in one sense, the canonic films do not typify the genre. They are drawn mainly from the A feature westerns made by the big studios or by prestigious independents rather than from the modest B pictures and series films which, in quantitative terms, constitute the bulk of the genre. In general, most westerns have come from outside the major studios, apart from certain periods such as 1939–42 and 1950–3, when almost as many came from the majors as from the independents. There is a sense, then, in which the real core of the genre, at least in statistical terms, lies in the B western, the staple series pictures, the Hopalong Cassidy films, the singing-cowboy pictures, and so on. *Pace* Bazin, *Stagecoach* and *My Darling Clementine*, as well as *Shane* and *High Noon*, only occupy a penumbraic position in the genre and (to continue the spatial metaphor) belong to a periphery.

Indeed, this bears upon the discussion of norms and deviations which often underpins analyses of the select canon of A features. For it can be argued that the norms, the basic conventions, the 'pure' versions of the genre, are really to be found only in the relatively self-contained world of the B western, whilst the A features were much more subject to the need to vary the conventions, to break the generic rules, and to conform, in certain respects, with the prevalent narrative and stylistic norms of the period. As Edward Buscombe has suggested, the 'A-Western . . . was always more of a risk financially; production was more erratic since each film had to sell itself on its merits. For this reason the A-Western was more susceptible to changes in fashion, more influenced by developments in other kinds of films and in Hollywood generally' (1988: 40–1). Accordingly, in the 1940s westerns such as *Pursued* (1947), *Blood on the Moon* (1948), *Station West* (1948), *Colorado Territory* (1949), and *The Furies* (1950), amongst others, reflect the Hollywood fashion for introspective psychologically oriented pictures and embody some of the stylistic and narrative features of the film noir. Generic definition, however, is a matter not simply of films themselves but also of the public discursive regimes that mediate between films and the audience and select certain examples for attention and ignore others. As a result, the focus upon the familiar and better-publicized A features—*My Darling*

Clementine, *The Searchers*, and so on—is not surprising. These, rather than the singing-cowboy films, are the ones discussed by critics and reviewers, analysed by film scholars, and used as the foundation-stones for the canonic edifice known as the western genre, which in turn constitutes the environment in which individual instances of the genre circulate and on which they depend for their currency.

The inclusive–exclusive distinction has been expressed in another way by David Bordwell, who claims that generic categories are 'core/periphery schema, with the more "central" members of the category creating a prototype effect' (1989: 148). While there are problems in using a core–periphery model of genre when it underpins an evaluative, rather than a descriptive, critical approach to genre (as is the case with critics such as Bazin), such a model nevertheless provides an opportunity for capturing the diversity of films traditionally rounded up under the familiar generic categories. Even the most sharply delineated genres include considerable variety, and, as Rick Altman has suggested, there is a 'need to recognise that not all genre films relate to their genre in the same way or to the same extent' (1984: 6–18). For example, the gangster film embraces both the urban settings of *Scarface* (1932) and *Little Caesar* (1930) and the rural mountain retreats of *High Sierra* (1941); the musical genre contains both the light touch of *Singin' in the Rain* and the darker themes of *A Star is Born* (1954). It is necessary to take account of such diversity in the defining of particular genres, and, indeed, to go further and acknowledge that part of this diversity reflects the hybrid generic qualities of many American films and a fluidity of generic boundaries which is, perhaps, best embodied in the film noir–women's picture–melodrama *Mildred Pierce* (1945). It might be suggested that both inclusive and exclusive definitions of individual genres are necessary and both, in their distinctive ways, represent particular aspects of the genre system. The notion of the broad, inclusive corpus alerts us to the extensive skein of relationships that encompass most Hollywood films. Although *Seven Brides for Seven Brothers* has many of the attributes of the western—it is set in the west, is about pioneers, has horses and guns, and so on—its syntactic structure, which relates romance to community, is characteristic of the musical. Indeed, with its singing and dancing and its focus upon romance, it is probably easier to relate the film to *Oklahoma!* (1955), another 'folk-musical', to use Altman's (1989) terminology, than to its western

contemporaries such as *The Searchers*. This does not mean that the film is not a western, but rather that it is more likely to be mentioned in inclusive definitions of the genre (as in encyclopaedias) than in focused discussion; also, it is more likely to be positioned on the periphery of the western while simultaneously occupying a place nearer the core of the musical.

Genre and the individual film

The discussion so far has focused upon generic systems and individual genres, abstract conceptual entities generated through a range of discourses and including extrafilmic elements such as advertising, press reviews, journal commentary, television and radio programmes on cinema, and other discourses often referred to as 'secondary' or 'subsidiary' to the films themselves which, of course, are at the centre of the critical project. The enterprise, in some respects, is one of classification: the construction and definition of generic systems and individual genres, the compilation of inventories of their characteristic subject-matter, themes, iconography, narrative syntax, and visual style. Problems occur, however, if the notion of classification is carried through to the ways in which the concept of genre functions in relation to individual films. This is especially the case when films appear not to settle easily into a category or, to put it another way, when a film offers elements which could be claimed by a number of genres, as the example of the 'western–musical' or 'musical–western' *Seven Brides for Seven Brothers* suggests. *Mildred Pierce*, to take another example, is centred on a woman played by one of the leading female stars (Joan Crawford), whose presence signals 'romantic drama' (Bourget 1971/1978); the film also begins with a crime, a murder, and has the investigative flashback structure of the film noir; a further generic strand (family melodrama) is evoked by the themes of female domesticity versus female career, children versus romantic relationships, from which the tensions surrounding the central character arise. In these cases, clear classification is impossible as both films relate in various ways to more than one genre; and this multigeneric quality is not confined to a few odd or unusual films as 'nearly all Hollywood's films were hybrids insofar as they tended to combine one type of generic plot, a romance plot, with others' (Neale 1990: 57).

If genre criticism were simply a matter of constructing taxonomies and allocating films to their places in the system, then the intellectual basis of the exercise would certainly be open to doubt. A shift in emphasis, however, to the activity of *reading* an individual film in the context of a notion of genre is one way of rethinking the entire concept and moving away from the somewhat static idea of genre criticism as taxonomy. Indeed, one of the central critical concerns with the notion of genre could be seen to be its provision of a background aid to the understanding of the individual film. Genre critics, as David Bordwell has suggested, '[f]ar from being concerned with definition or reasoning from genus to species . . . often identify the genre only to aid interpreting the particular work. The identification is transitory and heuristic, like that of nearly all the categories we draw upon in everyday life. Genres, and genre, function as open-ended and corrigible schemata' (1989: 148).

Thus, a notion of a particular genre or genres, sometimes accompanied by a sense of generic system, supervises the critical analysis and definition of the individual film. However, the critical work on that film may well rebound on the initial notion of the genre and/or of the generic system, transforming it and drawing attention to the 'open-endedness', the transitory status, of genres as conceptual entities. Looked at from this perspective, the notion of genre captures a process in which definitions—the western, the gangster film—are provisional, 'corrigible schemata', waiting upon the next instance of the genre which may balance confirmation of existing elements with their transformation, repetition with difference, in various and not entirely predictable ways.

A return to the individual film and its analysis enables us to find an appropriate role for the system-building, the taxonomic and inventory-oriented activity that characterizes genre criticism. Instead of asking the question 'To what genre does *Mildren Pierce* belong?', it is necessary to probe the consequences of positioning the film in relation to the various genres to which it has a family resemblance, and to think about genre in relation to the process of film comprehension, in relation to what literary theorist Jonathan Culler has called the 'operations of reading' (1975: 136). As Culler suggests, the process of reading requires background, context, a general reference-point against which the actual object of reading acquires sense and meaning. For Hollywood films this background is the generic system and its individual genres which constitute a framework for comprehension. The familiar constella-

tion of terms such as 'convention', 'iconography', 'horizon of expectation', 'audience expectation' acquires a specific sense in this context deriving from the 'ideal world' of the generic system which is constructed through a range of discourses including, of course, the individual films which make up the individual generic corpus (particularly as it emerges and definitions in exclusive terms are focused on a handful of films thought to be typical and/or regarded as prototypes). The individual viewer confronted with a genre film has already internalized a number of assumptions about the genre system and will have a perception of the 'world' implied by each genre with its characteristic iconography, situational conventions, and stock of characters. He or she will read the film against a 'horizon of expectations' derived from critical and journalistic discourse in the various media, marketing, and publicity activities, and from the memory of previous viewing of films which are sufficiently similar to act as guides in relation to the formation of the horizon of expectation. The notion of each genre evoking a 'world', a particular configuration of 'fictional reality' with its own rules of behaviour, its particular fictional trajectories, its distinctive visual surface, its overall verisimilitude or structure of plausibility, is useful if regarded as a background mental set which readers of genre cinema bring to the individual film and through which the film sustains at least some of its levels of comprehensibility and maybe its dominant level of comprehensibility.

Looked at in this light, questions of generic membership—'To what genre does this film belong?'—become less relevant. Indeed, alternative questions are required such as: 'What genre or genres constitute an effective and pertinent context for the reading of this film?' or 'What is/are the world/worlds invoked by aspects of this film which will enable it to be situated and understood, its narrative trajectory anticipated, its characters to be constructed, and so on?' If we return to *Mildred Pierce*, we can see that its sense and meaning derive from the ways in which it interweaves different generic strands which are, in many ways, in tension with each other. *Mildren Pierce* is not unique in its multigeneric character and the flexible world of genre identified in the work of Neale and Altman correlates with a flexible approach to the making of genre films in Hollywood itself. This is particularly the case with contemporary, 'postmodern' Hollywood and is exemplified in, for example, *The Silence of the Lambs* (1991), which combines elements of the police-procedural—the mechanics of detection, a focus on forensic detail—with the horror film.

Genre: a summary

The impulses behind the development of genre criticism included a sense of unease with traditional critical approaches which highlighted individuality and distinctiveness, and which were centred on the unconventional in film. It was argued, by Lawrence Alloway (1971) in particular, that popular American cinema required a different critical approach from those adopted for the more traditional art forms, an approach which recognized the positive role of formula and convention, stereotypical characterization, familiar narratives, and their centrality to Hollywood picture-making. It was suggested that audiences for Hollywood pictures read them according to a detailed set of assumptions—an intertextual consciousness—derived from a regular viewing of related films and an awareness of the various secondary discourses; and that their pleasures were derived from such qualities as the ritualistic predictability of the narratives and the nuancing of familiar conventions. The unacknowledged assumption was that other forms of cinema were different, non-generic, and subject to different and less restricted modes of reading.

However, the interplay of semiotics and genre in writers such as Neale and Altman suggests less of a difference between genre films and other forms of cinema at least in terms of the basic processes of communication and reading. All communicative forms, including all films, are underpinned by systems—arguably modelled on language—against which they acquire their significance and meaning. The audience for the films of Michelangelo Antonioni and Ingmar Bergman require a reading-context no less than the audience for the films of John Ford and Sam Peckinpah, and all films have woven into their texture at some level (narrative, style, iconography) signals that indicate the appropriate ways in which they might be understood and appreciated. American genre cinema becomes a special case from this perspective rather than a distinct form, and takes its place in a spectrum of cinematic types.

BIBLIOGRAPHY

Alloway, Lawrence (1963), 'Iconography and the Movies', *Movie*, 7: 4–6.
—— (1971), *Violent America: The Movies 1946–1964* (New York: Museum of Modern Art).
Altman, Rick (1984), 'A Semantic/Syntactic Approach to Film Genre', *Cinema Journal*, 23/3: 6–18; repr. in Grant (1986).
—— (1989), *The American Film Musical* (London: British Film Institute).
Bazin, André (1953/1971), Preface to J.-L. Rieupeyrout, *Le Western ou le cinéma américain par excellence*, in Bazin (1971).
—— (1971), *What is Cinema?*, 2 vols., trans. Hugh Gray, ii (Berkeley: University of California Press).
Bordwell, David (1985), *Narration in the Fiction Film* (London: Methuen).
—— (1989), *Making Meaning* (Cambridge, Mass.: Harvard University Press).
Bourget, Jean-Loup (1971/1978), 'Faces of the American Melodrama: Joan Crawford', in *Film Reader*, 3: 24–34.
Buscombe, Edward (1970), 'The Idea of Genre in the American Cinema', *Screen*, 11/2: 33–45.
—— (1974), 'Walsh and Warner Brothers', in P. Hardy (ed.), *Raoul Walsh* (Edinburgh: Edinburgh Film Festival and British Film Institute).
—— (ed.) (1988), *The BFI Companion to the Western* (London: Andre Deutsch and British Film Institute).
Culler, Jonathan (1975), *Structuralist Poetics* (London: Routledge & Kegan Paul).
*****Grant, Barry K.** (ed.) (1986), *Film Genre Reader* (Austin, Tex.: University of Texas Press).
Hardy, Phil (ed.) (1985), *The Encyclopedia of Western Movies* (London: Octopus Books).
Hess Wright, Judith (1974/1986), 'Genre Films and the Status Quo', *Jump Cut*, 1 (May–June), 1, 16, 18; repr. in Grant (1986).
Hutchings, Peter (1995), 'Genre Theory and Criticism', in Joanne Hollows and Mark Jancovich (eds.), *Approaches to Popular Film* (Manchester: Manchester University Press).
Jameson, Fredric (1975), 'Magical Narratives: Romance as Genre', *New Literary History*, 7: 135–63.
Kitses, Jim (1969), *Horizons West* (London: Thames & Hudson and British Film Institute).
Klinger, Barbara (1984/1986), '"Cinema/Ideology/Criticism": The Progressive Text', *Screen*, 25/1: 30–44; repr. in Grant (1986).
Lovell, Alan (1967/1976), 'The Western', in B. Nichols (ed.), *Movies and Methods*, 2 vols, (University of California Press).
McArthur, Colin (1972), *Underworld USA* (London: Secker & Warburg).

Maltby, Richard (1995), *Hollywood Cinema* (Oxford: Blackwell).

Movie, (1975), 'The Return of Movie', no. 20 (Spring) 1–25.

*****Neale, Steve** (1980), *Genre* (London: British Film Institute).

—— (1990), 'Questions of Genre', *Screen*, 31/1: 45–66.

Palmer, Jerry (1991), *Potboilers: Methods, Concepts and Case Studies in Popular Fiction* (London: Routledge).

Pye, Douglas (1975), 'Genre and Movies', *Movie*, 20: 29–43.

Rotha, Paul (1930/1967), *The Film Till Now* (London: Spring Books).

Ryall, Tom (1970), 'The Notion of Genre', *Screen*, 11/2: 22-32.

*—— (1975–6), 'Teaching through Genre', *Screen Education*, 17: 27–33.

Schatz, Thomas (1981), *Hollywood Genres* (New York: Random House).

Shklovsky, Victor (1927), 'Poetry and Prose in Cinematography', *Twentieth Century Studies*, 7–8: 128–30.

Todorov, Tzvetan (1975), *The Fantastic* (Ithaca, NY: Cornell University Press).

Warshow, Robert(1948/1970), 'The Gangster as Tragic Hero', in Warshow (1970).

—— (1954/1970), 'Movie Chronicle: The Westerner', in Warshow (1970).

—— (1970), *The Immediate Experience* (New York: Atheneum).

Williams, Alan (1984), 'Is Radical Genre Criticism Possible?', *Quarterly Review of Film Studies*, 9/2: 121–5.

Body genres

Linda Williams excerpted from Linda Williams, 'Film Bodies: Gender, Genre and Excess', *Film Quarterly*, 44/4 (Summer 1991), 2–13.

The repetitive formulas and spectacles of film genres are often defined by their differences from the classical realist style of narrative cinema. These classical films have been characterized as efficient action-centred, goal-oriented, linear narratives driven by the desire of a single protagonist, involving one or two lines of action, and leading to definitive closure. In their influential study *The Classical Hollywood Cinema*, David Bordwell, Janet Staiger, and Kristin Thompson call this the classical Hollywood style.

As Rick Altman has noted in a recent article, both genre study and the study of the somewhat more nebulous category of melodrama has long been hampered by

assumptions about the classical nature of the dominant narrative to which melodrama and some individual genres have been opposed. Altman argues that Bordwell, Staiger, and Thompson, who locate the classical Hollywood style in the linear, progressive form of the Hollywood narrative, cannot accommodate 'melodramatic' attributes like spectacle, episodic presentation, or dependence on coincidence except as limited exceptions or 'play' within the dominant linear causality of the classical.

Altman writes: 'Unmotivated events, rhythmic montage, highlighted parallelism, overlong spectacles—these are the excesses in the classical narrative system that alert us to the

Mildred Pierce (1945)—the fluidity of generic boundaries

Body genres continued

existence of a competing logic, a second voice'. Altman, whose own work on the movie musical has necessarliy relied upon analyses of seemingly 'excessive' spectacles and parallel constructions, thus makes a strong case for the need to recognize the possibility that excess may itself be organized as a system. Yet analyses of systems of excess have been much slower to emerge in the genres whose non-linear spectacles have centred more directly upon the gross display of the human body. Pornography and horror films are two such systems of excess. Pornography is the lowest in cultural esteem, gross-out horror is next to lowest.

Melodrama, however, refers to a much broader category of films and a much larger system of excess. It would not be unreasonable, in fact, to consider all three of these genres under the extended rubric of melodrama, considered as a filmic mode of stylistic and/or emotional excess that stands in contrast to more 'dominant' modes of realistic, goal-oriented narrative. In this extended sense melodrama can encompass a broad range of films marked by 'lapses' in realism, by 'excesses' of spectacle and displays of primal, even infantile, emotions, and by narratives that seem circular and repetitive. Much of the interest of melodrama to film scholars over the last fifteen years originates in the sense that the form exceeds the normative system of much narrative cinema. I shall limit my focus here, however, to a more narrow sense of melodrama, leaving the broader category of the sensational to encompass the three genres I wish to consider. Thus, partly for purposes of contrast with pornography, the melodrama I will consider here will consist of the form that has most interested feminist critics—that of 'the woman's film' or 'weepie'. These are films addressed to women in their traditional status under patriarchy—as wives, mothers, abandoned lovers, or in their traditional status as bodily hysteria or excess, as in the frequent case of the woman 'afflicted' with a deadly or debilitating disease.

What are the pertinent features of bodily excess shared by these three 'gross' genres? First, there is the spectacle of a body caught in the grip of intense sensation or emotion. Carol Clover, speaking primarily of horror films and pornography, has called films which privilege the sensational 'body' genres. I am expanding Clover's notion of low body genres to include the sensation of overwhelming pathos in the 'weepie'. The body spectacle is featured most sensationally in pornography's portrayal of orgasm, in horror's portrayal of violence and terror, and in melodrama's portrayal of weeping. I propose that an investigation of the visual and narrative pleasures found in the portrayal of these three types of excess could be important to a new direction in genre criticism that would take as its point of departure—rather than as an unexamined assumption—questions of

gender construction, and gender address in relation to basic sexual fantasies.

Another pertinent feature shared by these body genres is the focus on what could probably best be called a form of ecstasy. While the classical meaning of the original Greek word is insanity and bewilderment, more contemporary meanings suggest components of direct or indirect sexual excitement and rapture, a rapture which informs even the pathos of melodrama.

Visually, each of these ecstatic excesses could be said to share a quality of uncontrollable convulsion or spasm—of the body 'beside itself' with sexual pleasure, fear and terror, or overpowering sadness. Aurally, excess is marked by recourse not to the coded articulations of language but to inarticulate cries of pleasure in porn, screams of fear in horror, sobs of anguish in melodrama.

Looking at, and listening to, these bodily ecstasies, we can also notice something else that these genres seem to share: though quite differently gendered with respect to their targeted audiences, with pornography aimed, presumably, at active men and melodramatic weepies aimed, presumably, at passive women, and with contemporary gross-out horror aimed at adolescents careening wildly between the two masculine and feminine poles, in each of these genres the bodies of women figured on the screen have functioned traditionally as the primary *embodiments* of pleasure, fear, and pain.

In other words, even when the pleasure of viewing has traditionally been constructed for masculine spectators, as is the case in most traditional heterosexual pornography, it is the female body in the grips of an out-of-control ecstasy that has offered the most sensational sight.

There are, of course, other film genres which both portray and affect the sensational body—e.g. thrillers, musicals, comedies. I suggest, however, that the film genres that have had especially low cultural status—which have seemed to exist as excesses to the system of even the popular genres—are not simply those which sensationally display bodies on the screen and register effects in the bodies of spectators. Rather, what may especially mark these body genres as low is the perception that the body of the spectator is caught up in an almost involuntary mimicry of the emotion or sensation of the body on the screen along with the fact that the body displayed is female. Physical clown comedy is another 'body' genre concerned with all manner of gross activities and body functions—eating shoes, slipping on banana skins. None the less, it has not been deemed gratuitously excessive,

Body genres continued

TABLE 1. **AN ANATOMY OF FILM BODIES**

	GENRE		
	Pornography	Horror	Melodrama
Bodily excess	Sex	Violence	Emotion
Ecstasy—shown by	Ecstatic sex Orgasm Ejaculation	Ecstatic violence Shudder Blood	Ecstatic woe Sob Tears
Presumed audience	Men (active)	Adolescent boys (active–passive)	Girls, women (passive)
Perversion	Sadism	Sadomasochism	Masochism
Originary fantasy	Seduction	Castration	Origin
Temporality of fantasy	On time!	Too early!	Too late!
GENRE CYCLES 'Classic'	Stag films (1920s–1940s) *The Casting Couch*	'Classic' horror *Dracula* *Frankenstein* *Dr Jekyll and Mr Hyde* *King Kong*	'Classic' women's films Maternal melodrama *Stella Dallas* *Mildred Pierce* romance *Back Street* *Letter from an Unknown Woman*
Contemporary	Feature-length hard-core porn *Deep Throat* etc. *The Punishment of Anne* Femme Productions Bisexual Trisexual	Post-*Psycho* *Texas Chainsaw Massacre* *Halloween* *Dressed to Kill* *Videodrome*	Male and female 'weepies' *Steel Magnolias* *Stella* *Dad*

probably because the reaction of the audience does not mimic the sensations experienced by the central clown. Indeed, it is almost a rule that the audience's physical reaction of laughter does not coincide with the often dead-pan reactions of the clown.

In the body genres I am isolating here, however, it seems to be the case that the success of these genres is often measured by the degree to which the audience sensation mimics what is seen on the screen. Whether this mimicry is exact, e.g. whether the spectator at the porn film actually orgasms, whether the spectator at the horror film actually shudders in fear, whether the spectator of the melodrama actually dissolves in tears, the success of these genres seems a self-evident matter of measuring bodily response.

What seems to bracket these particular genres from others is an apparent lack of proper aesthetic distance, a sense of over-involvement in sensation and emotion. We feel manipulated by these texts—an impression that the very colloquialisms of 'tear-jerker' and 'fear-jerker' express—and to which we could add pornography's even cruder sense as texts to which some people might be inclined to 'jerk off'.

9

The star system and Hollywood

Jeremy G. Butler

The human body on screen ignites the desires of moviegoers. The actor's performance provides an essential pleasure in the film-viewing experience. The star's image dominates movie posters and appears on dozens of magazine covers; it is clearly one of the principal commodities that is used to market a film to an audience—equal in importance, in the minds of film producers and film viewers alike, to a compelling story or majestic scenery or a trendy director. And yet until the 1980s the presence of human bodies in motion, the impact of the actor's performance, and significance of the star's image were rarely discussed in film studies. Consequently, in order to understand the study of the star system, one must first ask: Why has the star system been ignored for so long by film studies?

The origins of this neglect lie in the very beginnings of film theory. Early theorists were sensitive to the charge that film, as a mechanical reproduction of reality, was not a true art form. They focused their attention on the aspects of filmmaking that separated it from reality and thereby provided the artist with tools for artistic expression. A particular camera angle could make someone look smaller or larger than he or she does in reality; a lighting style could make an actor appear grotesque; wide-angle lenses could distort perspective; and so on. Film could be justified as an art form, they argued, because the filmmaker did not just mechanically reproduce reality; he or she actually manipulated reality or even fabricated an entirely new

reality. Foremost among these first theorists was Lev Kuleshov (1975), who devised an editing experiment during the early 1920s. In the Kuleshov experiment, a shot of an expressionless actor was intercut with various significant objects—a bowl of soup, a baby in a coffin, and so on. (The actual components of the experiment are in doubt because no copies of it exist today.) Kuleshov maintained that spectators saw emotions in the actor's face (hunger, sorrow, and so on) that were generated through film technique rather than the work of an actor. Meaning did not exist in the actor's performance, but rather in the manipulation of performance through editing.

Thus, Kuleshov, founder of the world's first film school, devalued the significance of the actor's presence in his determination to fix the cinema's essence in editing (montage)—in which the actor's face is no more consequential than a bowl of soup. Other film theorists from the 1920s and 1930s were also uninterested in acting and stars, choosing instead to try and ascertain the components of film art and its impact upon viewers. Stars fared little better in subsequent decades. Film scholars in the 1940s–1960s often came to the cinema with a training in literary criticism. Such individuals were well equipped to analyse narrative forms common to film and literature, but could shed little light on the work of the star. They viewed the actor, instead, as simply the body that held the character's place on screen. It was the character's position within a narrative structure that mattered, not the star's embodiment of that character.

This emphasis on narrative and character over actors and their work also informs two of the major critical approaches to Hollywood cinema that are presented in this volume: genre and authorship studies (see Crofts and Ryall, Chapters 7 and 8). Most genres, with the major exception of the musical, are defined mainly by the stories they tell, and this leaves little room for the consideration of performance. And so it is not surprising that most critics have interpreted genre using narrative-based methods borrowed from structural anthropology and ideological criticism. Thus, despite several meaningful intersections of star and genre (as in the case of John Wayne and the western, Lana Turner and the melodrama, Fred Astaire and the musical), the impact of stars on genres has yet to be fully assessed. Britton (1984) and Gledhill (1991a), however, have offered some introductory thoughts.

In the case of authorship study (by which is meant, principally, the so-called 'auteur theory'), some concern with the star's impact upon a film might have been expected. After all, in common parlance, moviegoers characteristically identify a film in terms of its star—as if the star were its author. For example, despite the opening credits which declare *Pretty Woman* (1990) to be a 'Garry Marshall film' (referring to its director), most viewers are likely to refer to it as a 'Julia Roberts movie'. In some regard, then, the star is seen to be the central presence, the 'auteur', behind such a film. And, certainly, there are numerous examples of films being designed specifically for particular stars. In such cases, the star's image has determined the overall construction of the film, even if he or she didn't actually write the script or choose the camera angles. Even so, proponents of the auteur theory have seldom discussed the star as auteur, preferring instead to privilege the director as 'author' and to discuss his or her mise-en-scène, narrative structure, and thematics. This emphasis on the director over other members of the production team derives, à la Kuleshov, from a conception of the 'artist' as the man or woman in control of film technique (which is principally the director). Since the actor does not govern film technique—does not, in a sense, speak the language of the cinema—he or she cannot be considered a film artist.

In sum, analysis of the star system has been hampered by early film studies' reliance upon antiquated aesthetic traditions—particularly conventional literary criticism and Romanticism—that are ill-equipped to deal with the work of art in the age of mechanical reproduction (to invoke Walter Benjamin's telling phrase). The attempts in the 1920s–1940s to justify the cinema as an art form according to these traditions blinded theorists to the significance of the star system. More recently, however, analytical methods from semiotics, psychoanalysis, and cultural studies have been brought to bear upon the cinema, resulting in a re-evaluation of the position of stars in the cinematic apparatus. Leading the way in this regard was a slender volume entitled *Stars*, by Richard Dyer (1979). Following Dyer, there has been a growth of writing concerned with stardom and film performance, much of which may be found in two anthologies: *Star Texts* (Butler 1991) and *Stardom* (Gledhill 1991b).

The fundamentals of star studies

Central to Dyer's approach, and to that of many subsequent star studies, is the semiotics notion that stars should be studied as clusters of signs, as systems of signifiers or texts that communicate meaning to a spectator. These star texts are, of course, grounded in the lives of real human beings. There is no doubt that Mel Gibson and Demi Moore really exist. But Dyer stresses that these images are highly manipulated texts that have been fabricated, intentionally and unintentionally, through the work of the star, his or her representatives, and other cultural workers (e.g. gossip columnists, talk show hosts, and so on). Moreover, since there is no way to know a star except through media artefacts such as magazine articles and news reports, it is fruitless to search for the star's true identity 'behind' or 'beneath' the media-constructed façade. Few of us will ever meet Gibson or Moore in person, and even if we did there is little chance that we would penetrate their media shells and glimpse their 'true' identities. In so far as the viewer–analyst is concerned, the star's identity is his or her façade—our knowledge of him or her is always filtered through media accounts. Consequently, it is impossible to know the star in any other way. The study of stars, therefore, does not aim to reveal the truth behind a star's image—as is often the false claim of TV and magazine journalists—but rather seeks to bring out the meanings within a star's image and to contextualize them within larger discursive structures.

Having stressed the constructed, fabricated nature of star images—the existence of stars as texts—it is important to recognize that these texts do not exist in a hermetically sealed, nice-and-tidy, semiotic vacuum. Rather, star texts also exist within particular economic, ideological, and psychological contexts. Dyer and others, in this respect, recognize the importance of stars to both the cinema's mode of production and to a film's reception by viewers. To understand the star system fully, therefore, one must consider three interlocking elements:

1. star production: economic and discursive structures;
2. star reception: social structures and the theory of the subject;
3. star semiotics: intertextuality and structured polysemy.

Star production: economic and discursive structures

The star system is such an integral part of today's film and television industries that it is sometimes difficult to remember that this so-called 'system' did not always exist. The early cinema survived quite nicely for over a decade without it. Indeed, actor's names were not even listed in the credits of films at first. Using a star's image to promote a film would have been unthinkable around the turn of the century, but by 1910 the Hollywood mode of production had shifted and the actor had become a marketable commodity. Interestingly, quite a bit of controversy surrounds accounts of the star system's introduction into the Hollywood mode of film production. Examining that controversy can tell us much about the position of the star in the cinematic economic apparatus, as well as illustrating more general problems associated with the writing of film history.

The conventional history of the star system's evolution—a history which has been repeated in decades of film textbooks—constructs a convenient narrative of lone-wolf independent producers initiating the star system in order to outsmart the Motion Picture Patents Company (MPPC). (The MPPC was a protective trade association of the most powerful production companies formed by Thomas Edison in a monopolistic attempt to control film production and exhibition.) As the story is usually told, film producers initially resisted promoting actors' identities because they presumed a well-known actor would demand more money for his or her work. Also it is said that actors were ashamed of appearing in low-prestige 'flickers' and refused to have their names credited. However, the filmgoing public soon came to identify their favourites even without the aid of on-screen credits, lobby posters, or fan magazines. One such favourite was Florence Lawrence, identified by her public as the 'Biograph Girl' for her work in films produced by American Biograph, one of the members of the MPPC. In 1909 Lawrence was lured away from Biograph by an adversary of the MPPC, independent producer Carl Laemmle, of the Independent Motion Picture (IMP) Corporation. The following year, Laemmle mounted what is said to be the first promotional campaign for a film actor. Rumours were circulated—probably by IMP publicists—that Lawrence had been killed in a streetcar accident. Then Laemmle took out an advertisement in *Moving Picture World* declaring, 'We Nail a Lie' (reproduced by Staiger in Gledhill 1991*b*: 4). He heatedly denied these rumours and asserted that Lawrence was not only alive and well, but that, coincidentally, a film of hers was just about to be released. The success of promotions such as this, conventional wisdom maintains, led to the independent producers' triumph over the MPPC, which stodgily refused to promote its actors as stars.

Film historians such as Staiger (1983) and deCordova (1990) have challenged this conventional narrative. Attractive as this story is, it is undermined by several inaccuracies and misconceptions. As deCordova points out, an MPPC company (Kalem) publicized their actors a year before Laemmle and IMP did; and the Edison Company was probably the first (in 1909) to include a cast list in the film credits. Indeed, in 1910 most MPPC companies, with the notable exception of Biograph, began to promote their stars—at the same time as the independent producers did so. Thus, the independents were not alone in using stars as a marketing device. The emergence of the star system was not an instance of the underdog independents battling the bullying MPPC, but rather was the result of a more generalized shift in the mode of production and the discourses surrounding the medium. More significant

> **The star system is such an integral part of today's film and television industries that it is sometimes difficult to remember that this so-called 'system' did not always exist.**

to the emergence of the star system, contemporary historians (Bordwell, Staiger, and Thompson 1985) have argued, are other discursive and economic shifts.

First, in terms of aesthetic discourse, the introduction of major theatrical actors into the films of the Film D'Art and the Famous Players Film Company helped to legitimize film acting and to alter the discourse on film in general. Whereas early promotion of the cinema focused on the technology itself (objects in motion! on a screen!) and the stories presented (will the firemen rescue the endangered child?), a discourse on acting and the lives of actors began to intrude around 1909. When noted theatrical presence Sara Bernhardt appeared in *La Dame aux camélias* (France, 1912; *Camille*) it helped import a long tradition of performance discourse from the theatre into the movies and shifted the promotional spotlight from the technology and the narrative to the actor's body and the actor's life. For example, a 1912 advertisement for *La Dame aux camélias* focuses attention on the actor with some rather astonishing claims: 'Like the Noonday Sun Alone in the Blazing Majesty Giving Light and Life to Art Madame Sarah Bernhardt Illuminates the whole Motion Picture World Through Her Stupendous Genius Revealed in Her First and Only Photo Play "CAMILLE" In which she is taking the nations by storm and making a girdle of her pictured glory around the globe' (reproduced by Staiger in Gledhill 1991b: 13).

In deCordova's view, companies such as the Film D'Art and Famous Players changed the way actors were regarded in film. Adding to this were print media that began to publicize the off-screen existence of the performers. Although several film magazines initially slighted actors and stressed instead summaries of film stories—as the titles of *The Motion Picture Story Magazine* and *Photoplay* attest—by 1910 many of these magazines had begun running features on actors' off-screen lives. This journalist discourse was an essential component in the transition of the actor from nameless body on the screen to genuine film star—with a name and an identity that extended beyond the characters he or she played on-screen.

The construction of off-screen star identities, of true star images, had a significant economic impact on the cinema. Since by the time of the First World War actors had a presence larger than their individual characters, they could now be used to distinguish one film from another. The presence of a star such as Mary Pickford, for example, could set a film apart from the dozens of others competing for viewer attention. Thus, the Holly-wood mode of production quickly absorbed the star as commodity, as a source of product differentiation as significant as narrative-based genres and more powerful than studio identities. With the establishment of stars' extra-filmic identities and the arrival of the star as economic commodity, the star system was complete.

Star reception: social structures

Once the star system was in place and formerly anonymous actors had become stars, their images began to have a social presence. This presence became quite clear in the United States in the 1920s, when several scandals illustrated the new-found significance of the motion picture star. The enormous media attention paid to the murder of director William Desmond Taylor (involving actors Mary Miles Minter and Mable Normand), actor Wallace Reid's death from a drug overdose, and comedian Roscoe 'Fatty' Arbuckle's trial for rape and murder indicates the change in position of the film actor from turn-of-the-century anonymity to 1920s notoriety. It also suggests just how forceful the star's off-screen presence had become. It is tempting to read these events, and the images of the stars associated with them, as a reflection of the 'roaring twenties'—of an era of flappers, gangsters, and 'anything goes'. Indeed, it is a common presumption that star images are a reflection of society's values. Contemporary star studies, however, rejects this sort of 'reflectionism' as simplistic and reductive. Instead, the (many) meanings associated with a star are seen to form a part of the meaning system of that star's society, the ideology of that particular time and place.

From ideological criticism, star studies has fastened onto the basic presumption that ideology consists of the taken-for-granted values and concepts that underpin a particular society. Moreover, it is argued that these values exist in a systemic relationship to one another and that they have 'real' social causes and effects. Ideological values are presumed to be generated by a society's economic and social infrastructure and related to the ways that society treats individuals of different classes, races, and gender. As a result, star studies has sought to analyse the meanings of star images in relation to ideologies of class, race, and gender.

Eckert (1974), for example, incorporates Freudian notions of condensation, repression, and displace-

**Shirley Temple, child-
heroine of the Depression**

ment in his consideration of Shirley Temple's position within the class discourse of the United States during the Depression. He argues that the potentially disruptive, class-based topics of work and money are repressed in Temple's films, displaced into charity and love. Capitalist, bourgeois values, he argues, were under assault at the time of these films' production and Temple helps paper over the resulting ideological fissures: by bringing together the classes (Temple's character often romantically unites a wealthy man and a working-class woman, or vice versa) and embodying charity and love. She does not 'reflect'

1930s values so much as process them—repressing, condensing, and displacing.

Star studies often highlights this resolution of ideological conflicts by stars. Dyer adopts this approach when discussing the images of several stars. Marilyn Monroe (Dyer 1986) and Lana Turner (Dyer 1977–8), for example, are both discussed in terms of their reconciliation of conflicting gender values (innocent–sexy, ordinary–glamorous), while Paul Robeson's connections to conflicting racial discourses (African and European) form the basis of Dyer's (1986) analysis of his work. For Dyer and others, ideology is not a monolithic, hegemonic phenomenon that crushes all opposing viewpoints—as it might be for a traditional Marxist. Instead, ideology is explored for its conflicts and con- tradictions, many of which are inscribed on stars' images. The ideological function that stars such as Monroe, Turner, and Robeson serve is magically to resolve those contradictions. This is an essential allure of the star: the resolution of contradictions that cannot be resolved in the social sphere, in 'real life'. In this regard, stars operate in much the same way as genre narratives, which often relate mythic stories that man- age the unmanageable and 'resolve' the unresolvable. Genres and stars, it has been argued, comfort the viewer because they offer fantasy solutions to social problems that cannot be resolved in reality.

> This is an essential allure of the star: the resolution of contradictions that cannot be resolved in the social sphere, in 'real life'.

Stars and society: the special case of feminism

Feminism and gender studies hold a special place in star studies. Feminists were among the first film scho- lars to publish extended considerations of stars—not- ably, of women stars. Molly Haskell's *From Reverence to Rape* (1974) is filled with analyses of actors, although the consideration of stars is often eclipsed by her over- weening auteurism. Haskell discusses stars in terms of socially determined, patriarchal stereotypes that they do or do not fulfil. Mostly, she sees women stars as unique inflections of their society's gender roles. Her comments on Greta Garbo are illustrative: 'As actress, myth, and image of woman, Garbo, like any other star, was neither wholly unique nor wholly representative. She was not like the solitary and self-derived creation of the writer, on the one hand; nor was she a sponta- neous eruption of the national "anima", an archetypal heroine as might emerge from a truly "collective" art like television' (Haskell 1974: 106–7). The problem with Haskell's perspective for subsequent feminists is that she does not examine the complicated discursive operations by which the image of woman in film reflects and refracts social realities. As she contrasts

the star with the stereotype, she presumes that that stereotype is a stable, uncomplicated mirror of reality. In short, she does not develop an understanding of the star's and the stereotype's positions within ideological processes.

This 'image-of-woman' approach predominated in feminist film studies during its formative years, the later 1960s and early 1970s. Subsequently, this method of writing about women stars has been criticized for at least two reasons: first, its reliance upon the simple 'reflection' theory of ideology; and second, its naïve understanding of how the cinematic apparatus posi- tions the female image relative to the viewer. Since the publication of Laura Mulvey's seminal 'Visual Pleasure and Narrative Cinema' (1975), feminist film study has veered off into approaches grounded in Lacanian psy- choanalysis in an attempt to comprehend the process of film viewing. Informed by psychoanalytic film theory, the cinematic spectator has been renamed the 'sub- ject', who views and interacts with the on-screen human 'object'. This has had important implications for star studies because the 'theory of the subject' attempts to articulate the psychic mechanisms of desire behind the spectator's viewing of the star.

Star reception: the theory of the subject

It would seem self-evident that the relationship of the spectator-subject to the star-object is grounded in some form of visual desire, of pleasure in the image. We look at stars because it pleases us to do so. Nobody forces or coerces us to watch Brad Pitt or Marilyn Mon- roe. And yet, traditional film theory had little to say about visual pleasure and desire. Voyeurism has been the unspoken pleasure of the cinema. Mulvey's work in the mid-1970s opened the floodgates to analyses of cinematic pleasure based in Freud and the reworking of Freud by French psychoanalyst Jacques Lacan.

Even though Mulvey is less concerned with film star- dom *per se* than with the apparatus by which visual pleasure is orchestrated, her analysis does offer some specific thoughts on the star image of Marlene Dietrich and helps clarify (from a feminist psychoanalytic per- spective, at least) the star–spectator relationship. Mul- vey maintains that there are two aspects of visual pleasure in classical cinema: 'The first, scopophilic, arises from pleasure in using another person as an object of sexual stimulation through sight. The second, developed through narcissism and the constitution of the ego, comes from identification with the image seen' (Mulvey 1975: 10). Scopophilia, or voyeurism, is argued to be the key to understanding the representation of women in film. In this scenario, the viewing subject is specifically male and the viewed object is specifically female. Although the woman connotes 'to-be-looked-at-ness' (Mulvey's phrase), she also threatens to signify castration anxiety, which, according to Lacan, is the foundation upon which all language and signification is constructed. The classical cinema deals with the threatening object, the woman, by either investigating and demystifying her, or turning her into a safe 'fetish object'. By catering to the pleasure of the male spectator-subject, the classical cinema exists as 'an illusion cut to the measure of desire' (Mulvey 1975: 17).

It seems clear that many women stars are fabricated illusions cut to the measure of male desire: from Theda Bara to Jean Harlow to Lena Horne to Rita Hayworth to Kim Novak to Ann-Margret to Julie Christie to Bo Derek to Demi Moore. The castration anxiety that these women pose, in Freudian terms, is ameliorated by turning their bodies into fetish objects. Other, more threatening women are handled through containment or punishment in their story lines. Lana Turner's Cora, in *The Postman always Rings Twice* (1946), gets away with murder, but then perishes in a car crash. Jane Greer's Kathie Moffat, in *Out of the Past* (1947), betrays her lover but is killed at the end of the film. To psychoanalytic film theorists, the classical cinema is a phallocentric, patriarchal machine that has developed devices to check the peril embodied by women. Since stars are the most popular and the most powerful female figures in film, they are also the most capable of instigating both disruption and pleasure.

Recent considerations of women in film have been critical of Mulvey and other psychoanalytic film theor-

ists for their presumption of a male viewer and a masculine viewing position. What if, Hansen (1986) has queried, the viewing subject is female and the viewed object is male? Moreover, what if the viewing position for a film is designed for a feminine perspective? Hansen has written, specifically, on Rudolph Valentino, a star image successfully designed for a female audience. Her essay begins by noting the shifts in women's social position that accompanied the First World War—specifically, their integration into a consumer economy—and the first twentieth-century wave of the women's movement, the suffragettes. However, her central concern is the sexual politics of Valentino's films. She argues that the deep ambivalence of Valentino's sexuality, expressing a 'slippage of gender definitions', provides the opportunity for the taboo expression of female voyeurism. Further, Valentino also disrupts conventional sado-masochistic rituals; his masochistic femininity fissures patriarchal structures of dominance and submission. Hansen, like Mulvey, is concerned with the issue of desire and the movie star, but she inverts the genders of Mulvey's original structure.

Hansen's challenge to Mulvey still exists within the bounds of Freudian psychology, but other contemporary feminists go even further in their contesting of psychoanalytic interpretations of the image of woman in film. Stacey (1994) criticizes the psychoanalytic method for a number of reasons—not the least of which is that theorists such as Mulvey (1975/1989), Doane (1987), de Lauretis (1987), *et al.* seldom deal with actual film viewers. Their theories are developed from psychoanalytical principles, and they are never tested out on viewers in a screening situation. Stacey's approach, in contrast, grows out of ethnography, which uses interviews, surveys, viewers' letters and diaries, and so on, to study the discourse of real viewers. Like Hansen, Stacey is also dissatisfied with psychoanalytic film criticism's emphasis on the male viewer, but her book, *Star Gazing* (1994), does not merely invert the traditional viewing situation by studying female viewers and a male viewed. Instead, she focuses on how women look at women, at images of femininity, on screen. She does so by analysing letters and surveys from British viewers about US film stars from the 1940s and 1950s. This also allows her to study viewer discourse in a specific national and historical context. Another weakness of psychoanalytic theory, she contends, is that it presumes a universal subject, one outside the determinations of class, nation, and race.

> **It seems clear that many women stars are fabricated illusions cut to the measure of male desire: from Theda Bara to Jean Harlow to Lena Horne to Rita Hayworth to Kim Novak to Ann-Margret to Julie Christie to Bo Derek to Demi Moore.**

Rudolf Valentino, a star image successfully designed for a female audience (*The Sheikh*, 1926)

Star semiotics: intertextuality and structured polysemy

As has been noted, Dyer's *Stars* merges the sociological and ideological criticism outlined above with elements of semiotics. (And, although Dyer does occasionally borrow from Freudian psychology, his work skirts the Lacanian revision of Freud.) The semiotic approach that Dyer uses has provided the foundation for the analysis of stars as 'texts', as clusters of analysable signs, that informs much star analysis of the 1980s and 1990s. Dyer's semiotics is grounded in the notion that, at any one particular ideological moment, a star signifies a wealth of meanings, or a 'polysemy'. For Dyer, however, this polysemy is not infinite. It is seen as fabricated through a process involving 'media texts', as limited in its range, and as bearing a certain structure in the way that meanings relate systematically to one another. In his own words, 'From the perspective of ideology, analyses of stars, as images existing in films and other media texts, stress their structured polysemy, that is, the finite multiplicity of meanings and affects they embody and the attempts so to structure them that some meanings and affects are foregrounded and others are masked or displaced' (Dyer 1979: 3). It is worth stressing that Dyer does not see the range of meanings attached to a star as being unbounded. Doubtless it would be possible, for example, to find an individual who believes that Kevin Costner is descended from a race of space aliens, but such an individual exists outside the realm of contemporary ideology. Textual analysis, therefore, concerns itself with articulating the range of possible meanings that may be read in a star's image at a particular ideological moment (even if it does not speak to the actual interpretation of specific stars by real viewers—as is attempted in ethnographic work such as Stacey's).

For semioticians, the star image is constructed through media texts. These texts consist of a variety of phenomena: performances in films, articles in print publications, posters in theatre foyers, and so on. They have been grouped by Dyer into four types:

1. promotion;
2. publicity;
3. film roles/characters;
4. criticism and commentary on those roles.

Dyer seeks to distinguish promotion and publicity, although he recognizes that these two often overlap. Promotional texts consist of materials designed by the star and/or his or her minions in the deliberate attempt to manufacture a favourable image of the star. A poster for *Niagara* (1953), for example, proclaims 'Marilyn Monroe and "Niagara" a raging torrent of emotion that even nature can't control!' (in Dyer 1979: 123)—with an illustration that blends an enormous version of Monroe's body with Niagara Falls itself. Obviously, Twentieth Century-Fox's promotional department is here emphasizing the animal, 'natural' sexuality of Monroe's image.

Publicity texts, in contrast, are those that are uncontrolled by the star. When print media published reports that Roseanne, while a teenager, had given up a child for adoption, the star made public efforts to suppress this information. Despite her efforts, the story was released to the public. When articles about the incident appeared they affected how Roseanne's mothering skills (a central component of the meanings attached to her image) were understood. Though there is little doubt that Roseanne did not plant this piece of publicity, there are many cases in which the line between publicity and promotion are blurred or erased—such as when IMP spread rumours of Florence Lawrence's death.

Roseanne's perceived poor mothering skills ('abandoning' her child, in the parlance of the tabloid press) relate to other media texts: specifically, her role as a mother in a popular television sitcom. Although it might seem initially that, in this case, one element of the star's 'textuality' is conflicting with another, these two components actually fit together quite well. For the type of mother that Roseanne portrays in *Roseanne* is a sharp, sarcastic one who often makes disparaging remarks to her children. On television her maternal sarcasm is vitiated by her overarching ability to solve any domestic crisis and eventually provide each child with the nurturing he or she requires. The publicity about her as a bad mother does not contradict her on-screen role, although it does heighten one anti-nurturing component of it. Roseanne, as with all true stars, possesses an image constructed from interlocking media texts. Or, in other words, her polysemy is generated by the intertextuality of numerous media texts.

Intertextuality is a key component to understanding stars. According to Dyer, stars are separated from non-star actors by their presence in more than one area of the general media textuality. If an actor is only known for his or her character—as with many soap opera actors—then he or she has no intertextuality and is not truly a star. A star must appear in numerous texts, which play off one another. Thus, one could say that a star is defined by his or her intertextuality, by the ability to correlate various media texts.

The relationship of a star to the characters he or she plays is an interesting and complex one. Few viewers belive that the star actually is the character—even if they do bear the same name, as with Roseanne and her character Roseanne Conner—and yet characteristics of the character do align with characteristics of the star's image, and vice versa. Once a star is well established, the characters that he or she plays may fit the star image in one of three ways, according to Dyer (1979: 142–9):

1. selective use;
2. perfect fit;
3. problematic fit.

In the first instance, the character makes selective use of elements of a star's polysemy. During the 1940s, as Damico (1975) points out, Ingrid Bergman's polysemy contained seemingly contradictory sexual meanings. She was associated with a certain spiritual purity as well as a coarse sexuality. In her role as Joan of Arc (in *Joan of Arc*, 1948) her spirituality was 'selected' while her practically sordid earthiness was disregarded. Later, when her sexual liaison with Roberto Rossellini became public knowledge, other more sexually ambiguous elements of her polysemy were selected in roles such as Isabelle in Rossellini's *Viaggio in Italia* ('Voyage to Italy', Italy, 1953).

Dyer's perfect fit occurs when the character and the star's polysemy appear to be completely matched. It is almost as if the star has become the character. When Hugh Grant appeared in *Nine Months* (1995) he played Samuel Faulkner, an irresponsible playboy who was unable to commit to marriage. This fit closely with media texts describing his arrest with a prostitute just a few months previously. Indeed, in an odd juxtaposition of the fictional and the real, his police mug shot circulated in the media at the same time that previews for *Nine Months* were featuring a fictional mug shot. The sexual indiscretions of Grant the star perfectly fit the character of Grant in the film. The fit between Grant and Faulkner was often commented upon in various media texts and led to anecdotes such as this one, appearing in *People Online* (24 July 1995): 'Grant [as

Faulkner in *Nine Months*] is parked in his car with a sexy woman other than the woman with whom he shares his life. This hot number asks him if he would like to come up for coffee. He declines. "How about for sex, then?" she asks. At the screening I attended, an audience member yelled out, "I'll pay for it".' The implication that the *People* reporter is making is that viewers were finding humour in the blending of the behaviours and identities of the character and the star. Note also the use of Grant's, the actor's, name to refer to the *character's* conduct. Of course, it is common practice for popular magazines to refer to characters with the names of actors, but in this context *People*'s use of 'Grant' to refer to Faulkner further accentuates the perfect fit between star and character.

The problematic fit is the least common instance of character–star relations. In this case, the star is cast against his or her image. The role is the polar opposite of her or her image. One example is comedian Mary Tyler Moore's appearance in *Ordinary People* (1980). Her star image as a perky, upbeat, loving, and lovable woman had been firmly established through television roles in *The Dick Van Dyke Show* (1961–6) and *The Mary Tyler Moore Show* (1970–7), but in *Ordinary People* her character is a cold, remote mother of a troubled teenager. Very little of her star image was selected to construct that role. In Dyer's view, the problematic fit can have distinctive ideological significance as the star is called upon to reconcile social tensions. One could argue, for example, that the position of woman in the family was particularly unstable in 1980 in the United States after more than a decade of feminist activism, shifts in family economics that demanded more women working outside the home, and the landslide election of Ronald Reagan and the presumed endorsement of his conservative agenda. What better image to work through these tensions than a latter-day Mary Pickford, 'America's sweetheart' for the 1980s?

Dyer's use of semiotics contributes key elements to the study of stars, but it is not a systematic, global semiotics of the cinema. In fact, Dyer makes little use of the ground-breaking work of 1960s–1970s film semioticians such as Metz (1974a, b) and Heath (1981). Metz, Heath, and most conventional film semioticians have, in turn, been remarkably mute about the significance of the star. However, a few recent theorists associated with *Screen* and the British Film Institute have attempted to apply the rigour of semiotics to the study of stars. Thompson (1978) introduces the notion of the 'commutation test' to the study of performance. This concept is borrowed from early Barthes, and, although Thompson himself rejects commutation in a later article, we may still find it a useful method for contrasting stars' polysemies. In the commutation test, one alters one component of a text's signifiers and then examines what effect that change has on its signifieds. What if, for example, the character–performance signifiers created for the role of Scarlett O'Hara (*Gone with the Wind*, 1939) by Vivien Leigh had been generated by Bette Davis? Or what if Cary Grant, instead of Dustin Hoffmann, had played Ratso Rizzo (*Midnight Cowboy*, 1969)? The shift in meaning that these hypothetical recastings cause tells us something about the signifying power of those particular stars. This is particularly evident if the commutation test is grounded in actual recastings that can be compared and contrasted. A film and its remake provide such an opportunity. Although a remake frequently makes changes that are too broad for the commutation test, one can usually find individual scenes that are repeated verbatim and can be used to highlight the differences between two actors. For example, if you view the two versions of *Imitation of Life* (1934, 1959), you'll note sharp differences in the performance styles of Claudette Colbert and Lana Turner and you may draw conclusions about their star images based on those differences.

Another notable strain in the 1980s' *Screen*–BFI work is Barry King's (1985) 'cultural materialist' approach to performance and stardom. For King, the star text catalyses certain 'discursive resources' (meaning-generating phenomena) relevant to the cinema: 'the cultural economy of the human body as a sign, the economy of signification in film, and the economy of the labour market for actors' (King 1985: 27). Each of these 'economies' governs the production of meaning by star actors. King, significantly, does not limit himself to the discursive strategies of the film text, but also explores the influence of 'practical' matters (such as the availability of work for actors) upon the meanings associated with stardom.

Star studies: the current situation

Star studies is still in a rather embryonic state. It seems clear that the most productive approaches to stars are ones that will help us comprehend the economic significance, cultural meanings, and psychic pleasures associated with star images, but there is no one clear path to that goal. The ethnographic and ideological, semiotic, and psychoanalytic approaches to stars surveyed here are important attempts to rectify the decades of neglect that stardom has suffered. Until film studies comes to an understanding of the significance of stars and the star system it will have only a partial comprehension of the cinematic apparatus.

BIBLIOGRAPHY

Bordwell, David, Janet Staiger, and Kristin Thompson (1985), *The Classical Hollywood Cinema: Film Style and Mode of Production to 1960* (New York: Columbia University Press).

Britton, Andrew (1984/1991), *Katharine Hepburn: The Thirties and After* (Newcastle upon Tyne: Tyneside Cinema) excerpts in Gledhill (1991b).

*Butler, Jeremy G. (ed.). (1991), *Star Texts: Image and Performance Film and Television* (Detroit: Wayne State University Press).

Damico, James (1975/1991), 'Ingrid from Lorraine to Stromboli: Analyzing the Public's Perception of a Film Star', *Journal of Popular Film*, 4/1: 3–19; repr. in Butler (1991).

deCordova, Richard (1990), *Picture Personalities: The Emergence of the Star System in America* (Urbana: University of Illinois Press).

de Lauretis, Teresa (1987), *Technologies of Gender: Essays on Theory, Film and Fiction* (Bloomington: Indiana University Press).

Doane, Mary Ann (1987), *The Desire to Desire: The Woman's Film of the 1940s* (Bloomington: Indiana University Press).

Dyer, Richard (1977–8/1991), 'Four Films of Lana Turner', *Movie*, 25: 30–52; repr. in Butler (1991).

*—— (1979), *Stars* (London: British Film Institute).

—— (1986), *Heavenly Bodies* (New York: St Martin's Press).

Eckert, Charles, (1974/1985/1991) 'Shirley Temple and the House of Rockefeller', *Jump Cut*, 2: 1, 17–20; repr. in Butler (1991), Gledhill (1991b); and Peter Steven (ed.), *Jump Cut: Hollywood, Politics and Counter Cinema* (Toronto: Between the Lines).

Gledhill, Christine (1991a), 'Signs of Melodrama', in Christine Gledhill (ed.), *Stardom: Industry of Desire* (London: Routledge).

*—— (ed.) (1991b), *Stardom: Industry of Desire* (London: Routledge).

Hansen, Miriam (1986/1991), 'Pleasure, Ambivalence, Identification: Valentino and Female Spectatorship', *Cinema Journal*, 25/4: 6–32; repr. in Butler (1991) and Gledhill (1991b).

Haskell, Molly (1974), *From Reverence to Rape: The Treatment of Women in the Movies* (Chicago: University of Chicago Press).

Heath, Stephen (1981), *Questions of Cinema* (Bloomington: Indiana University Press).

King, Barry (1985/1991), 'Articulating Stardom', *Screen*, 26/5: 27–50; repr. in Butler (1991) and Gledhill (1991*b*).

Kuleshov, Lev (1974), *Kuleshov on Film*, ed. and trans. Ronald Levaco (Berkeley: University of California Press).

Metz, Christian (1974*a*), *Film Language: A Semiotics of the Cinema*, trans. Michael Taylor (New York: Oxford University Press).

—— (1974*b*), *Language and Cinema*, trans. Donna Jean Umiker-Sebeok (The Hague: Mouton).

Mulvey, Laura (1975/1989), 'Visual Pleasure and Narrative Cinema', *Screen*, 16/3: 6–18; repr. in *Visual and Other Pleasures* (Bloomington: Indiana University Press).

Stacey, Jackie (1994), *Star Gazing: Hollywood Cinema and Female Spectatorship* (London: Routledge).

Staiger, Janet (1983/1991), 'Seeing Stars', *The Velvet Light Trap*, 20: 10–14; repr. in Gledhill (1991*b*).

Thompson, John O. (1978/1991) 'Screen Acting and the Commutation Test', *Screen*, 19/2: 55–69; repr. in Gledhill (1991*b*).

10 Hollywood film and society

Douglas Kellner

Film emerged as one of the first mass-produced cultural forms of the twentieth century. Based on new technologies of mechanical reproduction that made possible simulations of the real and the production of fantasy worlds, film provided a new mode of culture that changed patterns of leisure activity and played an important role in social life. From the beginning, film in the United States was a mode of commercial activity controlled by entertainment industries that attempted to attract audiences to its products. Film production was accordingly organized on an industrial model and manufactured a mass-produced output aimed at capturing a secure audience share and thus realizing a substantial profit. As a commercial enterprise, American film developed as an entertainment industry, rather than as an educational instrument or art form (Horkheimer and Adorno 1972).

Film soon became the most popular and influential form of media culture in the United States (Sklar 1975; Jowett 1976). Indeed, for the first half of the twentieth century—from 1896 to the 1950s—movies were a central focus of leisure activity and deeply influenced how people talked, looked, and acted, becoming a major force of enculturation. The number of theatres grew from about 10,000 store-front nickelodeons with daily attendance of 4 to 5 million in 1910 to around 28,000 movie theatres by 1928 (May 1983). In the 1920s the average audience was between 25 and 30 million customers a week, while by the 1930s from 85 to 110 million people paid to go to the movies each week (Dieterle 1941). Consequently, films were a central form of entertainment and an extremely popular leisure activity.

Moreover, films became a major force of socialization, providing role models and instruction in dress and fashion, in courtship and love, and in marriage and career. Early films were produced largely for working-class, immigrant, and urban audiences and it was believed films could help to 'Americanize' immigrants and teach film audiences how to be good Americans (Ewen and Ewen 1982). Whereas some films from the silent and early sound era presented poverty and social struggle from progressive perspectives sympathetic to the poor and oppressed, many films focused on the rich and celebrated wealth and power, serving as advertisements for the consumer society and the ruling élites. Cecil B. de Mille's comedies and dramas of modern marriage, for example, can be seen as marriage and fashion models, and the romantic films of the 1920s can be read as 'manuals of desire, wishes, dreams' for those wanting to assimilate themselves to mainstream America (Ewen and Ewen 1982: 102). Consequently, films played an important socializing role by mobilizing desires into certain models. In particular, films helped socialize immigrant and working-class cultures into the emerging forms of the consumer society, teaching them how to behave properly and consume with style and abandon.

However, although films for the most part reflected mainstream American values, they also represented modern and urban social values, and as a result conservatives often attacked the alleged 'immorality' and 'subversiveness' of Hollywood films (Jowett 1976). Romantic dramas were attacked by the Legion of Decency for promoting promiscuity, while crime dramas were frequently criticized for fostering juvenile delinquency and crime. Due to pressure from civic groups and the threat of government regulation, a set of censorship boards was established with the co-operation of the film industry which produced a Production Code that was adopted by the film industry by the mid-1930s. Explicit limits were set on the length of allowable kisses and prescribed that no open-mouth kisses could be shown. No nudity or explicit sexuality was allowed, such things as prostitution and drugs could not be portrayed, criminals had to be punished, and religion and the church could not be criticized (the code is reproduced and discussed in Jowett 1976). The Production Code held sway until the 1960s (although it was challenged in the 1950s) and set firm ideological and social parameters to Hollywood films.

But the crucial determinants of the ideological functions of Hollywood film had to do with control of film production by major studios and the production of films primarily for profit. Since films had to attract large audiences, they needed to resonate to audiences'

dreams, fears, and social concerns, and thus inevitably reflected social mores, conflicts, and ideologies. Consequently, some of the first critical analyses of Hollywood film argued that films reflected American society, providing mirror images of its dreams, fears, and mode of life.

Film and society

The writings of Siegfried Kracauer provided one of the first systematic studies of how films articulate social content and was to influence the study of Hollywood. His book *From Caligari to Hitler* (1947) argues that German inter-war films reveal a fear of emerging chaos and disposition to submit to social authority. For Kracauer, German films thus reflect and foster anti-democratic and passive attitudes of the sort that paved the way for Nazism. While his assumption that 'inner' psychological tendencies and conflicts are projected onto the screen opened up a fruitful area of socio-cultural analysis, he frequently ignored the role of mechanisms of representation, such as displacement, inversion, and condensation in the construction of cinematic images and narratives. He posits film society analogies ('Their silent resignation foreshadows the passivity of many people under totalitarian rule'; 1947: 218) that deny the autonomous and contradictory character and effects of film discourse and the multiple ways that audiences process cinematic material.

Against this view, one could argue that the language of film does not find its exact analogue in social events, nor does film discourse exist as a parallel mirror to actual events. Rather, films take the raw material of social history and of social discourses and process them into products which are themselves historical events and social forces. Films, therefore, can provide information about the 'psychology' of an era and its tensions, conflicts, fears, and fantasies, but they do so not as a simple representation or mirroring of an extra-cinematic social reality. Rather, films refract social discourses and content into specifically cinematic forms which engage audiences in an active process of constructing meaning.

Sociological and psychological studies of Hollywood film proliferated in the United States in the post-Second World War era and developed a wide range of critiques of myth, ideology, and meaning in the American cinema. Parker Tyler's studies *The Hollywood Hallucination* (1944) and *Myth and Magic of the*

Movies (1947) applied Freudian and myth–symbol criticism to show how Walt Disney cartoons, romantic melodramas, and other popular films provided insights into social psychology and context, while providing myths suitable for contemporary audiences. In *Movies: A Psychological Study* (1950), Martha Wolfenstein and Nathan Leites applied psychoanalytical methods to film, decoding fears, dreams, and aspirations beneath the surface of 1940s Hollywood movies, arguing that '[t]he common day dreams of a culture are in part the sources, in part the products of its popular myths, stories, plays and films' (1950: 13). In her sociological study *Hollywood: The Dream Factory* (1950), Hortense Powdermaker studied an industry that manufactured dreams and fantasies, while Robert Warshow (*The Immediate Experience*, 1970) related classical Hollywood genres like the western and the gangster film to the social history and ideological concerns of US society.

> Films can provide information about the 'psychology' of an era and its tensions, conflicts, fears, and fantasies, but they do so not as a simple representation or mirroring of an extra-cinematic social reality.

Building on these traditions, Barbara Deming demonstrated in *Running away from Myself* (1969) how 1940s Hollywood films provided insights into the social psychology and reality of the period. Deming argued that '[i]t is not as mirrors reflect us but, rather, as our dreams do that movies most truly reveal the times' (1969: 1). She claimed that 1940s Hollywood films provided a collective dream portrait of its era and proposed deciphering 'the dream that all of us have been buying at the box office, to cut through to the real nature of the identification we have experienced there' (1969: 5–6). Her work anticipates later, more sophisticated and university-based film criticism of the post-1960s era by showing how films both reproduce dominant ideologies and also contain proto-deconstructive elements that cut across the grain of the ideology that the films promote. She also undertook a sort of gender reading of Hollywood film that would eventually become a key part of Hollywood film criticism.

Another tradition of film scholarship and criticism in the United States attempted to situate films historically and to describe the interactions between film and society in more overtly political terms. This tradition includes Lewis Jacob's pioneering history of Hollywood film (1939), John Howard Lawson's theoretical and critical works (1953, 1964), Ian Jarvie's sociological inquiries into the relation between film and society (1970, 1978), David M. White and Richard Averson's studies of the relation between film, history, and social comment in film (1972), and the social histories written by Robert Sklar (1975), Garth Jowett (1976), Will Wright (1977), Peter Biskind (1983), and Thomas Schatz (1988). While this tradition has produced useful insights into the relationships between Hollywood film and US society in specific historical eras, it has also tended to neglect the ways in which specific films or genres work to construct meaning and the ways in which audiences themselves interact with film.

More theoretical approaches to Hollywood emerged in the 1960s, including the ideological analyses of *Cahiers du cinéma* and the extremely influential work associated with *Screen* which translated many key *Cahiers* and other works of French film theory (see Metz 1974; Heath 1981). The *Cahiers* group moved from seeing film as the product of creative auteurs, or authors, to focus on the ideological and political content of film and how it transcoded dominant ideologies (see Crofts on auteurism, Part 2, Chapter 7). At the same time, French film theory and *Screen* focused on the specific cinematic mechanisms which helped produce meaning.

During this same period of ferment in film studies during the 1960s and 1970s, the Birmingham Centre for Contemporary Cultural Studies was discovering that gender, race, and subculture were also an important element of analysing the relationships between culture, ideology, and society. Encouraged by feminism to recognize the centrality of gender, it was argued that the construction of dominant ideologies of masculinity and femininity were a central aspect of Hollywood film (Kuhn 1982; Kaplan 1983). Studies of the ways in which Hollywood films constructed race, ethnicity, and sexuality also became a key aspect of film studies, and various post-structuralist-influenced theories studied the role of film and media culture in the social construction of ideologies and identities.

As the theory wars of the past two decades have proliferated, a tremendous range of new theories have in turn been applied to film. Consequently, structuralism and post-structuralism, psychoanalysis, deconstruction, feminism, postmodernism, and a wealth of other theoretical approaches have generated an often bewildering diversity of approaches to theorizing film which join and add complexity to previous critical stances such as genre theory, auteur theory, and historical–sociological approaches. My own take on the cacophony of contemporary approaches to film is that it is not a question of either/or and that a variety of approaches can be deployed to engage the relations of film to society. Consequently, in the following section I will discuss the genre approach to analysing the intersection of film and society, while in the concluding section I will note the use of auteur criticism and socio-ideological approaches to explain developments in contemporary Hollywood film. These approaches can be combined, I would argue, with the newer theoretical approaches to provide fuller and richer thematizations of the relations of Hollywood film to US society. Thus, analysing the connections between film and society requires a multidimensional film criticism that situates its object within the context of the social milieu within which it is produced and received (Kellner 1995).

Hollywood genres

Although much of the best European art film can be interpreted as a result of the creative vision and talent of individual directors, Hollywood film from the beginning was deeply influenced by the dominant genres in its studio system. The Hollywood mode of cinematic production formed an integrated system whose major studios not only controlled film production, but also distribution. This ensured a guaranteed exhibition site for Hollywood product. The system first emerged in the teens, took its distinctive shape in the 1920s, reached maturity in the 1940s, and began to disintegrate in the 1950s owing to antitrust legislation which caused the studios to divest themselves of their distribution and exhibition channels, and also to competition from other media of entertainment such as television (see Balio 1976; Schatz 1981, 1988; Gomery, Chapter 3).

Since the main Hollywood studios repeatedly reproduced the types of film that they thought were the most popular, Hollywood cinema became primarily a genre cinema in which popular formulas are repeated in cycles of genres that in turn deal with central societal

conflicts, problems, and concerns of its audiences (see Ryall, Chapter 8). The western, for example, deals with conflicts between civilization and threats to civilization, whereas the gangster film deals with threats to law, order, and social stability within an already established urban society. Melodramas, social comedies, and musicals deal with conflicts and problems within domestic arenas like the family and romance, whereas war films and adventure genres generally deal with conflicts in the public sphere outside the private realm.

In order to resonate to audience fears, fantasies, and experiences, the Hollywood genres had to deal with the central conflicts and problems in US society, and had to offer soothing resolutions, assuring its audiences that all problems could be solved within existing institutions. Western films, for example, assured their audiences that 'civilization' could be maintained in the face of threats from criminals, outsiders, and villains of various sorts, and celebrated individualism, white male authority figures, and violence as a legitimate way of resolving conflicts. In the westerns' mythologized version of American history, it was glossed over that the 'villains' in many westerns were the land's original inhabitants who had their property stolen by the white settlers, presented as being forces of civilization. This in turn generated ideologies of racism and imperialism whereby the 'enemies' of civilization (Indians, Mexicans, villains) were portrayed negatively, thus legitimizing the 'settlement' of the west by (white-male-dominated) forces of 'civilization'. In addition, women were stereotyped as either whores or submissive representatives of the domestic order, thus reproducing patriarchical ideologies.

Gangster films appealed to people's fear of crime and fascination with criminals; the classical Hollywood gangster films inculcated the message that 'crime does not pay' and showed the police and legal system able to contain crime and to deal with criminals. But gangster films also explored cultural conflicts and contradictions central to American capitalism. Gangsters are, in fact, prototypical capitalists who will do anything to make a buck and thus are allegorical stand-ins for capitalist energy and will. Gangster films explore the tensions within American life between making money and morality, between self-interest and legality, and between private and public interests. The gangsters are fantasy characters who act out secret audience desires to get ahead no matter what, although it is still not clear if their repeated punishment (mandated by the Production

A celebration of maternal sacrifice? Barbara Stanwyck, *Stella Dallas* (1937)

Code) actually helped prevent crime through drama-tizing what would happen if one broke the rules of the game and stepped outside the law, or promoted crime through making the gangsters—often played by pop-ular figures like James Cagney or Humphrey Bogart—extremely dynamic, attractive, and vital figures.

Melodramas, social comedies, and musicals in turn legitimized male-dominated romance, marriage, family, and moral rectitude as the proper road to hap-piness and well-being. Musicals followed formulas of boy meets girl, boy loses girl, and boy gets girl to celebrate the desirability of male-dominated romance. Melodramas dramatized what would happen to way-ward women or wilful men who failed to conform to dominant gender roles. They celebrated hard-working mothers who sacrificed their own happiness for their children, thus projecting the proper role for women (as, for example, in *Imitation of Life* (1934/1959), *Stella Dallas* (1937), *Mildred Pierce* (1945), and others), and intimated that life's greatest happiness derived from marriage and family. And social comedies, too, cele-brated marriage and family as the proper goals for men and women (Cavell 1982). Indeed, David Bordwell claims that in his random selection of 100 typical Hollywood movies, 95 made romance at least one important line of action while, in 85, heterosexual romantic love was the major focus (Bordwell *et al.* 1985: 16).

Hollywood genre films thus tended to promote the American dream and dominant American myths and ideologies. The Hollywood genres taught that money and success were important values; that heterosexual romance, marriage, and family were the proper social forms; that the state, police, and legal system were legitimate sources of power and authority; that violence was justified to destroy any threats to the system; and that American values and institutions were basically sound, benevolent, and beneficial to society as a whole. In this way, Hollywood film, supported by other forms of media culture, helped establish a certain hegemony or cultural dominance of existing institutions and values to the exclusion of others. As Raymond Williams has argued,

in any society, in any particular period, there is a central system of practices, meanings and values, which we can properly call dominant and effective . . . what I have in mind is the central, effective and dominant system of meanings and values, which are not merely abstract but which are organized and lived. That is why hegemony is not to be understood at the level of mere opinion or mere manipulation. It is a whole body of practices and expectations; our assignments of energy, our ordinary understanding of the nature of man and of his world. It is a set of meanings and values which as they are experienced as practices appear as reciprocally confirming. (Williams 1983: 8–9)

Hollywood film is thus implicitly 'political' in the way it tends to support dominant American values and institutions. The more explicitly political functions of Hollywood cinema generally emerge in times of social crisis.

During both world wars war films and other genres advocated patriotism and presented the 'enemy' in stereotypical terms. During the Cold War period Hollywood produced a genre cycle of anti-communist films that depicted the threat to democracy and the 'American way of life' by the 'communist conspiracy'. Whereas during the Second World War Russians were presented positively as US allies against fascism, from the late 1940s on through *Rambo* (1985) communists are generally presented as the incarnation of evil.

> Genre films could be used to contest ideological norms as well as reproduce them, and to provide ideology critique as well as legitimization.

Yet the Hollywood system was flexible enough to allow individual cinematic statements and social critique within the genre system. Hollywood films prized difference and variation within accepted boundaries and left a limited range open for artistic expression and social commentary. As a result, it is not certain that the genre films always resolved the social contradictions portrayed or successfully served as ideological advertisements for existing social institutions, discourses, and practices. As previously noted, the crime dramas often made the criminal's transgressions of societal norms more appealing and attractive than their punishment, and likewise women's transgressions of bourgeois norms in the melodrama often put in question established patriarchal institutions. The western could also be used to portray the victims of the conquest of the frontier sympathetically and could be used to attack the crimes and barbarism of the 'civilizing' forces. Genre films could thus be used to contest ideological norms as well as reproduce them, and to provide ideology critique as well as legitimization.

Hollywood today and into the future

During the 1950s the studio system, which had produced genre cycles as the mode of production of Hollywood film, began to break up, and the genre system was challenged, opening the way to new types of film. The result was a very fertile period of production in the 1960s, with film becoming more varied, diverse, and socially critical than in previous eras. The rise of new directors like Stanley Kubrick, Arthur Penn, and Robert Altman who had distinctive artistic visions and styles seemed to give credence to the notion of a 'New Hollywood' and provided a boost to auteur criticism that focused on the cinematic style and form of key directors and films (see Kramer, Chapter 6). However, a focus simply on the new freedoms granted to 'auteurs' is too one-sided; one also needs insight into the complex interaction of film, the production system, and more general social discourses and social struggles (Kellner and Ryan 1988).

It was widely perceived in the 1960s, for example, that youth constituted a major audience for Hollywood film and so more youth-oriented films and directors emerged, creating new cycles of films which cinematically inscribed the discourses of the New Left student movements, as well as the feminist, black-power, sexual liberationist, and counter-cultural movements, producing a new type of socially critical Hollywood film. These films transcoded (i.e. translated) representations, discourses, and myths of 1960s culture into specifically cinematic terms, as when *Easy Rider* (1969) transcodes the images, practices, and discourses of the 1960s counterculture into a cinematic text. Popular films intervened in the political struggles of the day, as when 1960s films advanced the agenda of the New Left and the counter-culture. Films of the 'New Hollywood' (such as *Bonnie and Clyde*, 1967, *Medium Cool*, 1969, and *Easy Rider*, 1969), however, were contested by a resurgence of right-wing films during the same era (e.g. *Dirty Harry*, 1971, *The French Connection*, 1971, and John Wayne films), leading many to conclude that Hollywood film, like US society, should be seen as a contested terrain and that films could be interpreted as a struggle of representation over how to construct a social world and everyday life.

In 1970s films, intense battles between liberals and conservatives were evident throughout the decade in Hollywood film, with more radical voices—of the sort that occasionally were heard in the late 1960s and early 1970s—becoming increasingly marginalized. As the 1970s progressed, conservative films became more popular (e.g. *Rocky*, 1976, *Star Wars*, 1977, *Close Encounters of the Third Kind*, 1977, *Superman*, 1978, and so on), indicating that conservative sentiments were growing in the public and that Hollywood was nurturing these political currents. This was linked to the growth of the 'blockbuster' syndrome begun by *Jaws* in 1975. Henceforth, 'high-concept' films that could be clearly described and marketed became a major focus of the Hollywood film industry, which sought blockbuster hits that would turn over a high profit (Wyatt 1994).

> Hollywood film, like US society, should be seen as a contested terrain and films could be interpreted as a struggle of representation over how to construct a social world and everyday life.

Indeed, during the 1970s even liberal films ultimately helped advance the conservative cause. A cycle of liberal political conspiracy films (e.g. *The Parallax View*, 1974, *All the President's Men*, 1976, *The Domino Principle*, 1977, *Winter Kills*, 1979, and so on) vilified the state and thus played into the hands of the conservative Reaganite argument that government was the source of much existing evil. And even the most socially critical films (such as the Jane Fonda films, *Network*, 1976, and other Sidney Lumet films) posited

individual solutions to social problems, thus reinforcing the conservative appeal to individualism and the attack on statism. Consequently, reading Hollywood films of the decade politically allowed one to anticipate the coming of Reagan and the New Right to power by demonstrating that conservative yearnings were ever more popular within the culture and that film and popular culture were helping to form an ideological matrix more hospitable to Reagan and conservatives than to embattled liberals (Kellner and Ryan 1988).

However, it is also worth noting that even seemingly conservative film genres such as the horror film, or seemingly anti-gay films like *Cruising* (1980), could contain critical moments, problematicizing hegemonic ideologies and putting in question dominant ideologies like the family (Wood 1986). Robin Wood argues that the 'incoherent text' is a dominant cinematic mode of the 1970s, full of ideological contradictions and conflicts that reproduce existing social confusion and turmoil. Thus, film, like society, was very much a contested terrain, with the future of society and culture up for grabs.

With the election of Reagan in 1980, the conservative wave of films continued throughout the decade, with the blockbuster syndrome remaining the predominant trend. Gender struggles were particularly intense with a return to the 'hard-body' masculine hero of an earlier era, replacing the more feminized male heroes of the late 1960s and early 1970s (Jeffords 1994). As part of the backlash against feminism, there was also a cycle of films that villainized independent women, showing single career women without families being driven into pathological behaviour. (*Fatal Attraction*, 1987, *Basic Instinct*, 1992, *The Hand that Rocks the Cradle*, 1992, and so on). On the other hand, conservative ideologies were contested by liberal and radical films like *Missing* (1982), *Reds* (1981), *Salvador* (1986), *Platoon* (1986), and other Oliver Stone films, as well as a wealth of films by independent filmmakers like John Sayles and Spike Lee. A cycle of gay and lesbian films expanded the representations of sexuality, and many films began to provide more complex, varied, and progressive representations of gender and ethnicity.

At the same time, a proliferation of new critical strategies emerged, including the multicultural approach of cultural studies. There was an especially intense focus on audience research, on how audiences produced meanings, on how films mobilized pleasure and influenced audiences, and on how audiences decoded and used the materials of media culture. Consequently, a wide range of positions appeared on the relationship between film, media culture, and its audiences (see the discussion in Staiger, 1991).

During the past decade globalization has made Hollywood film an ever more familiar and popular artefact throughout the world. Whereas Hollywood films have dominated the world market for decades, it is even more the case today with American global corporations playing an important role in distributing its products throughout the world. To some extent globalization equals Americanization, and Hollywood film is an effective arm of media culture to sell the 'American way of life' (see Cvetovich and Kellner 1997). However, the relationships between Hollywood film, US society, and the entire world are complex and require a multi-perspectival approach that dissects the political economy of the film industry and the production of film; provides critical and analytical readings of cinematic texts; and studies how audiences appropriate and use film and other cultural artefacts (see Miller, Chapter 12).

Finally, we are currently undergoing one of the most dramatic technological revolutions of all time with new entertainment and information technologies emerging, accompanied by unprecedented mergers of the entertainment and information industries (Wasko 1994). These new syntheses are producing novel forms of visual and multi-media culture in which it is anticipated that film will appear in seductive new virtual and interactive forms, accessible through computer, satellite, and other new technologies. There is feverish speculation that the Internet and its assorted technologies will create a new entertainment and information environment, and currently the major corporations and players are envisaging what sort of product and delivery system will be most viable and profitable for films and other entertainment of the future. Thus, one imagines that the relationships between film and society will continue to be highly significant as we approach a new century and perhaps a new era that will supply novel forms of film and new perspectives on the film culture of the past.

BIBLIOGRAPHY

Balio, Tino (ed.) (1976), *The American Film Industry* (Madison: University of Wisconsin Press).

Biskind, Peter (1983), *Seeing is Believing: How Hollywood Movies Taught us to Stop Worrying and Love the 50s* (New York: Pantheon).

Bordwell, David, Janet Staiger, and **Kristin Thompson** (1985), *The Classical Hollywood Cinema* (New York: Columbia University Press).

Cavell, Stanley (1982), *Pursuits of Happiness* (Cambridge, Mass.: Harvard University Press).

Cvetovich, Ann, and **Douglas Kellner** (1997), *Articulating the Global and the Local: Globalization and Cultural Studies* (Boulder, Colo.: Westview).

Deming, Barbara (1969), *Running away from Myself* (New York: Grossman).

Dieterle, William (1941), 'Hollywood and the European Crisis', *Studies in Philosophy and Social Science*, 9: 96–103.

Ewen, Stuart, and **Elizabeth Ewen** (1982), *Channels of Desire* (New York: McGraw-Hill).

Heath, Stephen (1981), *Questions of Cinema* (Bloomington: Indiana University Press).

Horkheimer, Max, and **T. W. Adorno** (1972), *Dialectic of Enlightenment* (New York: Seabury).

Jacobs, Lewis (1939), *The Rise of the American Film* (New York: Harcourt, Brace).

Jarvie, I. C. (1970), *Toward a Sociology of the Cinema* (London: Routledge & Kegan Paul).

—— (1978), *Movies as Social Criticism* (Metuchen, NJ: Scarecrow Press).

Jeffords, Susan (1994), *Hard Bodies* (New Brunswick, NJ: Rutgers University Press).

Jowett, Garth (1976), *Film: The Democratic Art* (New York: William Morrow).

Kaplan, E. Ann (1983), *Women and Film* (New York: Methuen).

Kellner, Douglas (1995), *Media Culture* (New York: Routledge).

*—— and **Michael Ryan** (1988), *Camera Politica: The Politics and Ideology of Hollywood Film* (Bloomington: University of Indian Press).

Kracauer, Siegfried (1974), *From Caligari to Hitler* (Princeton: Princeton University Press).

Kuhn, Annette (1982), *Women's Pictures* (London: Routledge & Kegan Paul).

Lawson, John Howard (1953), *Film in the Battle of Ideas* (New York: Mainstream).

—— (1964), *Film: The Creative Process* (New York: Hill & Wang).

May, Lary (1983), *Screening out the Past* (Chicago: University of Chicago Press).

Metz, Christian (1974), *Language and Cinema* (The Hague: Mouton).

Powdermaker, Hortense (1950), *Hollywood: The Dream Factory* (Boston: Little, Brown).

Schatz, Thomas (1981), *Hollywood Genres* (Philadelphia: Temple University Press).

Schatz, Thomas (1988), *The Genius of the System* (New York: Pantheon).

Sklar, Robert (1975), *Movie-Made America: A Social History of American Film* (New York: Random House).

Staiger, Janet (1991), *Interpreting Films: Studies in the Historical Reception of American Cinema* (Princeton: Princeton University Press).

Tyler, Parker (1944), *The Hollywood Hallucination* (New York: Simon & Schuster).

—— (1947), *Myth and Magic of the Movies* (New York: Simon & Schuster).

Warshow, Robert (1970), *The Immediate Experience* (New York: Atheneum).

Wasko, Janet (1994), *Hollywood in the Information Age* (Austin: University of Texas Press).

White, David M., and **Richard Averson** (1972), *The Celluloid Weapon: Social Comment in the American Film* (Boston: Beacon Press).

Williams, Raymond (1973), 'Base and Superstructure in Marxist Cultural Theory', *New Left Review*, 82: 6–33.

Wolfenstein, Martha, and **Nathan Leites** (1950), *Movies: A Psychological Study* (Glencoe, Ill.: Free Press).

Wood, Robin (1986), *Hollywood from Vietnam to Reagan* (New York: Columbia University Press).

*Wright, Will (1977), *Six-Guns and Society: A Structural Study of the Western* (Berkeley: University of California Press).

Wyatt, Justin (1994), *High Concept: Movies and Marketing in Hollywood* (Austin: University of Texas Press).

Hollywood and ideology

Robert B. Ray from Robert B. Ray, *A Certain Tendency of the Hollywood Cinema, 1930–1980*
(Princeton: Princeton University Press, 1985).

My work initially proceeded from a naïve reflection theory that sought to explain the evolution of the popular American cinema in terms of the movies' response to changing historical conditions. Eventually I realized that the movies not only reflected but also excluded the world, and that I needed an approach that would account for both a reflection more complicated than I had originally granted and an exclusion more systematic than I had reckoned on. In short, I needed theories of overdetermination and transformation. I found them in three schools of thought that have converged in recent film scholarship: Marxism (especially Althusser's discussions of ideology); myth study (especially Lévi-Strauss's notion that myths are transformations of basic dilemmas or contradictions that in reality cannot be solved); and psychoanalysis (especially Freud's dream work and its notions of condensation and displacement).

Each of these schools entails a particular assumption about film. For Marxism, movies are ideological formations, screened and shaped by political censorship. For myth study, movies are myths whose individual shapes arise from the 'rules of transformation'. For psychoanalysis, movies are dreams, screened and reshaped by a culture's collective psychic censorship.

The merger of these three methodologies (especially in *Screen* and the *Cahiers du cinéma*) derives from their two basic similarities: all three are theories of both overdeterminism and transformation. Althusserian Marxism proposes that any phenomenon at any level of society results from multiple determinations (economic, cultural, political, personal, traditional, aesthetic). Lévi-Strauss suggests that each version of a myth results from those multiple determinations that have shaped the rules of transformation—that flexibility which enables a single cultural anxiety to assume different shapes in response to an audience's changing needs. Freud refers to dream images as condensations and displacements resulting from multiple dream thoughts.

All three methodologies attempt to define the rules of transformation or censorship, the system that enables a message to cross a boundary and enter another domain. Thus, analysis in all three cases becomes an attempt to trace the path of that message back to its previous site. Marxism wants to discover the 'cause' of a culture's particular way of representing material conditions (i.e. its ideology)—in the case of Hollywood movies, for example, the material origins of melodrama. Lévi-Strauss asks why a body of myths has

appeal for a given culture: what dilemma does it attempt to solve? Freud wants to locate the repressed anxiety or wish behind the overdetermined dream images. Thus, according to these theories, *Casablanca* (1942), for example, becomes, as ideology, a representation of an unsolvable dilemma—the conflicting appeals of intervention and isolationism; as myth, an attempt to resolve that dilemma; as dream, a displaced condensation of the anxiety generated by that contradiction.

Since the beginning, however, film theory's particular preference for the psychoanalytic accounting (the movie-as-dream) has resulted in an impasse. Certainly, Freud's condensation and displacement (and his insistence on the dream's need for concrete representation) offered rules by which latent dream thoughts (wishes, anxieties) get transformed into dream images. But the associative chains by which Freud retraced these images to their unconscious sources were utterly private, available only to the particular dreamer (and, after enormous effort, to Freud himself). Dream images, in other words, are at best *subjective* correlatives whose import typically remains hidden from even the dreamer.

To the extent that movies do work like dreams, Hollywood's challenge lay in developing rules of condensation and displacement that would work for the audience as a whole, or, to put it another way, that would provide immediately (albeit unconsciously) recognizable objective (?) correlatives for the common wishes and fears of the mass audience. Hollywood's enormous commercial success proves that it met this challenge. It did so by becoming intuitively Lévi-Straussian: the American film industry discovered and used the existing body of mythic oppositions provided it by the local culture. In effect, the great Hollywood tsars became naïve, prodigious anthropologists.

The determinedly commercial nature of the American movie business, however, and its financial servitude to the politically powerful eastern banks, insured that Hollywood's elaborations of American mythology would not proceed according to the mathematically indifferent rules of transformation posited by Lévi-Strauss, but rather according to the ideologically censoring standards posited by Marx in a famous passage:

The ideas of the ruling class are in every epoch the ruling ideas, i.e. the class which is the ruling *material* force of society, is at the same time its ruling *intellectual* force. The class which has the means of material production at its disposal has control at the

Hollywood and ideology continued

same time over the means of mental production, so that thereby, generally speaking, the ideas of those who lack the means of mental production are subject to it.

Thus, each variation of what I will call the thematic paradigm (in westerns, musicals, gangster movies, etc.) could pose issues only in terms allowed by the prevailing ideology—or could refuse to acknowledge that ideological disposition only at its own commercial risk. *Casablanca*, as I will argue, could deal with the intervention–isolationism opposition only by displacing it into the ideologically favoured realm of melodrama, where (since such displacements were traditional to American culture) ample mythic types, images, and stories were available.

Have dissident variations (thematic or stylistic) *any* chance of disrupting or subverting a movie's intended ideological effect? This question seems to me the most interesting thing we can ask about the American cinema. Unfortunately, we still have to ask it on a case-by-case basis. I have not been able to develop a general theory that would account in the

abstract for a dissident thematic variation's ability to outfight the context that seeks to subdue it. I do not want to fall back on a lame imitation of Potter Stewart's famous 'I-know-it-when-I-see-it' definition of obscenity, but for the present, I can only suggest the value of a thesis proposed by Charles Eckert in an article that deserves to be far more famous than it is: writing about *Marked Woman* (1937), Eckert argues that truly effective challenges to Hollywood's prevailing ideology surface in those moments within a movie when the emotional quotient is simply excessive in terms of the narrative's needs—emotion, in other words, that remains inadequately motivated.

Significantly, some of the most abidingly interesting American movies display precisely these moments of excess. These same films have proved among the most popular ever made in this country, a fact suggesting that the mass audience in this country likes to live dangerously, likes to see the most privileged elements of its ideology sorely challenged, if not defeated.

11

Film policy: Hollywood and beyond

Albert Moran

Policy is a series of practices engaged in by an agency—whether government, private, or commercial—to achieve a particular set of outcomes. But although commercial agencies may engage in various market strategies such as restricted competition with rivals and price-fixing, they do not have the legislative force that the state can confer on its policy measures. The study of policy must therefore inevitably focus on the role of state apparatuses, even if it also attends to the capacity of private capitalist interests to influence the state in the establishment and maintenance of these mechanisms. The agencies, whether state or private, will follow different policy strategies, such as legislation, regulation, and financial assistance, as well as more general commercial strategies. Their goals may be short-term and specific as well as more long-term and general, and policy also may be at lower or higher level—a single measure or tactic, or an inter-linked group of strategies that merit the name 'policy'. Policy always exists in a complex field affected by factors such as constitutional and legislative arrangements, general economic conditions, the prevailing culture, social awareness, and technological capacities, as well as such human agencies as politicians, business entrepreneurs, white- and blue-collar labour, bureaucrats, and cultural and social workers. International forces have also become increasingly important. Given this variety of elements and players, policy may fall short of realizing its announced objectives, gener-

ating other, less anticipated results, and consequently requiring adjustment or major overhaul.

Film policy consists of measures that apply not only to the feature film exhibited in the hard-top cinema but also to several other forms of audiovisual product including television and video. It also applies across a series of areas and institutions including production, distribution, and exhibition, film education, film as visual art, and censorship. Film policy study may involve the investigation of any one or more of these areas. It may be prompted by an immediate practical need to analyse the effectiveness of existing policies, or it may be more removed from the various objects of its investigation and more concerned with gaining broader understanding of the historical and social context that produced particular policies. And film policy study will be undertaken by a range of practitioners, from those sharing pragmatic interests in immediate practical results, such as government officials and private consultants, to more dispassionate analysts, such as critical researchers and historians. Equally, the two groups can overlap.

These background remarks are necessary, not least because many areas of film study can legitimately be regarded as studies of film policy that are frequently denied that kind of recognition. For example, although there are individual entries under topics such as censorship and national cinemas in Richard MacCann and Edward Perry's *New Critical Film Index*, a summational bibliographical source for film scholarship and research published in 1972, there is no entry under the term 'film policy study'. Similarly, many actual studies of film policy pass without name in scholarly accounts of national cinema developments; for example, in the inaugural study of cinema in Ireland by Kevin Rockett, Luke Gibbons, and John Hill (1988), part 1 of the book, entitled 'History, Politics and Irish Cinema', by Rockett, traces the development of film production in Ireland and is in fact a sustained interrogation of the course of the film policies of the Irish state. In other words, although film policy is everywhere studied in its detail and in its operations, as well as in a broader, more historical context, and as such could be said to constitute a sizeable literature, the paradox remains that the field is little recognized. Given this, the aim here is to indicate rather than provide an exhaustive survey of the range of studies in the area of film scholarship that can be bracketed under the term 'policy'.

> **Although film policy is everywhere studied in its detail and in its operations, as well as in a broader, more historical context, and as such could be said to constitute a sizeable literature, the paradox remains that the field is little recognized.**

A good point of departure is the American cinema, for although it appears that Hollywood exists only as a private institution outside the apparatus of the state, this has not, in fact, been the case. The American cinema does not exist in a vacuum, either at the level of international relations or inside the United States itself. National cinemas throughout the rest of the world have long existed in the economic and cultural shadow cast by the American cinema, and state policies in relation to film implicitly address the American cinema as the 'other' of a national cinema. Nor has the American cinema existed autonomously within the United States. Although in private hands, Hollywood has been profoundly affected by legislation and regulation by municipal, state, and federal governments, by the activities of government departments and agencies, and by more general factors to do with the Constitution, labour relations, and moral legislation.

American cinema has also had to adopt policies in relation to other arenas, such as religion and politics, and these relationships, too, have attracted the attention of scholars. Given such an array of film policy areas, some of the more notable studies can be mentioned.

> **Although in private hands, Hollywood has been profoundly affected by legislation and regulation by municipal, state, and federal governments, by the activities of government departments and agencies, and by more general factors to do with the Constitution, labour relations, and moral legislation.**

US film policies

The Hollywood film companies established several mechanisms to control the film industry both in terms of its internal operations, such as controlling the costs of production, as well as in its external relationships with other American institutions. One key instrument was the establishment in 1922 of the Hays Office, which brought an important measure of self-regulation to the industry and which has been analysed both in an early study by Louis Nizer (1935) and more extensively by Raymond Moley (1945). Two other of the industry's own instruments for conferring general prestige on itself, as well as increasing the box-office appeal of individual films, are the Academy of Motion Picture Arts and Science, established in 1927, and, especially, the Oscar awards, whose development has been analysed by Emanuel Levy (1987). But these visible instruments are only the most external evidence of the oligopolistic nature of the motion picture industry. As antitrust action was initiated by the US Justice Department in the 1930s and 1940s, a series of studies analysed in detail the vertically integrated nature of the film industry and the practices pursued by the major studios in dominating it (Cassady 1956; Bertrand et al. 1941; Temporary National Economic Committee 1941; Huettig 1944).

If these studies are primarily concerned with distribution, the business policies of the industry in relation to film audiences have been given more attention elsewhere. Frank Ricketson's (1938) study of the management of film exhibition was an important codification of practices that obtained in film theatres across the country, and more recently the film historian Douglas Gomery (1975, 1978, 1979, 1981) has researched the history of changing exhibition policies and practices in the film industry. This research links with Gomery's earlier analysis (1975) of the coming of sound to the American film industry, a study that emphasized both the deliberate policy of technological innovation pursued by one of the major companies as well as the new policies relating to both production and exhibition that had to be adopted in the face of the innovation of sound. The coming of sound technology was one of the few occasions when oligopolistic arrangements among the film companies were broken. By the early 1930s this control was widely recognized, especially in government circles, and led to antitrust action. Scholars such as Michael Conant (1960), David Daly (1980), Gomery (1981), and, more recently, Asu Aksoy and Kevin Robins (1992) have investigated the distribution and exhibition policies adopted by the dominant groups following the success of this action.

Censorship is another aspect of film policy, and this too has been subjected to extensive analysis. Two important such studies by Ira Carmen and Richard Randall appeared in 1968 and both emphasized that censorship of film exhibition in the United States had been instigated by municipal and city authorities, with prohibitions and regulations being directed initially at exhibition venues and only later at movie content. However, the findings of these studies only echoed earlier work on film censorship such as that of Donald Young (1922). But, as is well known, the major film companies during the studio era also exercised their own form of censorship of film content in the form of a production code, and part of Moley's (1945) study of the Hays Office follows how the companies came to develop this production policy in the face of attack from moral pressure groups such as the Catholic church and as a safeguard against possible intervention in the film industry by the American government. However, if the company owners and executives were willing to accept the Hays Code, those further down the production line, such as producers, writers, and directors, often had a good deal of difficulty in producing films that would secure the seal of approval of the Office. Murray Schumach (1964) has collected a series of often hilarious case-studies of particular productions and the often complex and arcane accommodations

made to ensure films conformed to the letter of the law as far as this instrument of self-regulation was concerned.

In their internal relationships with their own production workers, the motion picture companies were perennially opposed to workers' rights, especially the right to unionize, and many bitter struggles ensued. The labour relations policies of the companies have been traced in detail in several studies, especially Ross (1945), Lovell and Carter (1955), and Jeter (1979). One particular aspect of the union relations between the motion picture companies and both their blue- and white-collar workers had to do with the policy of the blacklist that operated against suspected communists in the 1950s. This was a combined policy of the major and minor companies, another instance of joint action by groups that were in ostensible competition in the market-place. The standard study of this policy is Cogley (1956), but there have been several others, including a more full-length, historically informed book by the film star Robert Vaughan that began life as a Ph.D. dissertation (Vaughan 1972).

Finally we might briefly note some studies of various measures undertaken by the industry in relation to three particular institutions of American society: the Catholic church, the banking sector, and the federal courts. Moley's (1945) study of the pressures for censorship exerted by the Catholic church especially in the 1920s and 1930s and Martin Quigley's (1937) monograph demonstrate how one particular pressure group could marshal a case for censorship and articulate what it saw as appropriate policies by the industry. In turn, Paul Facey (1974) helps put Quigley's polemic in context. Secondly, although there had been much earlier work on the financing of the motion picture, both Edward Buscombe's (1975) study of Columbia's film production financing and, especially, Janet Wasko's (1982) analysis of Hollywood's relationship with American banks have introduced an important new area for consideration under the broad topic of film policy. Finally, the federal courts have been an important arena in which the US state has been involved in setting various aspects of film policy in place, and a full study of this subject would fill many volumes. Two crucial areas in which the courts reached important legal decisions for the industry can be mentioned. The first was a series of decisions concerning patents and copyright in the very early years of the twentieth century, decisions that were crucial to enabling the early cinema to be reorganized as a modern industry (Allen 1980; Bordwell *et al.*

1985). The second set of decisions which were equally profound in their effect were the antitrust actions and court decisions which ultimately resulted in the abandonment of involvement in production and exhibition by the film companies (Donovan and McAllister 1933; Conant 1960).

International film policies

If we turn to nation-states outside the United States, we are struck by the fact that, with the possible exception of national cinemas in India and China, by 1939 all other national cinemas had become directly dependent on state funding. This has led to a large body of studies of film policy in specific national settings.

In the case of Canada, America's closest neighbour, the study of film policy has assumed particular importance. The Canadian state has long been involved in the production and distribution of film through different film policy apparatuses—the Government Motion Picture Bureau, the National Film Board, the Canadian Film Development Corporation, and Telefilm Canada—and there is an impressive body of scholarship on the course of Canadian film policy. Studies by C. W. Gray (1973), Charles Backhouse (1973), David Jones (1980), Gary Evans (1984), and Peter Morris (1986, 1987) have done much to clarify not only the different policies concerning the production and circulation of documentary film but also the wider political and social context of these measures. Historical studies of Canadian cinema written in the past quarter-century, such as those by Pierre Berton (1975), Morris (1978), Manjunath Pendakur (1990), and Ted Magder (1993), have stressed the degree to which Canadian film policy has been contained within parameters set by the American film industry. The nationalist strain usually evident in these accounts of film policy has also been present in general collections on Canadian cinema such as those by Seth Feldman and Joyce Nelson (1977), Pierre Vronneau and Piers Handling (1980), Feldman (1984), Gene Walz (1986), and Douglas Fetherling (1988). Film policy has also been considered in the more general context of what has been called the Canadian culture industries by Susan Crean (1976), Dallas Smythe (1981), Paul Audley (1983), and Michael Dorland (1996). However, recent studies by Magder and Dorland have indicated a significant break with these nationalist accounts with analyses that are sensitive to recent debates in cultural studies and theories of state policy and power.

Of course, the operation, and therefore the study, of state film policy is by no means restricted to any one particular nation-state and further studies and bibliographies can be found in my collection of analyses of film policy (Moran 1996), which contains both national studies and studies of film policy at the regional and the international levels.

Although research on the international dimension of particular national film policies began as early as 1937 with the study by Donald Klingender and Stuart Legg of the economic impact of American film on the British market, itself a parallel to studies by the US Department of Commerce of the international market (Golden 1939), it was not until the end of the Second World War that research began on the international film industry (Bächlin 1945). However, Bächlin's pioneering study was available only in French and German. Another quarter-century passed before there was any English-language study of the international context of national film policies; Thomas Guback's (1969) analysis of the American film industry in Western Europe was the first. Adopting a comparative methodology, Guback analysed film policies instituted by national governments in Britain, France, Germany, and Italy in relation to policies pursued by the American film industry and the US State Department. The research started life as a thesis under the supervision of Dallas Smythe, the 'father' of political economy approaches to mass communications (Wasko et al. 1993). It was part of a wave that examined such areas as the overseas reach of American television and the cultural import of Disney comics and which used the concept of the 'national' in an unproblematic way in discussing the cultural and economic impact of US film and television programmes on national audiovisual systems. Guback's study was a major work of film policy research, whose continuing value lies in the detail and clarity of its analysis.

In 1985 Guback's work was joined by a complementary study by Kristin Thompson which analysed the policies pursued by the American film industry in the period from the turn of the century up to the mid-1930s that enabled it to dominate the international film business. One other major study in this tradition, by Armand Mattelart, Xavier Delacourt, and Michèle Mattelart, was published in France in 1983 and appeared in English in 1984. *International Image Markets* grew out of the report of a French government mission to explore the feasibility of a 'Latin audiovisual space' that would include several European and South

American countries. Like Guback's, the study is of most interest and continuing value in the details it produces about the international film and television industries in the 1980s. Conversely, it is at its weakest in its assumptions about the homogeneity of an audiovisual space, the latter being a modern label for 'national cinema' or 'national television' (Schlesinger 1987).

Summary

Film policy studies has a long lineage and features detailed scholarship and often passionate argument and advocacy. Although a cinema characterized by private ownership, Hollywood has long been aware of the domestic and international politics that underline its existence. National studies of film policy that focused on the key role played by Hollywood began in the 1930s while more dialectical studies of Hollywood and national cinemas date from the 1960s. Many of these studies are animated by cultural imperialist theory, although very recent accounts indicate new approaches based on notions of cultural pluralism rather than cultural nationalism.

BIBLIOGRAPHY

Aksoy, A., and K. Robins (1992), 'Hollywood for the Twenty-First Century: Global Competition for Critical Mass in Image Markets', Cambridge Journal of Economics, 16/1: 1–22.

Allen, Jeanne Thomas (1979), 'Copyright and Early Theatre: Vaudeville and Film Competition', Journal of the University Film Association, 31 (Spring), 5–11.

—— (1980), 'The Industrial Context of Film Technology: Standardisation and Patents', in Teresa de Laurentis and Stephen Heath (eds.), The Cinematic Apparatus (London: Macmillan).

Audley, Paul (1983), Canada's Cultural Industries: Broadcasting, Publishing, Records and Film (Toronto: James Lorimer).

Bächlin, P. (1945), Der Film als Wore (Basel: Burg).

Backhouse, Charles (1973), Canadian Government Motion Picture Bureau 1917–1940 (Ottawa: Canadian Film Institute).

Berton, Pierre (1975), Hollywood's Canada: The Americanization of our National Image (Toronto: McClelland & Stewart).

Bertrand, Daniel, W. Duane Evans, and E. L. Blanchard (1941), Investigation of Concentration of Economic Power, study for Temporary National Economic Committee.

Bordwell, David, Janet Staiger, and Kirstin Thompson (1985), The Classical Hollywood Cinema: Film Style and Mode of Production to 1960 (New York: Columbia University Press).

Buscombe, Edward (1975), 'Notes on Columbia Pictures Corporation 1926–1941', Screen, 16/3 (Autumn), 65–82.

Carmen, Ira H. (1968), Movies, Censorship and the Law (Ann Arbor: University of Michigan Press).

Cassady, Ralph, Jr. (1956), 'Impact of the Paramount Decision on Motion Picture Distribution and Price Making', Southern California Law Review, 32/4 (Summer), 325–90.

Cogley, John (1956), Report on Blacklisting, i: Movies (Santa Barbara, Calif.: Fund for the Republic).

Conant, Michael (1960), Anti-Trust in the Motion Picture Industry (Berkeley: University of California Press).

Crean, Susan (1976), Who's Afraid of Canadian Culture? (Toronto: General Publishing).

Daly, David A. (1980), A Comparison of Exhibition and Distribution Patterns in Three Recent Feature Motion Pictures (New York: Arno Press).

Donovan, William, and Breck P. McAllister (1933), 'Consent Decrees in the Enforcement of Federal Anti-Trust Laws: The Moving Picture Industry', Harvard Law Review, 46 (Apr.), 929–31.

Dorland, Michael (ed.) (1996), The Culture Industries in Canada (Toronto: James Lorimer).

Evans, Gary (1984), John Grierson and the National Film Board: The Politics of Wartime Propaganda (Toronto: University of Toronto Press).

Facey, Paul W. (1974), The Legion of Decency: A Sociological Analysis of the Emergence and Development of a Pressure Group (New York: Arno Press).

Feldman, Seth (ed.) (1984), Take Two: A Tribute to Film in Canada (Toronto: Irwin).

—— and Joyce Nelson (eds.) (1977), Canadian Film Reader (Toronto: Peter Martin).

Fetherling, D. (ed.) (1988), Documents in Canadian Film (Toronto: Broadview Press).

Golden, Nathan (1939), Review of Foreign Film Markets 1938 (Washington: US Dept. of Commerce).

Gomery, Douglas (1975), 'The Coming of Sound to the American Cinema: A History of the Transformation of an Industry', Ph.D. dissertation, University of Wisconsin.

—— (1978), 'The Picture Palace: Economic Sense or Hollywood Nonsense?', Quarterly Review of Film Studies 3/1 (Winter), 23–36.

—— (1979), 'The Movies Become Big Business: Public Theatres and the Chain Store Strategy', Cinema Journal, 18/2: 315–30.

—— (1981), 'The Economics of US Film Exhibition Policy and Practice', Cinetracts, 12 (Winter), 36–40.

Gray, C. W. (1973), Movies for the People: The Story of the National Film Board of Canada's Unique Distribution System (Montreal: National Film Board).

Guback, Thomas (1969), *The International Film Industry: Western Europe and America since 1945* (Bloomington: University of Indiana Press).

Huettig, Mae D. (1944), *Economic Control of the Motion Picture Industry* (Philadelphia: University of Pennsylvania Press).

Jeter, Ida (1979), 'The Collapse of the Federated Motion Picture Crafts: A Case Study of Class Collaboration', *Journal of the University Film Association*, 31 (Spring), 37–45.

Jones, David (1980), *Movies and Memoranda: An Interpretive History of the National Film Board of Canada* (Ottawa: Canadian Film Institute).

Klingender, D. F., and Stuart Legg (1937), *Money behind the Screen* (London: Lawrence & Wishart).

Levy, Emanuel (1987), *And the Winner Is: The History and Politics of the Oscar Awards* (New York: Unger).

Lovell, Hugh, and Tasile Carter (1955), *Collective Bargaining in the Motion Picture Industry: A Struggle for Stability* (Berkeley: University of California Institute of Industrial Relations).

MacCann, Richard, and Edward S. Perry (eds.) (1972), *The New Critical Film Index: A Bibliography of Articles in English 1930–1970* (New York: Dutton).

Magder, Ted (1993), *Canada's Hollywood: The Canadian State and Feature Films* (Toronto: University of Toronto Press).

Mattelart, A., C. X. Delcourt, and M. Mattelart (1984), *International Image Markets: In Search of an Alternative Perspective* (London: Comedia).

Moley, Raymond (1945), *The Hays Office* (New York: Bobbs-Merrill).

*Moran, Albert (ed.) (1996), *Film Policy: International, National and Regional Perspectives* (London: Routledge).

Morris, Peter (1986), 'Backwards to the Future: John Grierson's Film Policy for Canada', in Walz (1986).

—— (1987), 'Rethinking Grierson: The Ideology of John Grierson', in P. Vronneau *et al.* (eds.), *Dialogues* (Montreal: Mediatext).

—— (1978), *Embattled Shadows: A History of Canadian Cinema 1895–1936* (Kingston, Ont.: McGill-Queen's University Press).

Nizer, Louis (1935), *New Courts of Industry: Self-Regulation under the Motion Picture Code* (New York: Longacre Press).

Pendakur, Manjunath (1990), *Canadian Dreams and American Control: The Political Economy of the Canadian Film Industry* (Detroit: Wayne State University Press).

Quigley, Martin (1937/1971), *Decency in Motion Pictures* (New York: Macmillan; repr. New York: Jerome S. Ozer).

Randall, Richard S. (1968), *Censorship of the Movies: The Social and Political Control of a Mass Medium* (Madison: University of Wisconsin Press).

Ricketson, Frank H. (1938), *The Management of Motion Picture Theatres* (New York: McGraw-Hill).

Rocket, Kevin, Luke Gibbons, and John Hill (1988), *Cinema and Ireland* (London: Routledge).

Ross, Murray (1945), *Stars and Strikes: Unionization of Hollywood* (New York: Columbia University Press).

Schlesinger, Phillip (1987), 'On National Identity: Some Conceptions and Misconceptions Criticised', *Social Science Information*, 22/2: 219–64.

Schumach, Murray (1964), *The Face on the Cutting Room Floor* (New York: William Morrow).

Smythe, Dallas (1981), *Dependency Road: Communications, Capitalism, Consciousness and Canada* (Norwood, NJ: Ablex).

Temporary National Economic Committee (1941), *Motion Picture Industry: A Pattern of Control*, Monograph 43 (Washington: Government Printing Office).

Thompson, Kristin (1985), *Exporting Entertainment: America in the World Film Market 1907–1934* (London: British Film Institute).

Vaughan, Robert (1972), *Only Victims* (New York: G. P. Putnam's Sons).

Vronneau, Pierre, and Piers Handling (eds.) (1980), *Self Portrait* (Ottawa: Canadian Film Institute).

Walz, Gene (ed.) (1986), *Flashback: People and Institutions in Canadian Film History* (Montreal: Mediatext).

Wasko, Janet (1982), *Movies and Money: Financing the American Film Industry* (Norwood, NJ: Ablex).

—— Vincent Mosco, and Manjunath Pendakur (eds.) (1993), *Illuminating the Blindspot: Essays Honoring Dallas Smythe* (Norwood, NJ: Ablex).

Young, Donald R. (1922/1971), *Moving Pictures: A Study in Social Legislation* (Philadelphia: Westbrook; repr. New York: Jerome S. Ozer).

12

Hollywood and the world

Toby Miller

. . . When Saddam Hussein chose Frank Sinatra's globally recognized 'My Way' as the theme song for his 54th birthday party, it wasn't as a result of American imperialist pressure
(Michael Eisner)

. . . The Americans have colonised our subconscious
(Wim Wenders)

Hollywood history

We are all experts on American film. We have to be, since it comprises between 40 and 90 per cent of the movies shown in most parts of the world. The United States produced eighty-eight of the 100 top-grossing films in 1993, and in 1994 American cinema made more money overseas than at home for the first time (Rockwell 1994, H1). This is not to deny the importance of other screen cultures: people of colour are the majority filmmakers in the world, with much more diverse ideological projects and patterns of distribution than Hollywood (Shohat and Stam 1994: 27). But Los Angeles culture and New York commerce dominate screen entertainment around the globe, either directly or as an implied other, and the dramatic success of US film since the First World War has been a model for the export of North American music, television, advertising, the Internet, and sport. The spread of satellite television and the video cassette recorder,

combined with deregulation of national broadcasting, continues to increase the reach of audiovisual technology (Wasko 1994: 233). How did such dominance come about?

Economics has had difficulty theorizing the cinema. Unlike most forms of manufacturing, the production of film drama is dominated by a small number of large companies with limited, individually differentiated output. Most investments are complete failures, a pain that can only be borne by large firms. The absolute significance of story over cost for audiences goes against classical economics' standard assumptions about the role of price in balancing supply and demand and, because of a film's textual meaning, external factors play a crucial role in a film's economic performance.

Conventional economics explains Hollywood's historical success in terms of 'a flexible managerial culture and an open and innovative financial system' that has adapted to changing economic and social conditions. On this account, the silent era saw films made for the big American domestic market that also sold in other English-speaking countries. Because English was an international language, the coming of sound aided the process, whilst the diverse ethnic mix of the US population encouraged a more universal mode of storytelling than those of other cultures. The argument goes that these strengths have been built on since, under the guiding principle of free-enterprise competitiveness (Acheson and Maule 1994: 271–3). In contrast, a political economy approach would propose that this success has been a co-ordinated, if sometimes conflictual and chaotic, attempt by capital and the state to establish and maintain a position of market and ideological dominance in ways that find governments every bit as crucial as audiences and firms.

Indeed, the balance of textual trade was not always as we find it today: France sold a dozen films a week to the United States early in the century and in 1914 most movies and much movie-making technology in North America was imported, while Italy and France dominated exhibition in Latin America (Balio 1993: 32–3). But the Vitagraph Company was producing two negatives for every reel by 1907, one for European and one for domestic use (de Grazia 1989: 57). By 1909 North American companies could rely on the local market to recoup costs and were tailoring export prices to meet other markets (O'Regan 1992: 313). Between 1915 and 1916 US exports rose from 36 million feet of film to 159 million feet, while imports fell from 16 million feet before the First World War to 7 million by the mid-1920s (King 1990: 10, 22). As the feature film took off during those years, Hollywood began to sell to Asia and Latin America, almost wiping out Brazilian production, for example, by purchasing local distributors (Shohat and Stam 1994: 28). From 1919 overseas receipts were factored into Hollywood budgets, and in the 1920s Hollywood's leading export sites were Britain, Australia, Argentina, and Brazil (Armes 1987: 48). By the 1930s foreign sales provided between a third and a half of industry returns. When sound was standardized, non-English speakers were courted by the musical, and studios set up in different countries created foreign-language versions of domestic hits (Tunstall 1977: 91). The industry also achieved horizontal integration by linking the sale of radio and records to the musical film. In 1939 the Department of Commerce estimated that the United States supplied 65 per cent of the films exhibited world-wide (Harley 1940: 21).

Of course, some of this success was the result of textual appeal. In 1920s and 1930s Italy, for example, Hollywood projected fabulous modernity that appealed even to Mussolini. Beauty, youth, and wealth merged under the sign of fun. Local marketing played up the extraordinary pleasures of this world and its difference from traditional Italian life. At the same time, the local industry was held back by the growth of US-owned distribution, new government taxes, and a reliance on importing American technology (Hay 1987: 66–71).

But the two world wars complicate any notion of simple managerial sophistication or global consumer preferences explaining American dominance. The 1914–18 and 1939–45 conflicts left national production across Europe either shut down or at least slowed (Izod 1988: 61–3, 82, 118). A plenitude of unseen US 'inventory' waited to be unleashed (Italy was sent over 2,000 features in the four years from 1945), while the developing US shipping industry improved transport infrastructure. Hollywood's new Motion Picture Export Agency referred to itself as 'the little State Department' in the 1940s, so isomorphic were its methods and contents with US policy and ideology (Guback 1987: 92–3). This was also the era when the industry's self-regulating Production Code appended to its bizarre litany of sexual anxieties something requested by the 'other' State Department: selling the American way of life around the world (Schatz 1988: 160; Powdermaker 1950: 36). The compulsory dismantling of state film-making institutions among the Axis Powers complemented Hollywood profit plans with anti-fascist and anti-communist political agendas. For all its rhetoric of pure competition, therefore, the US film industry has been assisted by decades of tax-credit schemes, film commissions, State and Commerce Department representation, currency assistance, and oligopolistic domestic buying, while the US government has devoted massive resources to generate and sustain its 'private-sector' film industry in the interests of ideology and profits (Harley 1940: 3; Elsaesser 1989: 10–11).

With profits endangered at home by anti-monopoly laws and the arrival of television, the world market grew in importance for Hollywood during the 1950s (Armes 1987: 49). Vertical integration through ownership of production, distribution, and exhibition may have been outlawed at home, but not on a global scale. By the 1960s the United States relied on exports for half its film revenue. Britain and Latin America were Hollywood's most lucrative importers until the 1970s. In both cases, economic downturn and the failure to invest in multiplexes diminished attendances. As a result, Hollywood turned to new forms of internal commercial exploitation (as in the 'discovery' of the African American audience and the emergence of the 'blaxploitation' genre). Following recapitalization and the studios' acquisition by conglomerates, strategies were developed to regain world audiences (Mattelart 1979:

194). US government and industry set up cartels to market films everywhere, with special agencies created for anglophone and francophone Africa. Hollywood's African Motion Picture Export Company has dominated cinema sales to former British colonies since the 1960s, when the continent screened about 350 films a year, perhaps half of them American (Diawara 1992: 106, 1994: 385–6; Ukadike 1994: 63). Today, it is easier to find an African film screened in Europe or the United States than on home territory. Following the hyperinflation of the 1970s and 1980s, with film production in Mexico and Argentina decimated, the percentage of Hollywood films exhibited in Latin America has increased dramatically, while by the mid-1980s Japan was the principal source of foreign profit (Himpele 1996: 52; O'Regan 1992: 304). As we shall see below, shifts towards a neo-liberal, multinational investment climate over the past decade have aided Hollywood further through the privatization of media ownership, a unified West European market, openings in the former Soviet bloc, and the proliferation of video cassette recorders (Elsaesser 1989: 15; Guback 1987: 98–9; Wasko 1994: 220, 224).

However, if the growing economic dominance of world markets by Hollywood is clearly apparent, why has this dominance alarmed so many governments? Why have industrial issues about the balance of trade been matched by cultural concerns about the balance of meaning? What is the 'threat' which such dominance has been sent to represent, and what are the issues at stake?

Cultural imperialism

Countries on the periphery have exchanged ideas and goods for a millennium. Networks of information and trade connected the Pacific, Asia, the Mediterranean, and Africa until the fifteenth century, when the slavery, militarism, and technology of European imperialism began to wipe out these routes. Intracontinental communications came to rely on Europe as a conduit. New ideologies came too: racial supremacy and the conversion mission of Christianity (Hamelink 1990: 223–4). Culture and information were now imperial concerns.

Cinema technology and narrative emerged around the same time as some major transformations in colonial politics: the United States seized the Philippines and Cuba, the European powers agreed on a division of Africa, and Native American resistance was crushed.

While First Peoples' rights were being trampled, commercial cultural export and sovereign authority were synchronizing (with an array of genocidal stories being enacted on-screen). Hollywood exporters were aware as early as 1912 that where their films travelled, demand was created for other US goods. Will Hays told the J. Walter Thompson advertising agency in 1930 that 'every foot of American film sells $1.00 worth of manufactured products some place in the world' (Hays 1931: 15). By the late 1930s stories of heroic merchandising links between the cinema and sales were legion, such as the one that told of the new Javanese market for US sewing-machines following a screening of American factory conditions, Hollywood-style. The producer Walter Wanger even expressed delight at a strike by Paris stenographers in protest at the gap between their conditions and those of office workers in US films, the impact of what he called '120,000 American Ambassadors' (the number of prints exported each year) (Wanger 1939: 50, 45). Such links are encapsulated in two famous scenes involving Clark Gable. *It Started in Naples* (Melville Shavelson, 1960) finds him instructing a local boy on how to make a hamburger. This produced public controversy about compromising Mediterranean cuisine. A quarter of a century earlier a deputation of Argentinian businessmen had protested to the US Embassy about *It Happened One Night* (Frank Capra, 1934) because Gable was seen removing his shirt, revealing no singlet below and creating an inventory surplus in their warehouses (King 1990: 32).

Although an interest in screen stereotypes is often identified with a contemporary liberal sensibility, it has, in fact, been a long-standing concern of conservatives. Since the 1920s Hollywood has monitored how representations affect audiences. Mexico placed embargoes because of this issue in 1922 and official complaints from Germany, Britain, France, Italy, and Spain over cultural slurs also occurred during the same decade (Vasey 1992: 618, 620–1, 624, 627, 631). As different countries became profitable sources of income, their leverage over scripts increased. The industry's 1927 list of 'Don'ts and Be Carefuls' instructed producers to 'avoid picturizing in an unfavorable light another country's religion, history, institutions, prominent people, and citizenry'. The British insisted on the unrepresentability of Christ, so he was absent from *The Last Days of Pompeii* (Ernest B. Schoedsack, 1935), while Samuel Goldwyn complained that 'the only villain we dare show today

Culinary imperialism, or how to make a hamburger—Clark Gable in *It Started in Naples* (1960)

[1936] is a white American' (quoted in Harley 1940: 23). On the other hand, the Japanese were threatened with narrative stereotyping as criminals in the 1930s if they failed to give access to Hollywood films.

American advertising executives were quick to work on commodity tie-ins to film. This produced a negative response from many poorer nations, especially after the Second World War, when such exports were officially legitimized as part of making less-developed countries into modern ones. Widespread reaction against the racist and self-seeking—or at best patronizing—discourses of modernization foregrounded the international capitalist media as crucial components in the formation of public taste in commodities, mass culture, and forms of economic and political organization in the Third World. Examples include the export of US screen products and infrastructure as well as American dominance of international communications tech-

nology. Critics claimed the rhetoric of development through commercialism was responsible for decelerating economic growth and disfranchising local culture, with emergent ruling classes in dependent nations exercising local power only at the cost of relying on foreign capital and ideology.

These theories of dependency spread from Latin America across the globe during the 1960s and 1970s, finding agreeable surrounds in international cultural organizations and Group of Seventy-Seven alliances. But the position has declined politically and intellectually since then. Once adopted by Unesco, it became vulnerable to that agency's complex pluralism, which insisted on the equivalence of all cultures as well as the association of national identity with cultural forms. The United States and United Kingdom withdrew from the Organization in the mid-1980s, draining resources it had allocated towards a new world order of culture and communication. At the same time, the conceptualization of *dependencia* was attacked from the left for an inadequate theorization of capitalism, post-coloniality, internal and international class relations, the role of the state, and the mediation of indigenous culture (Tunstall 1977: 57; Reeves 1993: 30–5; Schlesinger 1991: 145; Mann 1993: 119, 132).

This last concern—the mediation of Hollywood's output by indigenous cultures—has been particularly important in qualifying the cultural imperialism thesis. Michel Foucault's story of a white psychologist visiting Africa is instructive in its detail of differing aesthetic systems: when the academic asks local viewers to recount a narrative he has screened, they focus on 'the passage of light and shadows through the trees' in preference to his interest in character and plot (Foucault 1989: 193). As the *Economist* magazine's 1994 television survey remarked, perhaps cultural politics is always so localized in its first and last instances that the 'electronic bonds' of exported drama are 'threadbare' (Heilemann 1994, Survey 4). In their study of the reception of the television series *Dallas* in Israel, Japan, and the United States, Tamar Liebes and Elihu Katz establish three prerequisites for the successful communication of US ideology: the text contains information designed to assist the US overseas, is decoded as encrypted, and enters the receiving culture as a norm. They 'found only very few innocent minds' across the different cultural groups that discussed the programme; instead, a variety of interpretive frames led to a multiplicity of readings (Liebes and Katz 1990: 3–4. p. v).

Indeed, anxieties about American entertainment are frequently expressed under the guise of concern for 'national cultures' that have themselves been repressive or phantasmatic. The extraordinary puritanism of some cultural protection denies the liberatory aspects of much US entertainment for stifling class structures, as in the case of Britain. Nor have national cinemas necessarily taken a critical distance from Hollywood as some damned other. Many seek to imitate it, notably the 1980s Si Boy cycle in Indonesia, with its youth culture of fast cars (and English-speaking servants) (Sen 1994: 64, 73, 129–30), while some countries have fused imported strands of popular culture with indigenous ones to rework notions of cultural identity, as in Irish cinema (Rockett *et al.* 1988: 147). Others indeed, may import Hollywood texts as buffers against cultural imports that are too close for comfort: Pakistan

may prefer the difference of North America to the similarity of India (O'Regan 1992: 343).

Armand and Michèle Mattelart, leading names in the discourse of cultural imperialism, today see it as an enabling alliance of intellectual engagement rather than a sustainable theory. Cultural imperialism mobilized people to think through the implications of international textuality via local audits of relations between states, especially the nexus between 'new' nations, their former colonizers, and the United States. It is not surprising that a concentration on the inequality of exchange emphasized directions in flow rather than signs and their reception. However, the accusation of cultural imperialism did bring local culture to bear in resistance to the assumptions of neo-classical economics and its heroization of the sovereign consumer (Mattelart and Mattelart 1992: 175–7). Moreover, the spread of such critiques exemplified the export of theory itself from the Third World to the First, contributing to and drawing upon the ideals of Third Cinema along with the Cuban Revolution, Peronism, and Cinema Nôvo (Shohat and Stam 1994: 28). Nor do revisions to the thesis mean film trade is a happily settled matter. The apparent domestication of exported culture sometimes merely offers a few signifiers of localism while the values of practice and genre are imported, as debates about Indian and Philippine cinema over the past twenty years indicate (McAnany 1989; Binford 1987: 146; David 1995: 33). In this sense, difference and a sensitivity to cultural specificity can be one more incorporative means to homogenize cultural production. This then leads us to cultural imperialism's 'successor'—the concept of globalization.

Globalization

I would argue that . . . the entertainment industry of this country is not so much Americanizing the world as planetizing entertainment. (Michael Eisner)

Global exchange has been with us for a long time, but since the 1970s financial and managerial decisions made in one part of the world have taken rapid effect elsewhere. New international currency markets sprang up with the decline of a fixed exchange rate, matching regulated systems with piratical financial institutions that crossed borders. Speculation brought greater rewards than production, as the trade in securities and servicing debt outstripped profits from selling cars or building houses. The world circulation of money created the conditions for imposing international creditworthiness tests on all countries. At a policy level, it meant an end to import substitution industrialization and the very legitimacy of 'national' economies, supplanted by export-oriented industrialization and the idea of an international economy. With productive investment less profitable than financial investment, and companies rationalizing production, marketing, labour, and administration were reconceived on a world-wide scale. The corollary of open markets and critiques of cultural protectionism is that national governments cannot guarantee the economic well-being of their citizens. The loan-granting power of the World Bank and International Monetary Fund has forced a shift away from local provision of basic needs and towards comparative advantage. In the domain of cinema, this means that 'if you aren't doing it profitably already, don't start or you will be punished'. However, we need to beware of interpreting globalization as a structural change that puts an end to centre–periphery inequalities, competition between states, and integrated macro-decision-making by corporations; it just cuts the capacity of the state system to control such transactions (McMichael 1996: 27–9; Marshall 1996; Connelly 1996: 12–13).

Economic, cultural, environmental, and political forces are increasingly world-wide in their scope and effects, dynamically interpenetrating local realities and practices. Theories of globalization put space and speed at the centre of both analytic and business concerns: social theory links commodification critique to advertising practice in a giddy process akin to the experience of watching an action-adventure film's climactic struggle. As capital moves at high velocity, it lights promiscuously on areas and countries, with materials and people exchanged across the globe. If the modern saw everyday life determined by events beyond the horizon in national institutions of the economy and polity, the postmodern sees these determinations across borders, languages, and skies via multiple diasporas, computerized technology, finance capital, media entertainment, international organizations, neo-classical economics, regional blocs, and democratic ideology. Put another way, the experience of empire for First Peoples is now experienced—in milder form—as corporate domination by former colonizers and colonized alike.

Globalization's meanings for screen studies vary between concerns over American-dominated cultural flow (as per cultural imperialism), the international spread of capitalistic production and conglomerates, and the chaotic, splintered circulation of signs across cultures (Jacka 1992: 5, 2). Ownership is concentrated in a diminishing number of increasingly large corporations. What used to be nationally dominated markets for terrestrial television have undergone vast changes. Companies like Disney are in a position to produce films, directly promote them across a variety of subsidiaries, screen them on an owned network, and generate television replicas—not to mention compact discs and reading-material—and all with an eye to external profits (McChesney 1996: 4) (but they may cower in the face of Marguerite Duras's condemnation of EuroDisney as 'cultural Chernobyl'; quoted in Van Maanen 1992: 26). Digital systems cut the cost and quicken the speed of communication and generic transformation. Some components of globalization theory are sanguine about such developments, stressing the skill of audiences in negotiating texts. Certain writers offer 'multicultural' business strategies, themselves a segment of US transnationalism extending its domain. Critics focus on the direction of multinational finance: the Hollywood studios have recently been French-, Japanese-, Canadian-, and Australian-owned and are increasingly beholden to cross-cultural audiences for their success. At the same time as this diversity appears, the means of communication, association, and political representation are seen to be converging (Jameson 1991, pp. xiv–xv; Reeves 1993: 36, 62; Sreberny-Mohammadi 1996: 3–8).

What is interesting about globalization is that all its theorists place culture at the centre. Whereas the phrase 'cultural imperialism' always seemed qualified by the power of the noun to conjure up structural domination, 'globalization' is more processual. It marks new forms of economic life in a decolonized, privatized world system that sees overlapping and mutually determining spheres of influence and flexible specialization in production and consumption. Unlike cultural imperialism, globalization allows for incoherent, multilateral forms and directions of power, celebrating them as market flexibilities or sites of popular resistance, depending on who is speaking (Tomlinson 1991: 175–6; Marshall 1996: 197).

Of course, part of the talent of international cultural commodities is their adaptability to new circumstances: the successes and meanings of Hollywood films need to be charted through numerous spatial, generic, and formatting transformations as they move through US release to Europe and Asia then domestic and international video, cable, and network television (Aksoy and Robins 1992: 14). Because culture is about discrimination as well as exchange, it is simultaneously a key to international textual trade and one of its limiting factors. The Ford Motor Company has long worked with the adage 'To be a multinational group, it is necessary to be national everywhere'. And General Motors translates its 'hot dogs, baseball, apple pie, and Chevrolet' jingle into 'meat pies, football, kangaroos, and Holden cars' in Australia. Each US film is allotted a hundred generic descriptions for individual use in specific markets. Kevin Costner's *Dances with Wolves* was sold to the 1990 French cinemagoer as a documentary-style dramatization of Native American life and *Malcolm X* (Spike Lee, 1992) was promoted there with posters of a burning Stars and Stripes (Wasser 1995: 433; Danan 1995). Such stories indicate the paradigmatic nature of the national in an era of global companies. New forms of rationalization standardize the acknowledgement of difference as part of capital's need for local marketability. What are the implications for the Hollywood film industry of this still-unfolding mode of multinational capitalism?

The new international division of cultural labour

We have created a product that by, say, putting the name of Warner Brothers on it is a stamp of credibility. But that could be an Arnon Milchan film, directed by Paul Verhoeven, starring Gérard Depardieu and Anthony Hopkins, and shot in France and Italy, and made with foreign money.
(John Ptak)

Hollywood is a place you can't geographically define. We don't really know where it is.
(John Ford)

Despite the US government's positive attitude to the movie business as ideology and trade, New Dealers opposed Hollywood's domestic cartels and vertical integration. A combination of antitrust decisions and the advent of television meant that the decade from 1946 saw a decrease of a third in the number of Hollywood-made films and more than a doubling of imports. Films went overseas—'runaway production'—as the world audience grew, while location shooting became a means of differentiating stories. Between 1950 and 1973, just 60 per cent of Hollywood

films began their lives in the United States, as studios purchased facilities across the globe to utilize cheap labour (Christopherson and Storper 1986). In 1949 there were nineteen runaway productions (Guback 1984: 56–7). Twenty years on, the figure was 183, mostly in Europe. Co-productions became a norm, with Dino De Laurentiis a pioneer of today's global pre-sales, which garner funds from distributors around the world in advance of production in Los Angeles. American film institutions are practised at purchasing foreign theatres and distribution companies and sharing risk and profit with local businesses (Izod 1988: 119). The 1990s have seen the emergence of truly global film distribution cartels, such as Warner and United International (Sorlin 1991: 93; Wasko 1994: 226). This may be seen to represent a possible new international division of cultural labour.

The concept of a new international division of cultural labour derives from revisions to the theory of economic dependency that emerged from West Germany in the late 1970s. The shift from the spatial sensitivities of electrics to the spatial insensitivities of electronics had pushed businesses away from treating the Third World as a source of raw materials. Instead, it set the shadow price of work, competing internally and with the First and Second Worlds. Production became split across continents in what Folker Fröbel and his collaborators christened a new international division of labour (Fröbel et al. 1980: 2–8, 13–15, 45–8). I am suggesting that, just as we have seen manufacturing flee the First World, which then depended for its employment base on the services sector, much cultural production has relocated around the world and may continue to do so at the level of creativity, marketing, and information. The factors determining this are a complex mix of legal and political frameworks, productivity, and skills. A peripheral group of suppliers can increase the profit margin of a centralized company that retains control of finance, research, and overall direction (Miège 1989: 41–3; Marshall 1996: 202; Mittelman 1995: 278).

Internationalization has quite different effects on stars and 'creative' people from its impact on artisanal workers. Unlike the vertically integrated studio system era, most Hollywood film production is now undertaken by small lighting, studio, and editing companies on behalf of independent producers who contract with major distributors or regional groups to show films around the world, sharing revenue through formulae that include non-recoverable advances to fund the movies (Christopherson and Storper 1986). Since the 1980s overseas firms have invested in Hollywood or lent money against distribution rights in their countries of origin. Joint production arrangements are well-established between US firms and Swedish, French, Italian, and British companies, with connections to video, cable, and theme parks (Buck 1992: 119, 123). So at the top and bottom end of the labour market, Hollywood has internationalized, while its large mid-section remains provincial (Briller 1990: 75–8). New technology problematizes the necessity for the collocation of financing, shooting, and editing, but it also reduces the need for 'authenticity', so filming abroad is mostly about cost. The diversity at production level, however, does not amount to dispersed power. Independents have always been part of the scene, but never sufficiently capitalized or vertically integrated either domestically or overseas to survive costly failures. Finance and distribution remain under the control of major studios (Acheson and Maule 1994: 279–80; Wasko 1994: 33; Miège 1989: 46; Aksoy and Robins 1992: 8–9).

We might consider the way the new international division of cultural labour can affect other countries through a brief case-study of *Kangaroo* (Lewis Milestone, 1952) and *The Return of Captain Invincible* (Philippe Mora, 1983). They provide chronological and conceptual limiting cases of US screen investment in a film industry. *Kangaroo* was the first of several Hollywood features shot in Australia during the 1950s. Twentieth Century-Fox dispatched a crew and most of the cast because its Australian-based capital reserves had been frozen to prevent foreign exchange from leaving the country. Shooting took place in Zanuckville, named to honour the studio head. A formulaic western, the film failed, but then the need to use money lying idle was probably the sole reason for its coming into being. Three decades on, *Captain Invincible* represented another outcome of the state producing conditions for foreign filmmaking. Taxation incentives designed to make the industry less dependent on canon-forming cultural bureaucrats and more attentive to the private sector saw the Australian Treasury subsidizing US producers to make a film set almost 'nowhere'. It concerns a lapsed American superhero, played by Alan Arkin, who migrates to Australia and dipsomania following McCarthyite persecution, reviving his powers and sobriety to thwart a villainous Christopher Lee. Recut by US producers following difficulties obtaining American distribution, the text

was disavowed by Mora and denied certification by the Australian government as insufficiently local by comparison with its original script. A court challenge against this ruling succeeded, but the tax haven designed to boost commercial production was politically and culturally compromised from that point.

The present and future

For all its lopsidedness, the contemporary trade in film is far from a unilateral exercise of power. When Congress was inquiring into foreign ownership of Hollywood in the late 1980s, Milos Forman expressed concern that if a German corporation bought Fox, 'all the war films could be "slightly corrected"' (quoted in Briller 1990: 77). The American Film Institute is anxious about the loss of cultural heritage to internationalism, and others ask what will become of US drama now that it is increasingly scripted with an eye to foreign audiences. Internationalization occurs at ancillary levels, as audience targeting becomes increasingly specific: Sean Connery is cast as a Hollywood lead because European audiences love him, while Michael Apted speaks with optimism of a gradual 'European-izing of Hollywood' (quoted in Dawtrey 1994: 75). George Quester laments that expensive British costume-history crowds out indigenous 'quality' fiction on US television, noting that there is more Australian high-end drama than locally produced material (Quester 1990: 57), while Paul Hirsch speaks of globalization displacing American dominance across the culture industries (Wasser 1995: 433; Danan 1995: 131–2, 137; Hirsch 1992: 677).

At the level of distribution and exhibition, the picture is unstable. As Chinese-language groups develop in many parts of the world, sometimes US exports do not even meet quota limits set on them in those territories, while Indonesia has seen a decline in Hollywood popularity since the mid-1980s (Sen 1994: 63–4). America blames this on government intervention but it may have more to do with the popularity of Hong Kong and Taiwanese film. Meanwhile, US government agencies pressure proprietors and politicians around the world to open up the audiovisual sector to additional imports, leading to bizarre acts of resistance such as Korean film industry people releasing snakes into theatres during screenings of *Fatal Attraction* (Adrian Lyne, 1987) to scare audiences away (Buck 1992: 129).

US film revenue from members of the European

Community increased throughout the 1980s, to 90 per cent of cinema receipts there by 1990. If we consolidate television, film, and video texts as at mid-1994, the American industry relied on exports for $8 billion of its annual revenue of $18 billion, with 55 per cent from Western Europe (*Daily Variety* 1994: 16). Europe imported $3.7 billion in 1992, compared to $288 million in reciprocal sales; and the disparity is increasing. Overseas hard-top exhibition is now a more significant source of Hollywood's revenue than domestic receipts, as the new multiplexes have massively increased attendances throughout Europe over the 1990s. US opposition to the single European market as a cultural producer is laughable given how much it benefits from the EC as a cultural consumer (Hill 1994: 2, 7 n. 4; Miller 1993: 102).

The television–film nexus has become increasingly critical. True to the style of the new international division of cultural labour, Turner Broadcasting, Time Warner, Disney, Viacom, NBC, and others are at the centre of the fast-growing West European industry, finding new sites of production as well as dumping-grounds for old material. Meanwhile, the US Department of Commerce offers policy materials on globalization to Congress that converge economic development and ideological influence, problematizing claims that Hollywood is free enterprise and its government uninterested in blending trade with cultural change. Business and the state luxuriate in the industry's 65 per cent share of the world box-office and an immeasurable share in emerging forms of life (Ferguson 1992: 83–4; Eisner, in Costa-Gavras *et al.* 1995: 9). Students of film need to blend our expertise in watching American films with an understanding of how and why they come before us.

BIBLIOGRAPHY

Acheson, Keith, and Christopher J. Maule (1994), 'Understanding Hollywood's Organization and Continuing Success', *Journal of Cultural Economics*, 18/4: 271–300.

*Aksoy, Asu, and Kevin Robins (1992), 'Hollywood for the Twenty-First Century: Global Competition for Critical Mass in Image Markets', *Cambridge Journal of Economics*, 16/1: 1–22.

Armes, Roy (1987), *Third World Film Making and the West* (Berkeley: University of California Press).

Balio, Tino (1993), *Grand Design: Hollywood as a Modern Business Enterprise 1930–1939* (New York: Scribner's).

Binford, Mira Reym (1987), 'The Two Cinemas of India', in John D. H. Downing (ed.), *Film and Politics in the Third World* (New York: Autonomedia).

Bordwell, David, Janet Staiger, and Kristin Thompson (1985), *The Classical Hollywood Cinema: Film Style and Mode of Production to 1960* (London: Routledge).

Briller, Bert R. (1990), 'The Globalization of American TV', *Television Quarterly*, 24/3: 71–9.

Buck, Elizabeth B. (1992), 'Asia and the Global Film Industry', *East–West Film Journal*, 6/2: 116–33.

Christopherson, Susan, and Michael Storper (1986), 'The City as Studio; the World as Back Lot: The Impact of Vertical Disintegration on the Location of the Motion Picture Industry', *Environment and Planning D: Society and Space*, 4/3: 305–20.

Connelly, M. Patricia (1996), 'Gender Matters: Global Restructuring and Adjustment', *Social Politics*, 3/1: 12–31.

Costa-Gavras, Michael Eisner, Jack Lang, and Benjamin Barber (1995), 'From Magic Kingdom to Media Empire', *New Perspectives Quarterly*, 12/4: 4–17.

Daily Variety (1994), 'After GATT Pique, Pix Pax Promoted', 8 June, 1, 16.

Danan, Martine (1995), 'Marketing the Hollywood Blockbuster in France', *Journal of Popular Film and Television*, 23/3: 131–40.

David, Joel (1995), *Fields of Vision: Critical Applications in Recent Philippine Cinema* (Quezon City: Ateneo de Manila University Press).

Dawtrey, Adam (1994), 'Playing Hollywood's Game: Eurobucks Back Megabiz', *Variety*, 7–13 (Mar.), 1, 75.

de Grazia, Victoria (1989), 'Mass Culture and Sovereignty: The American Challenge to European Cinemas 1920–1960', *Journal of Modern History*, 61/1: 53–87.

Diawara, Manthia (1992), *African Cinema: Politics and Culture* (Bloomington: Indiana University Press).

—— (1994), 'On Tracking World Cinema: African Cinema at Film Festivals', *Public Culture*, 6/2: 385–96.

Elsaesser, Thomas (1989), *New German Cinema: A History* (Basingstoke: Macmillan; London: British Film Institute).

Ferguson, Marjorie (1992), 'The Mythology about Globalization', *European Journal of Communication*, 7/1: 69–93.

Foucault, Michel (1989), *Foucault Live* (interviews, 1966–84), ed. Sylvère Lotringer, trans. John Johnston (New York: Semiotext(e) Foreign Agents Series).

Fröbel, Folker, Jürgen Heinrichs, and Otto Kreye (1980), *The New International Division of Labour: Structural Unemployment in Industrialised Countries and Industrialisation in Developing Countries*, trans. Pete Burgess (Cambridge: Cambridge University Press; Paris: Éditions de la Maison des Sciences de l'Homme).

Guback, Thomas H. (1984), 'International Circulation of US Theatrical Films and Television Programming', in George Gerbner and Marsha Siefert (eds.), *World Communications: A Handbook* (New York: Longman).

Guback, Thomas H. (1987), 'Government Support to the Film Industry in the United States', in Bruce A. Austin (ed.), *Current Research in Film: Audiences, Economics and Law*, iii (Norwood, NJ: Ablex).

Hamelink, Cees (1990), 'Information Imbalance: Core and Periphery', in John Downing, Ali Mohammadi, and Annabelle Sreberny-Mohammadi (eds.), *Questioning the Media: A Critical Introduction* (Newbury Park, Calif.: Sage).

Harley, John Eugene (1940), *World-Wide Influences of the Cinema: A Study of Official Censorship and the International Cultural Aspects of Motion Pictures* (Los Angeles: University of Southern California Press).

Hay, James (1987), *Popular Film Culture in Fascist Italy: The Passing of the Rex* (Bloomington: Indiana University Press).

Hays, Will (1931), Speech, 12 May, J. Walter Thompson Collection, Duke University, Creative Staff Meeting File, Monday Evening Meetings.

Heilemann, John (1994), 'A Survey of Television: Feeling for the Future', *Economist*, 330/7850, Survey 1–18.

Hill, John (1994), Introduction, in John Hill, Martin McLoone, and Paul Hainsworth (eds.), *Border Crossing: Film in Ireland, Britain and Europe* (Belfast: Institute of Irish Studies; London: British Film Institute).

Himpele, Jeffrey D. (1996), 'Film Distribution as Media: Mapping Difference in the Bolivian Cinemascape', *Visual Anthropology Review*, 12/1: 47–66.

Hirsch, Paul (1992), 'Globalization of Mass Media Ownership', *Communication Research*, 19/6: 677–81.

Izod, John (1988), *Hollywood and the Box Office 1895–1986* (New York: Columbia University Press).

Jacka, Elizabeth (1992), Introduction, in Elizabeth Jacka (ed.), *Continental Shift: Globalisation and Culture* (Sydney: Local Consumption).

Jameson, Fredric (1991), *Postmodernism; or, The Cultural Logic of Late Capitalism* (London: Verso).

King, John (1990), *Magical Reels: A History of Cinema in Latin America* (London: Verso).

Liebes, Tamar, and Elihu Katz (1990), *The Export of Meaning: Cross-Cultural Readings of Dallas* (New York: Oxford University Press).

McAnany, Emile G. (1989), 'Television and Cultural Discourses: Latin American and United States Comparisons', *Studies in Latin American Popular Culture*, 8: 1–21.

McChesney, Robert W. (1996), 'The Global Struggle for Democratic Communication', *Monthly Review*, 48/3: 1–20.

McMichael, Philip (1996), 'Globalization: Myths and Realities', *Rural Sociology*, 61/1: 25–55.

Mann, Michael (1993), 'Nation-States in Europe and Other Continents: Diversifying, Developing, not Dying', *Daedalus*, 122/3: 115–40.

Marshall, Don D. (1996), 'Understanding Late-Twentieth-Century Capitalism: Reassessing the Globalization Theme', *Government and Opposition*, 31/2: 193–215.

Marvasti, A. (1994), 'International Trade in Cultural Goods: A Cross-Sectional Analysis', *Journal of Cultural Economics*, 18/2: 135–48.

Mattelart, Armand (1979), *Multinational Corporations and the Control of Culture: The Ideological Apparatuses of Imperialism*, trans. Michael Chanan (Sussex: Harvester Press; Atlantic Heights, NJ: Humanities Press).

—— and Michèle Mattelart (1992), *Rethinking Media Theory: Signposts and New Directions*, trans. James A. Cohen and Marina Urquidi (Minneapolis: University of Minnesota Press).

Miège, Bernard (1989), *The Capitalization of Cultural Production*, trans. Josiane Hay, Nicholas Garnham, and Unesco (New York: International General).

Miller, Toby (1993), *The Well-Tempered Self: Citizenship, Culture, and the Postmodern Subject* (Baltimore: Johns Hopkins University Press).

Mittelman, James H. (1995), 'Rethinking the International Division of Labour in the Context of Globalisation', *Third World Quarterly*, 16/2: 273–95.

O'Regan, Tom (1992), 'Too Popular by Far: On Hollywood's International Popularity', *Continuum*, 5/2: 302–51.

Powdermaker, Hortense (1950), *Hollywood the Dream Factory: An Anthropologist Looks at the Movie-Makers* (Boston: Little, Brown).

Quester, George H. (1990), *The International Politics of Television* (Lexington, Mass.: Lexington).

Reeves, Geoffrey (1993), *Communications and the 'Third World'* (London: Routledge).

Rockett, Kevin, Luke Gibbons, and John Hill (1988), *Cinema and Ireland* (Syracuse, NY: Syracuse University Press).

Rockwell, John (1994), 'The New Colossus: American Culture as Power Export', *New York Times*, 30 Jan. H1, H30.

Schatz, Thomas (1988), *The Genius of the System: Hollywood Filmmaking in the Studio Era* (New York: Pantheon).

Schlesinger, Phillip (1991), *Media, State and Nation: Political Violence and Collective Identities* (London: Sage).

Sen, Krishna (1994), *Indonesian Cinema: Framing the New Order* (London: Zed).

Shohat, Ella, and Robert Stam (1994), *Unthinking Eurocentrism: Multiculturalism and the Media* (London: Routledge).

Sorlin, Pierre (1991), *European Cinemas, European Societies 1939–1990* (London: Routledge).

Sreberny-Mohammadi, Annabelle (1996), 'Globalization, Communication and Transnational Civil Society: Introduction', in Sandra Braman and Annabelle Sreberny-Mohammadi (eds.), *Globalization, Communication and Transnational Civil Society* (Cresskill: Hampton Press).

*Tomlinson, John** (1991), *Cultural Imperialism: A Critical Introduction* (London: Pinter).

Tunstall, Jeremy (1977), *The Media are American: Anglo-American Media in the World* (London: Constable).

Ukadike, Nwachukwu Frank (1994), *Black African Cinema* (Berkeley: University of California Press).

Van Maanen, John (1992), 'Displacing Disney: Some Notes on the Flow of Culture', *Qualitative Sociology* 15/1: 5–35.

Vasey, Ruth (1992), 'Foreign Parts: Hollywood's Global Distribution and the Representation of Ethnicity', *American Quarterly*, 44/4: 617–42.

Wanger, Walter (1939), '120,000 American Ambassadors', *Foreign Affairs*, 18/1: 45–59.

*Wasko, Janet** (1994), *Hollywood in the Information Age: Beyond the Silver Screen* (Cambridge: Polity Press).

Wasser, Frederick (1995), 'Is Hollywood America? The Trans-Nationalization of the American Film Industry', *Critical Studies in Mass Communication*, 12/4: 423–37.

Weinraub, Bernard (1993), 'Directors Battle over GATT's Final Cut and Print', *New York Times*, 12 Dec., L24.

Wenders, Wim (1991), *The Logic of Images: Essays and Conversations*, trans. Michael Hofmann (London: Faber & Faber).

List of Picture and Reading Sources

PICTURES

Unless otherwise stated all photographic material was reproduced courtesy of the Kobal collection. Whilst every effort has been made to identify copyright holders that has not been possible in a few cases. We apologize for any apparent negligence and any omissions brought to our attention will be remedied in any future editions. 2.2 Courtesy of the British Film Institute 2.5 Courtesy of the British Film Institute 2.7 Universal City Studios, Inc. a division of MCA 2.8 Turner Entertainment Co. 1942 2.9 Warner Brothers 1967 2.10 Lucasfilm 1977 2.11 Universal City Studios, Inc. a division of MCA 1975 2.12 Twentieth Century Fox 1939 2.13 Metro Goldwyn Mayer 1954 2.14 Warner Brothers 1945 2.15 Courtesy of the British Film Institute 2.17 Metro Goldwyn Mayer 1937 2.18 Paramount 1960

READINGS

Richard Maltby: 'Casablanca' from Richard Maltby, *Harmless Entertainment: Hollywood and the Ideology of Consensus*, Metuchan, NJ: Scarecrow Press 1983. Rick Altman: 'Casablanca' from 'Dickens, Griffith, and Film Theory Today' in *South Atlantic Quarterly*, 88(2) 1989, © 1989 Duke University Press, 1992. Reprinted with permission. Peter Wollen: 'John Ford' from Peter Wollen, *Signs and Meaning in the Cinema*, Secker & Warburg, 1992. Linda Williams: 'Body genres' excerpted from Linda Williams, 'Film Bodies: Gender, Genre and Excess', *Film Quarterly*, 44(4), © 1991 by The Regents of the University of California. Robert B. Ray: 'Hollywood and Ideology' from Robert B. Ray, *A Certain Tendency of the Hollywood Cinema, 1930–1980*, © 1985 Princeton University Press. Reprinted with permission from Princeton University Press.

Index of Selected Films and Names

McArthur, Colin 95, 101, 102, 105
MacCabe, Colin 5, 47, 49
McCann, Richard Dyer 67–8
Maltby, Richard 57–60, 73, 75, 80
Man who Shot Liberty Valance, The 99–100
Mann, Antony 88
Marked Woman 138
Marx Brothers 89, 106
Marx, Karl 137
Mattelart, Armand 142, 146, 149
Mattelart, Michèle 142, 149
May, Lary 8
Mayer, Michael 23
Mayne, Judith 35
Medium Cool 134
Mekas, Jonas 69
Méliès, Georges 37
Metz, Christian 32, 47, 48, 50, 125, 130
Mildred Pierce 109, 110, 115, 132
Minnelli, Vincente 87, 91, 92, 95
Missing 134
Mitchell, Juliet 54
Mitry, Jean 107
Modleski, Tania 54, 61, 95
Monroe, Marilyn 120, 121, 124
Movie 73, 74, 88, 89, 95, 103
Mulvey, Laura 5, 51, 52, 53–4, 95, 121–2
Murnau, F.W. 5, 73
Musser, Charles 4, 8, 32, 33
My Darling Clementine 99–100, 106, 108
Myles, Lynda 76, 77, 78

Narboni, Jean 47–8, 49, 50, 55, 90, 91
Neale, Steve 14, 63, 74, 75, 80, 104, 106, 107, 109, 110, 111
Negt, Oskar 35
Neilsen 32
Nichols, Bill 50
Nowell-Smith, Geoffrey 46, 63, 80, 89, 90, 93, 94

Ophuls, Max 92, 95
O'Regan, Tom 146, 147, 149

Paisà 64
Parallax View, The 134
Pearson, Roberta 39, 40
Peckinpah, Sam 111
Penn, Arthur 69, 71, 78, 88, 133
Perkins, V.F. 88, 103
Pickford, Mary 119, 125
Platoon 140
Porter, Edward S. 32, 33, 35, 40
Positif 87, 88
Powdermaker, Hortense 130, 146
Pudovkin, Vsevolod 86
Pye, Douglas 106
Pye, Michael 76, 77, 78

Quiet Man, The 99–100

Rabinowitz, Lauren 35, 40
Rafelson, Bob 73
Raiders of the Lost Ark 92
Ramsaye, Terry 2, 3
Ray, Nicholas 87, 95
Ray, Robert B. 75, 137–8
Red River 108
Renoir, Jean 87
Rivette, Jacques 87
Robbins, Kevin 141, 152
Robeson, Paul 120, 121
Robins, Kevin 151
Robinson, David 2, 8
Robinson, Edward G. 106
Rockett, Kevin 140, 149
Rogers, Ginger 106
Rohmer, Eric 87
Rome, Open City (Roma, città aperta) 65
Roseanne 124–5
Rosen, Phillip 47
Rosenbaum, Jonathan 88
Rossellini, Roberto 49, 88, 125
Rotha, Paul 2, 86, 96, 101
Rowe, Kathleen 36, 63, 80
Ruiz, Paul 96
Ryan, Michael 75, 133

Salt, Barry 13–14
Sarris, Andrew 69, 70, 71, 73, 85, 88, 94, 95
Saussure, Ferdinand de 93
Sayles, John 134
Schatz, Thomas 63, 64, 76, 78, 103–4, 130, 131, 146
Schlesinger, Philip 143, 149
Scorsese, Martin 77, 78, 88
Screen 5, 47, 49, 74, 80, 95, 126, 130, 137
Searchers, The 94, 99, 103, 108, 109
Seldes, Gilbert 66, 68, 73
Sen, Krishna 152
Seven Brides for Seven Brothers 104, 107, 109
Shklovsky, Victor 103
Shohat, Ella 91, 146, 149
Silence of the Lambs 110
Singer, Ben 33, 39, 40
Sirk, Douglas 52, 87, 91, 92, 95
Sklar, Robert 2, 3, 31, 128, 130
Slide, Antony 2
Spellerberg, James 4, 14
Spielberg, Steven 73, 75, 77, 78, 92, 95
Stacey, Jackie 122
Stagecoach 64, 103, 108
Stahl, John M. 52
Staiger, Janet 5, 7, 8, 14, 20, 24, 26, 31, 33, 35, 36, 47, 49–50, 55, 63, 64, 80, 81, 84–5, 87, 94, 113, 118, 119, 135, 141
Stam, Robert 50, 91, 146, 149
Stanwyck, Barbara 105
Star Wars 13, 21, 75, 134
Stella Dallas 52, 54, 115, 132
Sternberg, Joseph von 92, 95

INDEX OF SELECTED FILMS AND NAMES—VOLUME 2